The

New England
Bed and Breakfast
Book

Corinne Madden Ross

The East Woods Press
Charlotte, North Carolina

Library of Congress Cataloguing-in-Publication Data
Ross, Corinne Madden.
   The New England bed and breakfast book.

   Rev. ed. of: The New England guest house book. 3rd ed. ©1984.
   Includes index.
   1. Bed and breakfast accommodations—New England—Directories. I. Ross, Corinne Madden. New England guest house book. II. Title.
TX907.R588   1986   647'.9474   85-45691
ISBN 0-88742-060-5

Cover design by Talmadge Moose

Inside illustrations and photographs provided by bed and breakfast inns
   of New England
Typography by Raven Type
Printed in the United States of America

East Woods Press Books
Fast & McMillan Publishers, Inc.
429 East Boulevard
Charlotte, NC 28203

Contents

Introduction

When I was a child growing up in New England, my family and I had few choices in the way of interesting overnight travel accommodations. Mostly there were roadside cabins (some—in the really rural areas—still proudly advertising "flushies," or flush toilets!), and tourist homes, also known as guest houses. If we could find them we preferred the latter because they were usually spotlessly clean, very inexpensive, and offered a homey alternative to the often elusive charms of tourist cabins.

After World War II, with the advent of the modern highway system, motels began to appear in great numbers and were an instant success. The older forms of lodging suffered: tourist cabins were abandoned to decay, and many tourist homes, usually located on the old back-country roads, were forced out of business. In the late 1970s, when I compiled the first edition of *The New England Guest House Book*—because I wanted to share my fondness for these nice, comfortable homes—they were difficult to find. Clusters of them still remained in the most visited seacoast areas, but inland they had become rarities. And few guest houses served breakfast.

Since then the idea of "bed and breakfast," a familiar one to travelers throughout Great Britain and parts of Europe, has become increasingly popular in the United States, and the number of bed-and-breakfast guest houses has grown to astonishing proportions. Nowadays one can travel almost anywhere in New England and stay in a different house each night. And although many travelers still choose motels, an ever-growing number of people are discovering the unique pleasures of "bed and breakfast."

Basically, a bed-and-breakfast guest house is a privately owned home with several rooms for guests; usually, breakfast is the only meal served. The meal may be a simple continental repast of juice, muffins or toast and a hot beverage, or a full "country" breakfast replete with regional specialties. The price of breakfast is generally included in the rates which are, on the average, moderate. Many guest houses offer a range of rates, lower for rooms that share a bath and higher for those with a private bath and other extra amenities. Even the most expensive guest house rates compare favorably with chain motels and hotels.

Guest houses are often conveniently located in or near a town, so that vacationers can easily walk to restaurants, shops, historic sites and other local points of interest. Others, offering a welcome respite from the tensions of the road, are situated in scenic rural areas far away from the hustle and bustle of the usual tourist routes. Most owners welcome families with children. Businessmen enjoy guest houses as a change from the ubiquitous motels; women traveling alone find them a safe, quiet haven, and out-of-towners waiting to move into a new house can live there temporarily in comfortable and relaxed surroundings.

The greatest appeal of bed-and-breakfast guest houses for most travelers, though, lies in their individuality. Some are still the simple, small homes of yesteryear, but many nowadays are downright luxurious. In New England, their ranks include some of the region's loveliest homes, often centuries old with fascinating histories and a gratifying diversity of architectural styles. You may stay in a handsome restored Colonial house built by a sea captain in the eighteenth century, or in an elegant Federal or Victorian mansion listed on the National Register of Historic Places. Other choices include contemporary mountain chalets, beach cottages large and small, and comfortable old farmhouses surrounded by acres of meadows and woods. All of the houses reflect the personality of their owners, and the decor is often one of great imagination and flair.

Magnificent antiques abound in many homes, along with polished wide-board floors, intricate moldings and other fine architectural details. Some of the guest rooms may have working fireplaces. A pleasant parlor or lounge is usually available, with books, magazines and games, and sometimes with a cheerful blaze crackling away in the fireplace or wood stove. Some thoughtful hosts place fresh flowers, fruit or wine in each guest chamber; others serve afternoon tea or sherry to their guests. Breakfast may be served on a shady porch or terrace, in a cozy kitchen, or perhaps in a splendid formal dining room. Guests are always invited to enjoy the house's grounds, too, often with lovely gardens to admire.

Guest house owners are as individual as their homes, except for one shared characteristic: they all truly enjoy their guests, and often form lasting friendships with them. Guests often are greeted upon arrival with a welcoming cup of tea or cooling glass of lemonade, and are made to feel instantly at home. Your hosts will be delighted to direct you to the best places to eat or shop in the vicinity and to offer helpful suggestions on things to do, such as visiting country fairs or attending a bean supper at a nearby church. Personal, friendly service and gracious extra touches are the keynotes of bed-and-breakfast hospitality.

The descriptions of the houses in this book are as accurate and detailed as possible. Sometimes, however, situations and/or owners change, and if you should find any of the accommodations not measuring up to your expectations I will very much appreciate your letting me know so that we can re-evaluate the listing for the next edition. (I would also like to hear about any new bed-and-breakfast houses you think would make good additions.)

It should also be mentioned that attractive as most travelers find it, the bed-and-breakfast experience is not necessarily for everyone. Not all of the houses offer private baths, and most do not provide a private phone or TV set in each room. Because the houses are private homes, guests need to be considerate of others in the matters of noise and privacy. They should try not to monopolize a shared bathroom, or allow children to run about unaccompanied. Some travelers do not enjoy sharing breakfast with others, although most people discover that the communal meal is a splendid way to meet interesting fellow guests and often consider breakfast the highlight of the day.

As the houses are generally small with only a few rooms for guests, making reservations in advance by phone or letter is a good idea, and sometimes required. Some owners also request an advance deposit; a few ask for a minimum stay of two or three days, especially over holiday weekends. Credit cards are not usually accepted; cash or traveler's checks are preferred. Personal checks are often acceptable, but it is advisable to ask ahead of time. The rates for each house (for double occupancy) are listed under one of four general categories:

Inexpensive	(under $25)
Moderate	($25–$45)
Moderately expensive	($45–$65)
Expensive	($65 and up)

Most guest houses stay open year-round; some may close in the off season or for a brief holiday. Information on dates open, which if any credit cards are accepted, and whether or not the owner welcomes children and/or pets has been included for each house. Unless otherwise stated, breakfast is complimentary. As many of New England's bed-and-breakfast houses are older and of traditional architecture, the guest rooms often are reached via a steep staircase. For travelers who do not feel up to managing stairs, lower level guest quarters are mentioned where they are available.

The aim of this book is to offer travelers a wide and entertaining choice of bed-and-breakfast accommodations throughout New England. In addition to describing the individual houses, descriptions of the various states and regions, their history, and suggestions for places to see and things to do are included. New England attracts visitors from all over the world. Its six states are similar in many ways, all of them offering travelers a wealth of historical sites, cultural and sports activities galore, and spectacular scenery. Yet each of the six—Maine, New Hampshire, Vermont, Massachusetts, Connecticut and Rhode Island—has its own distinctive character and appeal.

Excellent highways crisscross every state, fine for reaching a destination rapidly. But the best way to discover the real charm of New England is to follow the secondary routes and back roads. Just keep in mind that although distances look short on the map, the roads are winding and often narrow, so allow plenty of time to get wherever you are going. These scenic byways will take you through picturesque Colonial villages, inland valleys and forested wilderness areas, over rugged mountain passes and along the jagged, rockbound seacoast. They will also lead you to the delightful bed-and-breakfast guest houses of New England, where you are cordially invited to linger and get to know both the region and the people.

Maine

Evergreen trees, their thickly needled tips stabbing skyward against the horizon—these are the very essence of Maine. More than ninety percent of the fittingly nicknamed Pine Tree State is covered by vast tracts of dark-green forests. Pointed firs march in massed ranks down to the ocean's edge, somehow managing to thrive atop the tumbled granite ledges that form Maine's ragged coastline.

It is the seacoast that attracts the majority of visitors to New England's, and the country's, northeasternmost state. Millions of years ago the mighty peaks of a gigantic mountain range loomed along this coast. During the Ice Age, massive glaciers ground down the mountains, allowing the ocean to rush in. The glaciers left behind one of the most irregular seacoasts in the world. And the tops of those drowned mountains are now offshore islands, hundreds and hundreds of them.

If a straight line were drawn directly up Maine's seaboard, the distance covered would be only 228 miles. The actual shoreline, however, measures 3478 miles! Although Route 1 is the nearest thing to a coastal highway, you can't just merrily roll along in your car and expect to be awed by splendid vistas of sea and rock. They're there, all right, but most can be discovered only by making a trek eastward from Route 1, sometimes for a good many miles. To see the sea you must study your map and then choose which of the innumerable capes, coves and long, narrow peninsulas you wish to explore.

In the early 1600s, both France and England founded short-lived settlements along the coast. The English Popham Colony, near the mouth of the Kennebec River, was abandoned after one bitter Maine winter. The colonists informed the Mother Country that no one could ever survive in that climate. Some modern-day State of Mainers agree with this opinion and spend their winters in Florida if they can manage it.

Most of the inhabitants, however, relish the cooler months with their clear, crisp air, and the return to leisurely, slow-paced living. Snug harbors are emptied of their summertime jams of pleasure craft; only the fishing boats remain. An atmosphere of serenity pervades the coastal villages. Snow drifts quietly down upon beaches and gray rock, clinging to tree branches and piles of lobster pots. For a growing number of travelers, this is the best time of all to come. There's not

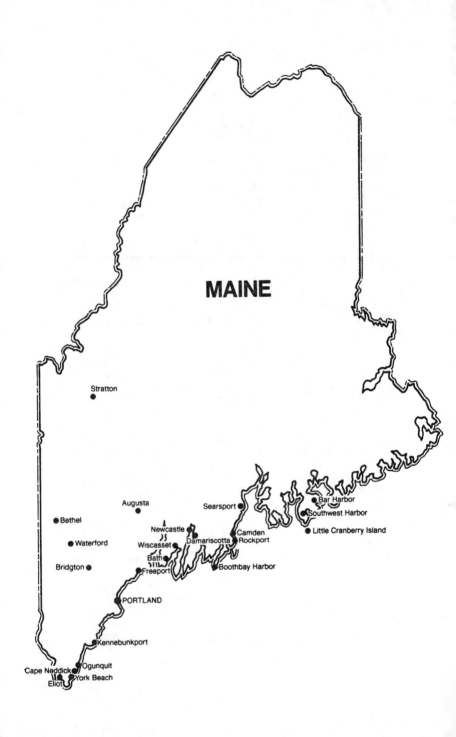

MAINE

Stratton ●

Augusta ●   Searsport ●   ● Bar Harbor

● Bethel   Newcastle ●   Camden   ● Southwest Harbor

● Waterford   Wiscasset ●   Damariscotta ● Rockport   ● Little Cranberry Island

Bath ●

Bridgton ●   Freeport ●   ● Boothbay Harbor

● PORTLAND

Kennebunkport ●

Cape Neddick ● ● Ogunquit
Eliot ● ● York Beach

as much activity, perhaps, but winter's dazzling beauty, and the joy of having it all to yourself, are enticement enough.

In summer, the seacoast swarms with tourists. Things to do include sightseeing, antiquing, clambakes, boat trips to the islands, seal watching, exploring tidal pools, and ocean swimming—if you can tolerate the frigid Maine water. The sun doesn't always shine, of course. Rain falls occasionally; some days fog rolls softly in from the sea. A walk along the sands or rocks in swirling salt mist, all sound muffled except for the constant boom of the surf, can become an unforgettable memory. Eating is also a popular occupation, and Maine boasts a well-deserved reputation for good food. Freshly caught, boiled lobsters are the state's most famous offerings; blueberry pie, made with the tiny native berries, comes in a close second.

Whatever time of the year you choose to come, try to strike up a conversation with the local people whenever possible. Maine folk are proud, direct and—despite their reputed taciturnity—downright chatty when given a chance. Don't attempt to imitate the twangy accent, though. You will only amuse the natives and run the risk of earning the derisive sobriquet, "summer complaint."

Heading north up the coast (or "Down East" to those in the know), you will find a profusion of intriguing towns, villages and seaside resort areas. York Beach, Ogunquit, Kennebunkport, Portland and the Boothbay Harbor region are all within as easy drive from Boston. Camden, with its uniquely appealing harbor, and Bar Harbor, the grand old summer watering place of the wealthy near spectacular Acadia National Park, are farther along. The nation's easternmost point, Quoddy Head State Park, is way up near Lubec, across Passamaquoddy Bay from New Brunswick, Canada. A bridge leads out to Campobello Island and Franklin D. Roosevelt's summer home, which is open to the public.

Although Maine is as large as the other five New England states combined, its population numbers a mere 1.1 million. A look at a map will give you an idea of the awesome expanse of uninhabited wilderness, slashed by whitewater rivers, that spreads over most of the state's northern regions. This rugged area includes Baxter State Park and, to the southwest, Moosehead Lake—Maine's largest, forty miles long and twenty miles wide. Away from the coast the state's topography ranges from flat, potato-growing Aroostook County to gently rolling countryside and low mountains, with some 2500 freshwater lakes and 5000 streams. Summertime activities include swimming, canoeing, rafting, fishing, hunting and hiking; in winter visitors can enjoy downhill or cross-country skiing and snowshoeing. Central and southwestern Maine are dotted with attractive small towns and villages, with fine old houses to look at and a host of antique shops to explore.

Coastal Maine

The Yorks/Eliot/Cape Neddick

The southernmost tourist area on Maine's seacoast is known as The Yorks—York Village, York Harbor and York Beach—all on Route 1A. York Village, originally called Agamenticus, was settled in 1624. It was incorporated in 1642 as Gorgeana, named after Sir Ferdinando Gorges, English soldier and mariner, then proprietor of the Province of Maine. Massachusetts seized the province in 1652, and Gorgeana, known as the first English "city" in America, was reduced to a town and renamed York.

Indians frequently attacked the town, almost destroying it in 1692, killing or capturing about half of the inhabitants. Old Snowshoe Rock, where the Abenaki Indians were supposed to have left their snowshoes before the deadly raid, is one of the area's many interesting historic sites. York Village offers several well-preserved Colonial houses, and the Old Gaol Museum, known as the King's prison, is noted for its gloomy dungeons and fine collections of china and furniture. In York's Old Burying Ground you'll find a witch's tomb. Four excellent beaches and a deep, landlocked harbor provide surf- and deep-sea fishing, boating and swimming, and a tidal pool for children. A short drive west from York Harbor brings you to the small country town of Eliot; heading north from York you come to Cape Neddick. Out on the tip of the cape is scenic Nubble Light, immensely popular for picnicking and photo taking.

The Jo-Mar, Bed and Breakfast on the Ocean. Named for its proprietors, Joan Curtis and her mother, Mary Della Puletra, the Jo-Mar is an attractive house on a quiet street in York Beach. A cross between Colonial and mid-Victorian architecture in style, the house

sits on a bluff and has a spectacular view of cliffs and ocean, especially from the landscaped terrace. Six large, comfortable guest rooms, with shared baths, are decorated in Colonial style; most of the rooms face the ocean. There is also a one-bedroom cottage, with private bath, available for guests. The cottage, called the Depot, was once an old railroad station! All guests are invited to use the Jo-Mar's coffee room and the living room, with a fireplace; outdoors there are picnic tables, charcoal grills and lawn chairs. House guests are offered a continental breakfast of English muffins or toast, homebaked coffee cake or pastry (blueberry muffins are the house specialty), and coffee or tea, served in the Gathering Room or on the porch.

The Jo-Mar, Bed and Breakfast on the Ocean, 41 Freeman St., P.O. Box 838, York Beach, ME 03910; (207) 363-4826; in winter and early spring call (203) 377-4756. (From I-95 take exit for "The Yorks" to Rte. 1; turn left and go north 3.4 miles to junction with Rte. 1A. Turn right and go 1.4 miles; as you enter the town of York Beach, Freeman Street is on the left.) Rates are moderate, lower by the week. Children are welcome, but there are no cribs for babies; no pets, please. Open mid-May to mid-October.

High Meadows Bed & Breakfast. A few miles west of the seacoast, in Eliot, travelers will find High Meadows, a handsome Colonial structure built in 1736 by Elliott Frost, a merchant shipbuilder and captain. When Elaine Raymond bought the house in the early 1960s it had no heat, no lights and no running water except for a free-flowing spring. Today High Meadows, while maintaining its old Colonial charm, offers all modern amenities. For guests there are three large double upstairs rooms, sharing one and a half baths, and one bedroom on the ground floor with queen-size bed, a private bath and a working fireplace. All of the accommodations are pleasantly furnished, with many antiques. Guests are invited to enjoy the den with TV and a large porch and terrace. Breakfast, served in the attractive country kitchen or out on the terrace, consists of fresh fruit compote, choice of juice, homemade muffins and coffee or tea. You will need a car to reach restaurants and shops. Historic York and the York beaches are within a short drive as is Portsmouth, New Hampshire, and its famous restored Strawbery Banke area. Your hostess also recommends boat trips to the Isles of Shoals and whale-watching expeditions in summer, and leaf watching in the fall. Golfing is available nearby; ski areas are one and a half hours away.

High Meadows Bed & Breakfast, Rte. 101, Eliot, ME 03903; (207) 439-0590. (Ask for directions when you call or write for reservations.) Rates are moderate to moderately expensive. No children or pets, please. Open year-round.

Wooden Goose Inn. Jerry Rippetoe and Anthony Sienicki are your proud hosts at the Wooden Goose Inn in Cape Neddick, north of York. To quote their own words: "We find it difficult to be objective

Wooden Goose Inn

about the house; guess we're too modest. All we can say is that our guests are overwhelmed with the place!" Built in 1850 by a sea captain, the Wooden Goose is a typical Maine farmhouse, set on four acres along the Cape Neddick River just one mile from the ocean. There are six air-conditioned rooms for guests (three are on the ground floor) including one single and five doubles. Two have private baths, the others share two baths. The living room, dining room, and terrace dining room offer comfortable areas for quiet reading or socializing. The house is decorated in an eclectic Victorian/Country style with pastel color schemes, the rooms furnished with antiques and the owners' collections of porcelain, crystal and bronze. According to Jerry and Tony, their guests spend hours just browsing around. A full breakfast is served, and there will be juice or a fresh fruit dish such as berries in heavy cream, fruit with sherbet or broiled grapefruit, homemade muffins or breads, and an entree of corned beef hash with poached eggs, eggs Benedict or Florentine, shirred eggs and sausage, or perhaps quiche Lorraine or French toast Amaretto. Afternoon tea is also included, and your hosts always provide something special like liver pate or almond croissants. For other meals, a restaurant is within walking distance, as are beaches and a spectacular ocean walk.

Wooden Goose Inn, Rte. 1, Box 195, Cape Neddick, ME 03902; (207) 363-5673. (After junction of rtes. 1 and 1A, continue north on Rte. 1 and you'll see four small houses; the next house is the Wooden Goose.) Rates are moderately expensive. Children over 12 are welcome; no pets, please. Open daily Feb. 1–Dec. 31. From the weekend after Columbus Day in October through mid-May, a Winter/Spring holiday weekend package for two is offered, including two nights at the inn, breakfast and afternoon tea, and dinner at the Cape Neddick Inn.

Ogunquit

One of my favorite memories of Ogunquit is not of a lazy summer's day on the beach but rather of a nasty night in late September. Heavy winds and drenching, chilly rain—the backlash of a hurricane—made going outside a misery. My friends and I, however, sat snug and warm beside a roaring fire, feasting on seafood and wine at Perkins Cove. A British companion, more or less enjoying her first experience of tearing apart a whole boiled lobster, mopped at the butter dripping from her chin. She announced that the Maine seafood was excellent, if a bit messy. "However," she added tartly, "when you come to England, just don't dare make any adverse comments about *our* weather."

The name Ogunquit means "beautiful place by the sea." It is, especially along the winding roads that lead to the ocean. The beach is fabulous—a stretch of clean white sand that extends for three miles. Maine's coast is so rocky that a beach of this magnitude is rare. Usually there are tidal pools, too, where children or adults can paddle in shallow, warm, salt water.

Meandering along the craggy cliffs between Ogunquit Beach and Perkins Cove is the Marginal Way. A winding path about a mile long, the Way is bordered by blueberry and bayberry bushes, bittersweet vines and storm-twisted, stunted trees. Below are coves with masses of gray rocks; if you like solitude these tiny coves are perfect for sunbathing—when the tide is out. A sneaky incoming tide can quickly fill them up, and unless you can scale a cliff rapidly, you might be taking an unexpected swim.

Perkins Cove at the other end of the Marginal Way is a picturesque little harbor stuffed with boats, both pleasure and working. Shops and galleries offering a broad range of things to look at or buy have taken over the once busy fishing shacks on the narrow peninsula alongside. Several good places to eat include some that specialize in steamed clams and lobsters, served indoors or out. Up behind the cove, beautiful old houses look benignly down over the hillsides of green lawns or brilliantly blooming gardens.

The Captain Lorenz Perkins House. This splendid three-story Colonial house in Ogunquit Village is more than 200 years old. Captain Perkins bought the place a century ago, when he retired from the sea. Today's owners, Ron and Jean Mullenaux, have thirteen attractive rooms for guests, including six doubles and seven triples; three are on the ground floor. The eight rooms in the main house, each decorated individually with period wallpapers and antiques, share two baths. Several of the rooms boast quilts made by your hostess, and unusual handmade rectangular braided wool rugs cover the halls and stairs. The other five rooms, more modern in decor and all with private baths, are located in the century-old attached carriage

The Captain Lorenz Perkins House

house and garage, which are graced with wide pine plank flooring. Three of these rooms have their own sun deck.

Breakfast consists of homemade fruit and nut breads (the zucchini bread is very popular, according to Jean), juice, coffee or tea. At cocktail time, guests are offered a complimentary glass of wine. A parlor on the first floor of the main house has a fireplace, game table and reading area; a small sitting room on the second floor offers a collection of local restaurant menus. There's also a shop on the premises, operated by Jean and called "The Captain's Mistress Emporium." (According to local history, Captain Perkins kept a mistress in nearby Portsmouth, creating a juicy morsel of gossip among the Ogunquit citizenry.) The shop, which contains a fine collection of antique glassware and collectibles, represents more than two dozen New England artists and craftspeople.

The Captain Lorenz Perkins House, N. Main Street, P.O. Box 1249, Ogunquit, ME 03907; (207) 646-7825. (Two blocks north of main intersection.) Rates are moderate to moderately expensive, lower off season. Children over 4 are welcome; no pets, please. Open April–October.

Hartwell House. An elegant blend of old and new, Hartwell House is of contemporary design with skylights, French doors, stained glass and greenery, furnished in Early American and English antiques. Owned by Jim and Trish Hartwell, the house is managed by resident innkeepers. For guests there are seven rooms and two apartments, all with private baths and air conditioning; two of the rooms are on the ground floor and most include a private balcony overlooking the lawn and gardens. A glassed-in, air-conditioned and heated porch offers easy chairs in spring and fall and antique wicker furniture in summer. Breakfast consists of homemade breads, a variety of fruit salads, juices, and coffee or tea. Tennis, golf and a swimming pool are available close by; Perkins Cove and Ogunquit Beach are within easy walking distance.

Hartwell House, 116 Shore Rd., Ogunquit, ME 03907; (207) 646-7210. Rates are expensive. Visa and MasterCard are accepted. Children over 14 are welcome; no pets, please. Open early spring to late fall.

Seafair Inn. Jeff Walker is your host at the Seafair, just one-half block away from Ogunquit's village center. Built in the late 1800s as the private summer residence of a wealthy New England family, the Seafair was converted to an inn during the 1930s and has been in continuous operation ever since. Now completely renovated, the inn has been refurnished with period Victorian antiques. Each of the twenty guest rooms (including seventeen doubles and three triples)

is individually appointed. Sixteen of the rooms have private baths; four share baths. Nine of the rooms, all with private baths, are on the ground floor. For relaxation there are a library with color TV, a living room with a fireplace and a baby grand piano, a glass-enclosed porch and a landscaped garden. Breakfast offers homemade muffins and breads, juice, coffee or tea, and on chilly days during the off season there will also be afternoon tea. The inn is conveniently close to Ogunquit's many fine restaurants and shops, the beach and Marginal Way. *Seafair Inn, 24 Shore Rd., Box 1221, Ogunquit, ME 03907; (207) 646-2181. Rates are moderately expensive, lower off season (April–June 20 and Labor Day–November.) Visa and MasterCard are accepted. Well-behaved children (those respectful of antique furniture) are welcome; pets are accepted on an individual basis. Open mid-April–November.*

Kennebunkport

From the Yorks, it's only a short drive north to the Kennebunk region. You can take either Route 1 or the Maine Turnpike (I-95) and watch for the turnoff signs. If you are interested in antiques, this stretch of Route 1 will delight you—virtually every barn, garage, stable and house along the way advertises old things for sale. The Maine Turnpike, on the other hand, is faster and is pleasantly lined by nothing but trees. The turnpike has another good point: just before reaching the turnoff for the Kennebunk region you will pass underneath a road with a most intriguing name . . . Cat Mousam.

According to knowledgeable folk at the Brick Store Museum in Kennebunk, there's a story connected with this road, which may or may not be true. Seems there was once a sawmill on the Mousam River. One day a cat chasing a mouse caught—and lost—his tail in one of the saws. The mill thereafter became the Cat Mill, and the road the Cat Mousam.

Exit 3 from the Maine Turnpike will take you east to the Kennebunks. They consist of Kennebunk itself, on the west bank of the Kennebunk River; Kennebunkport and Arundel on the east; and Kennebunk Beach, Cape Porpoise and Goose Rocks Beach nearby. The region has been a popular summer colony since the Civil War. Even the Indians of earlier times appreciated its charms, regularly setting up summer encampments along the shore. Among the area's many attractions nowadays—including long, broad beaches and excellent fishing—is the Seashore Trolley Museum in Arundel where visitors can take an old-time trolley ride.

Kennebunk was, long ago, a shipbuilding town. On Route 9A/35 you will find a row of splendiferous mansions built by shipyard owners and sea captains. They're all frilled and gussied up in true Victorian style; the most outstanding is the famous Wedding Cake House, not—unfortunately—open to the public. Kennebunkport, an exceptionally attractive town, was the home of Kenneth Roberts, author of many New England historical novels. Dock Square, just beyond the river, teems with specialty shops and galleries. Ocean Avenue, leading out of the square, takes you past some magnificent scenery, including Spouting Rock and Blowing Cave. The town also boasts a superb collection of beautiful old houses, a number of which offer overnight accommodations to travelers, year-round.

The Chetwynd House Inn. Capt. Matthew Seavey of Kennebunkport built this house around 1840; in later years it was owned by artist Abbott Graves, known for his scenes of Kennebunkport social life in the early 1900s. (His work is on view at the Brick Store Museum in Kennebunk.) Today the blue-shuttered house is owned by Susan Knowles Chetwynd. Mrs. Chetwynd, a personable lady and creative cook, has a well-deserved reputation for serving her guests fabulous breakfasts. A few of her unusual specialties are boned chicken in cheese sauce, baked haddock, mushrooms on toast, and oyster stew. Egg dishes are served with a colorful vegetable: a mushroom-capped tomato, broccoli, spinach or eggplant. There's fresh fruit, too, beautifully presented—such as melon filled with strawberries or blueberries. Visitors come to Chetwynd House from all over the world, and the breakfast table is a favorite place to meet and share experiences over the delicious food. Guests may help themselves to coffee, tea or cocoa during the day, and on rainy afternoons there may be a full tea with little sandwiches and cakes. All of these delightful amenities are included in the rates!

The inn has five upstairs guest rooms, two with private baths. All are cheerful and very comfortable, furnished with antiques and period pieces. The Gable Room, for example, contains a handsome cannonball bed and blue velvet chairs. Touches of blue, Mrs. Chetwynd's favorite color, may be seen throughout the house, which is graced with long windows and the original, wide pine floorboards. The pleasant living room/library offers a wall of well-filled bookshelves for guests' enjoyment. Outside there is a lovely little garden; even though all the activity of the village is only steps away, a feeling of seclusion and peacefulness pervades.

The Chetwynd House Inn, Chestnut Street off Ocean Avenue, P.O. Box 130, Kennebunkport, ME 04046; (207) 967-2235. (From Dock Square, take a right on Ocean Avenue and go 2 blocks.) Rates are moderately expensive to expensive; special winter rates are available. Children over 16 are welcome during the off season; no pets, please. Open year-round; in winter, please be sure to call ahead for reservations.

The Captain Lord Mansion. With its unbeatable combination of comfort, elegance, charm and gracious hospitality, the Captain Lord Mansion in Kennebunkport is certain to delight even the choosiest of travelers. The Mansion, listed in the National Register of Historic Places, is a beauty.

Nathaniel Lord (just between us historians) was not actually a sea

captain. He was a merchant and shipbuilder, a prominent citizen of Kennebunkport. In 1812, when the British blockaded the harbor, Lord's shipwrights had little to do. To keep the men occupied, he had them build the most magnificent mansion in town. The Federalist-type structure contains twenty-five rooms, twelve fireplaces and a museum's worth of other splendid touches. Some of the light fixtures are of real silver; several of the bathrooms have marble sinks and clawfoot tubs. There are a graceful four-story spiral staircase, a three-story suspended elliptical staircase, an octagonal cupola with a widow's walk on the roof, blown-glass windows and hand-painted *trompe l'oeil* doors. Floors are the original wide "pumpkin pine."

Host Rick Litchfield and wife Bev Davis, "refugees from the corporate world of advertising," as they describe themselves, purchased the house in 1978. They then worked diligently for several years to refurbish the place, which is now authentically restored to its proper 1812 ambiance. In addition, Rick and Bev produced two daughters and acquired a Maine Coon Cat named "Aggie." There are sixteen rooms for guests, including eight deluxe corner rooms. The accommodations are exceptionally spacious, and each of the bedrooms is individually appointed and furnished with antiques and period reproduction wallpapers. Eleven of the rooms have working fireplaces, which guests are encouraged to use. One guest room even has its own private little elevator. Windowseats, handmade quilts, braided rugs, color-coordinated linens and live plants all add to the charm of this remarkable house. There is also a ghost.

Her portrait hangs over the fireplace in one of the two downstairs guest rooms. Sally Buckland was her name; she was the daughter of Charles P. Clark, grandson of Nathaniel Lord and president of the New York/New Haven Railroad. Sally loved the house with a passion and wanted all of its glories preserved forever. Her grandchildren recall being frequently admonished not to step on the rugs or damage any of the furniture. Since her death there have been, so it is said, a number of spooky incidents, the sound of footsteps, lights mysteriously going on and off and the like. The obvious explanation is that Grandmother Buckland stalks the house, checking to see that all is well. To be on the safe side, please be sure to wipe your feet when you enter.

Breakfast, served at a big, long table next to the huge wood stove in the homey kitchen, includes juice, homemade muffins, hot breads and soft-boiled eggs. Bev's collection of recipes for muffins (including banana, blueberry bran, cranberry, pineapple nut, oat and jam) and hot breads (apple raisin, rhubarb nut and many more) are available on printed cards for guests to take home. Afternoon tea is also offered, with ten varieties of Twinings tea in winter and ice tea—served from an antique ceramic crock—in summer. For relaxing, guests are invited to use the Gathering Room with its working fireplace and many books, puzzles and games of chess, backgammon, Chinese checkers and cards. There's a gift shop, too, on the premises.

At Halloween, your hosts celebrate with a pumpkin-carving contest and a masked scavenger hunt. Between December 1 and April 30, Bev and Rick offer a winter weekender "Fireside Special": three nights at a special discount rate (including holidays). Designed for guests who would like to savor the pleasures of the Maine winter season, the package includes breakfast each morning and a specially prepared room with a bottle of wine and stack of firewood for cozy nights. *The Captain Lord Mansion, P.O. Box 800, Kennebunkport, ME 04046; (207) 967-3141. (Corner of Pleasant and Green streets; from Dock Square, go right on Ocean Avenue. The mansion is on the second block on the left. Park behind building and follow brick walk to office.) Rates range from expensive to very expensive. Children over 12 are welcome; no pets, please, and no smoking in the halls or common rooms. Open year-round.*

The Captain Jefferds Inn. Vying in elegance with the Captain Lord Mansion across the street, the Captain Jefferds Inn is a large, white clapboard house with black shutters. Of Federal design with later nineteenth-century additions, the gracious old home was built in 1804 by an affluent sea captain, William Jefferds, Jr. Your cordial hosts today are Warren Fitzsimmons and Don Kelly. Antique dealers and designers (a former residence and the inn have both been featured on the covers of *House Beautiful*), they have decorated the mansion with unusual American antiques. Included are brass beds, handmade quilts, wicker and rattan, folk art and special collections such as majolica and tramp art. And nothing is behind glass! In the adjoining antiques barn, guests may browse through an array of intriguing collectibles.

The main house contains eleven guest bedrooms: eight doubles and three triples. Two are on the ground floor. One two-room suite shares a bath; the other rooms all have private baths. Some offer fireplaces and harbor views; most have Laura Ashley wallcoverings,

and each room has been done in a different mood. The "Belle Watling" room, for example, is reminiscent of *Gone With the Wind*. In addition, three apartments in the attached eighteenth-century carriage house, each with a living room, private bath and kitchen, may be rented either as separate bedrooms or as efficiencies by the day, week, month or season.

The inn's public rooms include a large living room, with fireplace, decorated with colorful chintz-type fabrics; the walls are a warm, misty yellow. A comfortable sun porch is filled with plants and looks out to the harbor. Two terraces and a spacious lawn are also pleasant places for relaxing, with attractive wicker furniture arranged in conversational settings. A generous country breakfast features homebaked breads or muffins, fruit in season, and Warren's special blueberry or banana crepes or dropped eggs on corned beef hash. The meal is served on Staffordshire china, with beautiful crystal and silver, in the gracious formal dining room. In wintertime, your hosts also offer afternoon tea, served by a crackling fire.

The Captain Jefferds Inn, Pearl Street, Box 691, Kennebunkport, ME 04046; (207) 967-2311. (Follow Ocean Avenue .3 mile; at Arundel Wharf go left to Pearl Street.) Rates are expensive. Children over 12 are welcome, as are friendly pets (those that like other animals. Your hosts have three dogs and one cat. Many guests, they say, vie with one another as to which animal will share their rooms with them!) Open April–October.

North Street Guest House. John and Glenda Consla welcome travelers to their pleasant old farmhouse in Kennebunkport. The 1850 structure, recently renovated, sits on a half acre of land just a short walking distance from the town center. Glenda, who has taken

time off from practicing law in Boston to operate the guest house, has repainted the house in Williamsburg colors and added charming period wallpapers to the rooms. There are two guest rooms, one with a double bed and one with two double beds; each has a private bath. One of the rooms is on the ground floor. The decor is simple but comfortable, with a few nice antiques; one of the baths is exceptionally large and boasts a classic old tub with legs. For relaxation guests may use the living and dining rooms and the front porch, with its wicker furniture. Breakfast features fresh fruit, freshly squeezed orange juice, blueberry pancakes or cheese omelets, apple or blueberry muffins or toast and coffee. Glenda herself picks the blueberries and apples!

North Street Guest House, North Street, P.O. Box 1229, Kennebunkport, ME 04046; (207) 967-4452. (One-third of a mile north of town.) Rates are moderately expensive, lower off season (Dec. 1–June 1.) Well-behaved children are welcome; no pets, please, and no smoking. Open year-round.

Dock Square Inn. Situated on a quiet, one-way street just off Dock Square, this gracious old Victorian house was built in 1856 by Captain Newell of Kennebunkport. Newell was widely acclaimed for his rescue of a British vessel and was presented with a spyglass and letter of commendation by the British government—both of which items may be seen at the Historical Society on North Street. The house was later purchased by David Clark, the town's busiest shipbuilder. His

shipyard, which was located directly across the street on the Kennebunk River, produced almost 100 sloops, schooners and barks from 1852 to 1901. The present-day owners of the house, Frank and Bernice Shoby, have six rooms for guests, including one single and five doubles, all with private baths. Two of the rooms are on the ground floor. The comfortable, attractively furnished accommodations all have TVs and contain many interesting family Victorian antiques and collectibles. Each of the rooms is named after one of the ships built by David Clark. A pleasant sitting room offers books and magazines, and there are always bowls of fresh fruit and assorted candy for nibblers. Bernice loves flowers, and throughout the house guests will find green plants or fresh bouquets in season. Breakfast, served at the call of an old schoolhouse bell, consists of juices or fresh fruit compote, cereals, freshly baked breads or muffins (Bernice says her old-fashioned blueberry muffins are the favorite), and homemade jams and jellies, freshly ground imported coffee, or tea. Some mornings there will be a breakfast surprise prepared by Frank: waffles, pancakes or French toast served with Maine maple syrup and sausages. Afternoon tea, a delightful amenity, is also offered if guests wish it, with homemade goodies to munch.

Dock Square Inn, Temple Street, P.O. Box 1143, Kennebunkport, ME 04046; (207) 967-5773. (Follow Rte. 9 over the drawbridge, through Dock Square; Temple Street is the first left.) Rates are moderately expensive, lower from April 1 through June 15 and Oct. 15 through Dec. 1 and for longer stays. Visa and MasterCard are accepted. Children over 12 are welcome; no pets, please. (Guests will be greeted by Riiki-Shaw of Ching Ling, the Pekingese "sentry dog.") Open year-round.

English Meadows Inn. Helene and Gene Kelly, and their daughter Claudia, thoroughly enjoy showing guests around their comfortable old Victorian home just outside of Kennebunkport. Buttons, a lovable lump of a sort-of-sheepdog, will be there, too, to greet you at the

door. The house is situated on seven acres of meadow, with fruit trees and pine groves, flower gardens, and forty or more hundred-year-old lilac trees. Come, if you can, when the lilacs are in bloom . . . the scent is downright breathtaking! And deer sometimes come to graze in the pines and meadows in the early morning.

There are fifteen rooms for guests, including two suites with cooking facilities for longer stays. Four of the rooms are in the main house; the comfortable accommodations include brass and iron beds, in-room sinks and semi-private baths. Braided or hooked rugs cover the wide pineboard floors; old prints, handmade quilts and coverlets, hanging plants and fresh flowers add further welcoming notes. The other rooms and suites, some with private baths, are in the attached "Carriage House." An attractive, informal place to stay, the paneled Carriage House includes a large central room with stone fireplace and early wicker furniture. Seven of the rooms are on the ground floor.

A hearty breakfast is served in the cozy old kitchen in the main house. There'll be lots of good conversation with the friendly Kellys and your fellow guests, and probably one of the house specialties such as "Eggs McMeadows," sourdough French toast with fresh berries, or—to quote Helene Kelly—"the best omelets ever!"

Although only a mile from the ocean and a half-mile walk to town, the "Meadows" has the nice feeling of being way out in the country. Bicycling is a great way to explore the area; bring your own or the Kellys will tell you where you may rent one. Antique enthusiasts don't even have to leave the grounds: the Kellys operate their own shop at English Meadows—Whaler Antiques—where you will find country furniture and accessories, quilts, hooked rugs, baskets, wicker, folk art and unusual collectibles.

English Meadows Inn, RFD 1, Rte. 35, Lower Village, Kennebunkport, ME 04046; (207) 967-5766. (From the Maine Turnpike take Exit 3 to Kennebunk; turn left on Rte. 35 south and go 5 miles; English Meadows will be on your right.) Rates are moderately expensive. Children over 12 are welcome; sorry, no pets. (Besides Buttons, there are two nice cats in residence.) Open April 1–Nov. 1.

Portland/Freeport

Portland, overlooking an island-studded bay, is Maine's largest city. Walking tours (maps are available at the Chamber of Commerce, 142 Free St.) take you through several historic areas and past stately mansions of Federal, Greek Revival and Italianate architecture. Early in its history, Portland was often attacked by Indians, and the British bombarded and burned it in 1775. In the 1800s, the largest commercial sailing fleet on the Eastern Seaboard operated out of the harbor. Fire destroyed much of the city in 1866, but its citizens quickly rebuilt. The Old Port Exchange, the beautifully restored nineteenth-century waterfront area, offers a fine collection of interesting shops and restaurants. Don't miss paying a visit to the recent addition to the Portland Museum of Art, on Congress Street downtown. The building is almost a sculpture all by itself, intriguing inside and out.

Another point of interest in the area is Portland Head Light out near Cape Elizabeth. One of the oldest lighthouses in the country, it was erected on the orders of George Washington and beamed out its first warning beacon in 1791. A somewhat different attraction not far away is L.L. Bean's famed emporium of outdoor apparel and gear in Freeport. To get there, drive eighteen miles northeast from Portland on Route 1. Bean's is open 24 hours a day, 365 days a year.

The Inn on Carleton/Bed & Breakfast. Greg Dismore and Gretchen Henn own this handsome 1869 three-story Victorian town-house in Portland. The quiet residential neighborhood in which the house is located boasts one of the largest collections of Victorian homes in the country. The Museum of Art is a short walk away; Portland's Old Port Exchange with its many excellent restaurants and shops, and the waterfront, are a twenty-minute walk. The inn's seven guest rooms are on the second and third floors, reached by a magnificent open staircase. There are six doubles (two also have a cot and may be used as triples) and one single. Currently two of the rooms have private baths and five share baths. The private bath on the third floor is new and notable, strikingly done in gray and white tile. Large and comfortable, the guest bedrooms are furnished with local antiques; most contain a marble-topped washstand. In wintertime your hosts thoughtfully add flannel sheets and warm comforters to the beds. There is a front parlor for guests' use with reading material and information on things to do and see in the area; no TV is available except for special occasions such as major sports events, political conventions and the like. Breakfast at the inn offers juice and fruit, muffins (Greg's banana bran muffins are renowned), breads and toast, coffee or tea. Occasionally there may be cheese or hard-boiled eggs in addition, and in cold weather, hot cereal.

The Inn on Carleton, 46 Carleton St., Portland, ME 04102; (207) 775-1910. (Ask for directions when you call or write for reservations.) Rates are moderate to moderately expensive. Children are welcome; no pets, please, and no smoking. Limited (3 spaces) parking is available. Open year-round.

Bed & Breakfast in the White House. A spacious sixteen-room home built in 1900, the White House in Portland belongs to Lorraine Marion. Your hostess lives upstairs; five double guest rooms, two baths (one with tub, one with shower), the dining room and kitchen are all on the first floor. The guest bedrooms include the Rose, Orchid and Blue rooms, the Oval Room and the East Room. There is also a large family room in the basement, with color cable TV, for guests to use. Breakfast consists of coffee with cream, orange juice, home-made muffins, cold cereal and fruit. Mrs. Marion says that she usually goes downstairs around 7 a.m. and sets everything up; her guests arise when they wish and help themselves. The White House is one mile from downtown Portland, a fifteen-minute drive from the beach.

Bed & Breakfast in the White House, 62 Roberts St., Portland, ME 04102; (207) 772-6257. (Directions will be given when you call or write for reservations.) Rates are moderate. Children and pets are welcome, as long as they are well behaved. Parking is available. Open year-round.

The Isaac Randall House. A half-hour's drive north from Portland will bring you to Freeport, and the convivial Isaac Randall House.

Constructed in 1823 as a wedding gift for Isaac Randall, Jr., and his bride, Betsy Cummings, the Federal-style farmhouse has been a stop on the "Underground Railway" by which escaped slaves made their way to Canada, a dairy farm, a prohibition-era dance hall, and an apartment house. Today, beautifully restored as a bed-and-breakfast country inn, the house is owned by Jim and Glynrose Friedlander. Glyn says: "Running the place has been the nicest sort of experience . . . with the nicest guests and just good things happening."

Six guest rooms include four doubles, one triple and one that sleeps four; four of the rooms have private baths and two share a bath. Three of the bedrooms, all with private baths, are on the ground floor. Antiques, Orientals and colorful old quilts grace the guest quarters, which include the Violet Room, with richly carved dark furniture, a double brass bed and ornate chandelier; the Blue Room, with Victorian golden oak furnishings and a bathroom with claw-footed tub; the rustic Pine Room, decorated with Navajo rugs and Western paintings; the romantic Rose Room containing a harpsichord desk and framed antique valentines; the cozy Green Room overlooking a landscaped terrace, and the Ivory Room, with country garden prints and an old pine dresser.

A Common Room with comfortable places to sit offers cable TV, books and magazines, and games. Breakfast, served family-style on a long table in the cozy beam-ceilinged country kitchen, features melon or mixed fresh fruit, prunes, homemade granola, homebaked breads—banana, lemon or perhaps sticky buns—with cream cheese and butter, and milk, tea or Amaretto-flavored coffee. In addition, there'll be a hot dish such as scrambled eggs with diced ham and freshly made biscuits and jam, or wild blueberry pancakes with real maple syrup. Glyn and Jim do things just right, even to the extent of always using cloth napkins and placing fresh flowers on the breakfast table.

The Isaac Randall House has a spring-fed pond on its five wooded acres; you may roam among the wildflowers, play horseshoes or badminton, or broil a steak on the outdoor grill. Hiking trails and golfing are nearby. L.L. Bean's is about five blocks north; Freeport also has a fine selection of distinctive shops offering designer fashions, shoes, pottery and the like, all at outlet prices. The ocean and Wolfe's Neck State Park are one mile away; Bowdoin College in Brunswick is fifteen miles away.

The Isaac Randall House, Independence Drive, Freeport, ME 04032; (207) 865-9295. (Ask for directions when you call or write for reservations.) Rates are moderately expensive, lower off season (June 15–Nov. 1) and for longer stays. Children are welcome; no pets, please. Open year-round.

Bath/Wiscasset

The old seaport of Bath, on the Kennebec River, has been a shipbuilding center for more than 200 years. And the Bath Iron Works, which began building ships in the late 1800s, still launches new vessels regularly. You will want to take the time to explore the fascinating Maine Marine Museum, located at four separate sites in town. During the summer months visitors can take a boat cruise along the river from one display to another, including a shipyard where wooden sailing vessels are still being built. Washington Street, lined with magnificent eighteenth-century mansions, is another Bath attraction not to be missed.

From Bath, follow Route 1 north to Wiscasset. Wiscasset claims to be Maine's prettiest village, and may well be. It comes as a surprise: you crest a hill and there it is. Picturesque Main Street with its brick sidewalks and handsome old homes begins at the curve, slants sharply downward and ends abruptly at the broad Sheepscot River. Just to the right of the bridge you'll see two derelict sailing ships—the four-masted schooners *Luther Little* and *Hesper*. Photographers seem to like them, and they *are* old. I find them depressing. But Wiscasset is not, and the hilly little town offers a number of interesting things to see. The Old Jail and Jailer's House are fun to explore, and the Nickels-Sortwell Mansion, an 1807 sea captain's home, contains a large display of period furnishings.

Grane's Fairhaven Inn. This exceptionally attractive guest house, situated in peaceful country surroundings not far from Bath, has a lengthy history. The original house was built in 1790 by Pembleton Edgecomb for his bride, and the Edgecomb family occupied the house for 125 years. In 1926, the house was purchased by the Gillies, who named it Fairhaven. They added more rooms on the west side in the 1940s, but the east facade was left virtually unchanged. The George Millers took ownership in 1969 and for almost a decade worked at restoring and refurbishing the place. In 1978, Jane Wyllie and Gretchen Williams bought Fairhaven and have been welcoming guests to their pleasant country home ever since.

Your cordial hostesses have nine guest bedrooms, including one on the ground floor with its own private bath. The upstairs rooms share three nicely appointed baths. All of the accommodations are spacious and very comfortable, decorated with handmade quilts and some antiques. The rooms in the front have a splendid view of the Kennebec River; 300 feet of the inn's property edge the water. Rooms at the rear look out on a wooded hillside. Guests may enjoy the Tavern, a BYOB bar with a fireplace and piano, and the comfortable Library with a large collection of books, color TV, stereo and another fireplace. Menus from restaurants in the area are provided to help you choose a good place for lunch or dinner. Outdoors, the flagstoned patio and tree-edged lawn are delightful spots to sit, contemplate the view, and soak up the country silence.

Breakfast at Grane's Fairhaven is a memorable experience, thanks to your hostesses' creative flair with food. A modest extra sum is charged for the feast, which is served in two charming dining rooms. Homemade muffins and breads are house specialties, along with delicious jams and jellies, also homemade. There will also be juices, fruits in season such as melon or bananas in French cream, hot and cold cereals, and one or two of the following: bacon, sausage or ham, scrapple, hash, a variety of egg dishes or a souffle of cheese or ham, an omelet or quiche, fruit pancakes, orange French toast or pecan waffles. And an "endless" cup of excellent coffee, tea or hot chocolate!

For activities, guests can start right at the house, which is surrounded by twenty-seven acres of lawns, woods and fields offering sunning, hiking, picnicking, cross-country skiing and snowshoeing. Reid State Park not far away has a fine beach for swimming, and picnic facilities. Golfing, boating and fishing are easily accessible, as are duck and deer hunting in the fall. The nearby towns of Bath, Brunswick, Wiscasset and Boothbay Harbor provide a wealth of shops, galleries and restaurants. (You'll need a car.) In addition there are the Performing Arts Center and Maine Marine Museum in Bath, and the Music Theater in Brunswick, for entertainment.

Grane's Fairhaven Inn, Bath Road, Bath, ME 04530; (207) 443-4391. (From Rte. 1 north of Brunswick, before reaching Bath, take New Meadows exit and follow signs about 3 miles north to Grane's Fairhaven. Look sharp for the last sign; it's at a sudden left turn just past the golf course.) Rates are moderately expensive; 4th, 5th and 6th nights $5 off for double room; one free night for a week's stay. Well-behaved children and pets (with advance notice) are welcome. Advance notice is also required for reservations. Open year-round.

The Roberts House. Situated right on Wiscasset's Main Street up a few steps from the old red brick sidewalk, this historic building dates

The Roberts House

back to approximately 1799. Francis Blyth, a trader, built the house for his wife on land provided by her father, Capt. Ebenezer Whittier (John Greenleaf Whittier's uncle). During the War of 1812, Captain Binney, leader of the regiment at Fort Edgecomb, occupied the place.

In the early 1970s, a local bank purchased the house, planning to raze it and erect a new bank building on the site. But irate depositors threatened to withdraw their money if such desecration were carried out, and so the handsome old Federal home was sold instead to Edward and Alice Roberts. They took ownership in 1973, and in 1981 (their two daughters grown up and away at school), the Robertses opened the house to guests.

There are three upstairs guest bedrooms done in blue and white, all with working fireplaces. Two baths are shared, one with tub and one with shower, and one room also has a sink. Guests are invited to use the pleasant downstairs sitting room with its comfortable chairs, a music room with a grand piano and books, and the spacious screened porch.

A full breakfast includes fresh fruit, homemade breads or muffins— perhaps including Alice Roberts' specialty, sourdough biscuits—and eggs, coffee, tea or cocoa. Your hostess always provides delicious extras, too, like stuffed mushrooms or tomatoes, or sausage. Native Maine blueberries are usually part of the repast. The hearty meal, served on English Wedgwood and Royal Worcester china, is offered in the dining room with its colorful Oriental rug or on the porch. Afternoon tea is also available, if requested. Mrs. Roberts will be delighted to recommend one of the area's many excellent restaurants for other meals. As the house is located right in the village, most of Wiscasset's shops and sites of interest are within easy walking distance.

The Roberts House, Main Street, P.O. Box 413, Wiscasset, ME 04578; (207) 882-5055. (Look for the blue and white sign out front.) Rates are moderately expensive, lower in winter and early spring. School-age children are welcome; no pets, please. Open May 15–Oct. 12, winter and spring by chance.

The Boothbay Region:
Boothbay Harbor/Damariscotta/Newcastle

The Boothbay Region lies east of Route 1 and is made up of several vacation communities. The main hub of activity is Boothbay Harbor, out at the end of one of the region's many peninsulas. To get there, turn right off Route 1 onto Route 27, shortly after crossing the bridge from Wiscasset. Thronged with visitors in summer, Boothbay Harbor is studded with boutiques and restaurants, and several types of boat excursions leave from its docks. The *Balmy Days* will take you to Monhegan, farthest out of the bay's chain of islands. The *Argo* offers shorter cruises around some of the other islands and a chance to see lobstermen at work, seals, and with luck, a rare bird such as an osprey. In early July an impressive parade of old sailing vessels takes place, along with other events, during Windjammer Days.

The twin villages of Newcastle and Damariscotta, separated by the Damariscotta River, are reached by returning to Route 1 and heading north for a few miles. The 1754 Chapman-Hall House in Damariscotta is open to the public and offers a fascinating glimpse into eighteenth-century life; the town also offers several good restaurants. From Damariscotta, take routes 129 and 130 out to Pemaquid Point, one of the most scenic Atlantic overlooks on the coast. There you will find rugged cliffs, granite ledges like a giant staircase down to the sea, sea gulls wheeling overhead and possibly a seal or two basking upon the rocks.

Kenniston Hill Inn. A charming country inn two miles north of Boothbay Harbor, Kenniston Hill is a 200-year-old Colonial house on three and a half acres of land. Hosts Ellen and Paul Morissette have eight rooms available for guests. Each of the rooms has been individually decorated with lovely antiques, poster beds and quilts. Four have working fireplaces and private baths; the other four share two baths. One room is on the ground floor. Guests may relax in a

living room with piano and fireplace, a large porch with rockers, a patio and several elaborate gardens. A full country breakfast features popovers, blueberry muffins, eggs Benedict or fritatta specialties, and brandy! The country club, a church, a general store and a post office are within walking distance of the house, and Boothbay Harbor is a short drive away.

Kenniston Hill Inn, Rte. 27, Boothbay Harbor, ME 04537; (207) 633-2159. Rates are moderately expensive; lower off season from April through June and November through December; 7-day packages and weekend specials are also available. Visa and MasterCard are accepted. Children over 12 are welcome; no pets, please. Open April–December.

The Brannon-Bunker Inn. Joe and Jeanne Hovance are the new owners of this attractive bed-and-breakfast inn in a quiet country setting about five miles south of Damariscotta. Your hosts are in the process of redecorating most of the rooms, adding antiques and other appropriate touches. Work on the Carriage House is completed, with stenciled walls, antique furniture and handmade quilts. The inn has ten rooms for guests including twins and doubles, plus a two-bedroom efficiency apartment, located in the Carriage House and barn. Three have private baths, and three of the rooms are on the ground floor. One of these is new, with a queen-size bed and private bath. Also new to the house is a large collection of military documents and pictures on the second floor. Three of the bedrooms and one bath offer views of the Damariscotta River. Guests are invited to enjoy the Publyk Room, a large lounge with TV and a fieldstone fireplace. Breakfast is served, family style, in the dining area: a variety of juices, fruits in season, homemade muffins and coffee cakes or breads, and coffee, tea or milk. There is a pond behind the house, and plenty of land for children and pets (well-behaved, please) to run off steam. Golf, tennis, ocean swimming, fishing, boating and canoeing are all available nearby. And last but by no means least, seals may sometimes be observed in the Damariscotta River at low tide.

The Brannon-Bunker Inn, Rte. 129, H.C.R. 64, Damariscotta, ME 04543; (207) 563-5941. (Take Rte. 1 to Business Rte. 1, Newcastle-Damariscotta, then go south on rtes. 130/129. When they split, about 3 miles from town, stay on Rte. 129 for another mile and a half.) Rates are moderately expensive. Visa and MasterCard are accepted. Children are welcome; pets are allowed but only in the Carriage House. Smoking is permitted only in the Publyk Room. Open year-round.

The Newcastle Inn. This large, turn-of-the-century New England inn is beautifully situated on the tidal Damariscotta River in Newcastle. Your hosts, Sandra Thomas and her family, have twenty guest rooms, including singles, doubles, one triple and one quadruple. Three are on the ground floor. Seven of the rooms have private baths; the others share four baths. All of the individually decorated accommodations are furnished with antiques. For relaxing, there are a pleasant living room with fireplace, a TV room, and a spacious enclosed porch that overlooks the gardens and bay. A full breakfast is served in the dining room each morning: juice, eggs, bacon, French toast or Sandra's famous buttermilk pancakes, and coffee or tea.

The nearby towns of Newcastle and Damariscotta offer shops of all kinds and several good restaurants; Pemaquid Point and Boothbay Harbor are less than a half hour away. And for guests who would like to experience a sail along the rocky coastline of Maine, charter sailing is available nearby.

The Newcastle Inn, Rte. 1, Newcastle, ME 04553; (207) 563-5685 or 563-8878. Rates are moderate, lower off season. Well-behaved children are welcome; no pets, please. Open year-round.

The Captain's House. The Captain's House in Newcastle, perched on a hill overlooking the Damariscotta River, was constructed in 1840 by Capt. Farley Hopkins. His descendants lived in the house until Cathy and Kirk Schlemmer purchased it in 1983. Your friendly young hosts have four bedrooms for guests, including one on the ground floor, sharing two baths. Two have double beds, one has a double and a twin, and one—suitable for four persons—offers two double beds. The accommodations are spacious, bright and airy with handsome hardwood floors downstairs and wide pine floors on the second story. The guest rooms are nicely furnished in antiques refinished by your hosts, antique quilts and handmade afghans.

For cool nights, two working fireplaces and a wood stove on the first floor add a comforting touch. Guests are welcome to share the pleasant sitting room with TV and stereo, cards, games and a small

library. In warmer weather, the wide front porch—with a swing—is a delightful place to sit and admire the view. A full breakfast is served on a wide wooden table in the breakfast room. You'll find juice, fresh fruit, homemade granola, eggs, freshly baked breads and homemade jam. Kirk is renowned for his cinnamon raisin bread; Cathy's specialties are fruit muffins and breads (blueberry, banana or datenut), and Scottish scones. The attractive village of Damariscotta is within easy walking distance for restaurants and shops.

The Captain's House, Rte. 1, Box 19, River Road, Newcastle, ME 04553; (207) 563-1482. (From Rte. 1 going north, exit River Road/Newcastle and go .8 mile. From Rte. 1 going south, exit Newcastle and follow Rte. 215 south ½ mile to River Road.) Rates are moderate; no charge for children up to 3. Well-behaved children are welcome; no pets, please, and no smoking. Open year-round.

South Thomaston/Rockport/ Camden/Searsport

Continuing northeast on Route 1 you'll come to the small city of Rockland, Maine's foremost lobster-catching port. A four-day seafood festival is held here each August, with parades, bands, and— naturally—lobsters to eat. From the Maine State Ferry Terminal you can take a ferry ride out to the islands of Vinalhaven and North Haven. South Thomaston is south of Rockland, out on yet another scenic peninsula. Just north of Rockland, off Route 1, is the tiny community of Rockport, home of Andre the seal. Famous Andre was found abandoned as a pup by Harry Goodridge of Rockport, who raised the seal to stay wild. But proximity to people appealed to Andre more than life with other seals out in the open sea. Eventually he grew too fond of human company and overturned a few small boats in his efforts to make friends. Now Andre spends his summers in a special water pen in Rockport's harbor and winters in the Mystic Marine Life Aquarium in Mystic, Connecticut. Each spring the plump gray harbor seal is flown to the tip of Cape Cod, from where he embarks on his annual swim back home to Rockport, a distance of some 230 miles. Andre usually makes the trip in five or six days. Thousands of tourists come to Rockport Harbor every summer to watch the seal perform an extensive routine of tricks for his old friend Goodridge.

Camden, eight miles north of Rockport, vies with Wiscasset for the title of Maine's prettiest town. Camden's waterfront is unusually striking, even for Maine. A mountain stream tumbles headlong down from the rounded hills behind, becoming a full-fledged waterfall as it crashes thunderously into the harbor below. Next to it a grassy park offers a perfect spot to sit and observe the scene. In summer, visitors can admire Camden's famous Windjammer fleet and take sailing trips along the coast on several of the old-time schooners. The town also offers a wide choice of good restaurants and appealing shops. For a splendid view of Penobscot Bay, drive up 1300-foot Mt. Battie, just northeast of town. The only ski area on the coast is nearby, too—the Camden Snow Bowl.

Searsport is a famous old seafaring town, about twenty miles north of Camden on Penobscot Bay. Still active in marine commerce today,

Searsport ships out massive quantities of potatoes as well as a host of other Maine products. The excellent Penobscot Marine Museum—comprising six separate historic structures—houses collections of ship models, Oriental and American furnishings, nautical memorabilia and portraits of almost 300 sea captains, all of whom lived in the town.

Sign of the Unicorn Guest House. Unicorns (stuffed), and bears, sheep and other appealing creatures are very much in evidence in Winnie Easton's guest house in Rockport. You'll also find books and flowers galore, and prints, paintings, photographs and sculpture. Your hostess, a teacher, photographer, musician, artist and poet, has traveled extensively, lived in France for five years and speaks French, she says, "with gusto and grammatical errors!" Her house, built in the 1870s by a sea captain, is a modified Down East Victorian, overlooking Rockport Harbor. There are four rooms for guests (five in the off season) and three baths.

The upstairs Front Room, with a peach carpet, has a grand view of the harbor and is furnished with a double bed, wicker, antiques and old quilts. The Twin Room, also upstairs, has twin beds, a pine chest, a desk and comfortable chairs. Downstairs, the White Room boasts a grand piano and other musical instruments, floor-to-ceiling (well-filled) bookshelves, a double bed and a twin, old family quilts, white carpeting, and a harbor view. The Great Room, which is mostly used as a gathering room for guests, may be rented as a four-person sleeping room. With a spectacular twenty-four-foot glass wall overlooking the harbor and a sleeping loft, the Great Room is done in California contemporary with a deep sun-color carpet and diagonal pine boards, books (of course!) and plants. Sound-insulated, the room is perfect for families with infants or a young child.

Breakfast at the Unicorn is an occasion: Winnie Easton claims, "We spoil people rottener than they are!" Guests will enjoy homemade breads or muffins (blueberry, apple, orange, spice, bran and others); "French Toast-with-Orange-and-a-Nip"; "Snail Eggs" (eggs done in snail butter sauce with parsley, garlic and cognac) or perhaps blueberry pancakes or omelets with onions, cheese and tarragon or dill; hot, old-fashioned "overnight" oatmeal or homemade granola; fresh fruit salad; coffee or tea. Herb iced tea, lemonade or iced coffee will cool you off after a day's sightseeing, or perhaps there'll be wine and cheese as a sunset snack. A hearty supper soup may be offered in wintertime. Guests, by the way, are encouraged to use the kitchen, which has—in addition to more than 150 cookbooks—everything a cook could wish in the way of appliances. Cook-ins are a regular happening, according to Winnie, who adds, "We love celebrating *anything!*"

An excellent restaurant right on the harbor, a gourmet shop, and (in summer) Rockport's renowned Andre the seal are within walking distance. Your hostess will tell you about nearby boat rentals, horseback riding, freshwater or ocean swimming, concerts and much more.

Sign of the Unicorn Guest House, P.O. Box 99, Rockport, ME 04856; (207) 236-8789 or answering machine (207) 236-4042. (End of Mechanic Street; ask for directions when you call or write for reservations.) Rates are moderately expensive, lower Nov. 1–April 1 and for longer stays. Children (civilized, kind, considerate ones) are very welcome; no pets except by prior arrangement. Non-smokers preferred, but considerate smokers are accepted. Open year-round except for Thanksgiving and Christmas.

Goodspeed's Guest House. Don and Linda Goodspeed may hold the record for swift accomplishment of a goal. In 1981, while touring New

England, the couple discovered Camden and were captivated by the town's charm. The Goodspeeds had spent three years in Europe, where they traveled extensively and developed a fondness for that continent's delightful bed-and-breakfast establishments. Finding that none existed in Camden at that time, they decided to open one of their own. Moving purposefully, they located just the house they wanted—a handsome old place built in 1879—and bought it in only one hour's time! The couple then proceeded to shift rooms around and extensively remodel the interior, re-creating its original appearance as closely as possible. Goodspeed's Guest House, hosted by Don and Linda and their daughter Lisa, began welcoming guests in June, 1982.

Tastefully furnished throughout in period decor, the house now offers ten guest rooms including two singles, six doubles and a two-room suite; the rooms share five baths. Five of the guest bedrooms are on the ground floor. Wide-plank white oak floors set off attractive country-style wallpaper and stained-glass windows; wicker furniture and antique beds, greenery and crisp white linen curtains add to the ambiance. A collection of antique clocks is displayed in the three common rooms. There's also an outside deck for sunbathing. Breakfast, served in the pleasant dining room, consists of freshly squeezed juice, homemade muffins and breads, Danish and coffee or tea.

Goodspeed's Guest House, 60 Mountain St. (Rte. 52), Camden, ME 04843; (207) 236-8077. Rates are moderately expensive; extra cot in room available

for a small extra fee. Children over 12 are welcome; no pets, please. Open June 1–Oct. 15.

Edgecombe-Coles House. Set on a hillside overlooking Penobscot Bay, the Edgecombe-Coles House in Camden is a beautiful place. The oldest part of the house, the wing that contains the kitchen, was originally a farmhouse built in the mid-1800s. The rest of the spacious house was added in 1890, creating an elegant summer "cottage" for a wealthy Chicago family. A broad expanse of lawn fronts the house; at the rear there are a flower garden and view of the woods.

Your hosts, Terry and Louise Price, have restored the house and have furnished it throughout with antiques, original artwork and Oriental rugs. There are five upstairs guest rooms: four doubles and one triple. Three of the rooms have private baths and two rooms share a bath. The largest guest room offers a king-size brass bed, a working fireplace and a stunning view of the Bay and islands. Another has pineapple-top four-poster twin beds, and a third has an ornate brass and iron bed with a queen-size mattress. A "suite," with sitting room, is furnished with country painted pieces. All of the guest beds have antique handmade bedspreads, quilts or coverlets. Small black-and-white TVs are available for the rooms if guests desire. And you will find the added amenities of bedside candy, fresh flowers and potpourri, and fluffy towels.

Downstairs are a large living room with a fireplace, baby grand piano and ocean view, and a small library/den also with a fireplace and view of the water. A full breakfast, served in the dining room or in the garden, consists of a choice of juices, fruit, homebaked breads and muffins, egg dishes, sausage, bacon or ham, or seafood. The Prices sometimes offer a house specialty called "Dutch Babies," a cross between a giant popover and pancake, crab and almond or fiddlehead fern omelets, and Mimosas (champagne and orange juice). Freshly ground coffee, a choice of brewed teas or milk rounds out the delicious fare.

Edgecombe-Coles House, 64 High St., Rte. 1) Camden, ME 04843; (207) 236-2336. (Six-tenths of a mile north of town center on Rte. 1.) Rates are moderately expensive to expensive, lower from the end of October through the end of June, approximately, and for longer stays; ski packages and weekday discounts are available in winter. Visa and MasterCard are accepted. Children over 8 are welcome; pets are allowed by prior arrangement only. Open year-round.

J. Sloan Inn. Mary DuRoss is your warmly welcoming hostess at this friendly bed-and-breakfast inn in Camden. An 1870 Victorian, consisting of the house and remodeled barn, the J. Sloan Inn is named after Mary's young son. Five rooms are available for guests: the Skylight Room with double bed and semi-private bath; the New England Room with double bed and semi-private bath; the Parlor Room with double

J. Sloan Inn

bed and semi-private bath; the Victorian Two-Seater Room with double bed and semi-private bath, and the Loft Suite with two double beds, sitting areas and a private bath. The rooms are furnished with antiques, and, as Mary DuRoss puts it, "are laidback, very elegant fun!" Guests are invited to share the comfortable living room and enclosed sun porch. The house is right at the foot of Mt. Battie; a hiking path starts from the back yard. Camden's many attractions are within walking distance, and your hostess will be pleased to offer suggestions on all manner of things to do or see in the area.

From Monday through Saturday breakfast is served buffet style at 8 a.m., with choices of sweet rolls, muffins and breads, fresh fruit, orange juice, cheese, an egg dish and Mary's excellent coffee. On Sundays there is a lavish 10 a.m. champagne brunch, buffet style, with a choice of croissants, sweet rolls, breads or bagels; an egg dish or waffles with sausage, ham or bacon; seafood and chicken salads; fresh fruit; coffee, and a glass of champagne.

J. Sloan Inn, 49 Mountain St. (Rte. 52), Camden, ME 04843; (207) 236-8275. (At junction of rtes. 1 and 52—blinking light—turn left onto Rte. 52 and go up hill 3½ blocks; the inn's blue sign will be on the right.) Rates are moderately expensive to expensive, lower in winter and for longer stays. Well-behaved children over 5 are welcome; no pets, please. Open May–March.

The Carriage House Inn. Set well off the road at the end of a long, circular driveway, this stately Victorian mansion in Searsport was built in 1874 by John McGilvrey, a clipper ship captain. Waldo Peirce, a renowned Maine artist, later owned the house and established his studio there. Ernest Hemingway, a friend of Peirce's, stayed at the house on several occasions during the 1950s. The gracious old mansion, listed in the National Register of Historic Places, is now owned by Nancy and Susan Nogueira. Your hostesses have six large, comfortable guest bedrooms including three doubles, two triples and a suite. Two rooms have a private bath; the others share. The front sitting room with a fireplace and view of Penobscot Bay is a nice place to relax any time of the year; in winter the room is especially appealing with a cheerful log fire blazing away. A shop on the premises, located below Waldo Peirce's old studio in the attached carriage house, offers antiques, collectibles and contemporary gifts. Guests receive a courtesy discount. Breakfast at the Carriage House consists of a choice of juice, fresh fruit, homemade muffins and breads, and coffee, tea or

hot chocolate, served in the candlelit dining room. Afternoon tea, a pleasant custom, is also served.

The Carriage House Inn, East Main Street (Rte. 1), Box 238, Searsport, ME 04974; (207) 548-2289. (Just north of town.) Rates are moderately expensive, lower for children and for longer stays. Visa, MasterCard and American Express are accepted. Well-supervised children and pets are welcome, but pets must be under strict supervision. Open year-round.

Acadia National Park/Bar Harbor/ Southwest Harbor/Little Cranberry Island

Maine folk don't ordinarily take to superlatives, but even they would probably describe Acadia National Park as "finest-kind." The startling beauty of Maine's seacoast is so concentrated here that it almost hurts the senses. It's not a gentle beauty, the meeting of mountains, forest and sea—it is awesome, and unforgettable.

To reach the park, and Bar Harbor, take Route 3 off Route 1 in Ellsworth to Mt. Desert Island. The park extends over some fifty square miles; follow Ocean Drive and Loop Road for a twenty-mile drive up Mt. Cadillac, out to Great Head—a sheer headland jutting over the Atlantic—and past Thunder Hole where the sea surges in, booming and echoing against the ancient rocks. At the Visitor Center, three miles northwest of Bar Harbor off Route 3, you will find park rangers who give guided walks and cruises. Hikers and horseback riders can roam over 100 miles of woodland trails. From the peak of 1530-foot Mt. Cadillac, highest point on the East Coast, early risers can be the first in the United States to greet the morning sun.

The French explorer Samuel de Champlain discovered the island in 1604, and named it *L'Isle des Monts Deserts*. "Desert," pronounced with the accent on the second syllable, means "uninhabited and wild." Bar Harbor, on the eastern shore of the island, was once a small, sleepy fishing village. In 1844, a visiting artist who was captivated by the area carried back word of its spectacular beauty. Affluent families from Boston and Philadelphia began to journey north in ever-growing numbers to spend their summers. Sprawling hotels were built to house them, and a vast number of mansions almost as opulent as the "cottages" of Newport were constructed.

Bar Harbor's solid gold way of life, at its peak around the turn of the century, slowly went into decline in later years. The Depression, two World Wars, the imposition of income taxes and the lack of servants pretty much put an end to the glorious era of lavish living. The Great Fire of 1947 was the final blow. All of the grand old hotels and seventy of the mansions were destroyed. The fire also devastated the forests along a great stretch of the coast. The trees have come back; the glittering, leisurely life of the late 1800s has not, and never will. But Bar Harbor and Acadia National Park are now accessible to more people than ever. Different people . . . like us. Bar Harbor today is as pretty as it ever was, with its hills and views of water and fir-covered islands. And many of the surviving splendid old mansions now welcome overnight guests.

In addition to famous Bar Harbor, Mt. Desert Island offers a number of smaller, quieter towns such as Southwest Harbor. Only a short drive from the bustle of Bar Harbor, the tiny village is authentic Maine, with a lobster wharf and a boat building industry. Just beyond Mt. Desert Island, Little Cranberry Island—reached by a ferry from Northeast Harbor—provides another peaceful haven for travelers.

The Manor House Inn. Col. James Foster, a builder and veteran of the Civil War, began construction of this striking twenty-two-room Victorian mansion in 1887. Frank and Jan Matter purchased the house in 1977; their restoration efforts were rewarded in 1980 when the mansion was included in the National Register as a significant part of the West Street Historic District—the only lodging place in Bar Harbor to be so honored. For guests the Matters have fourteen double bedrooms and suites, including one on the ground floor. All have

40

private baths, four of the rooms have working fireplaces, and all are beautifully furnished with circa 1880 antiques. The accommodations are located in "Boscobel," the mansion itself, and the restored original chauffeur's cottage. There are also two completely equipped cottages on the landscaped grounds. Five gardens, including a double crescent formal garden and a shade garden, are delightful to see. For relaxation, guests are invited to share two first-floor parlors, each with antique furnishings and a fireplace boasting a fine Victorian mantel, and a third-floor sitting room with TV. In hot weather, the spacious veranda provides a cool retreat. Breakfast at the inn consists of juice, cereal, in-season fruits, native blueberry muffins and homebaked breads, and a wide selection of coffees and teas.

The Manor House Inn, 106 West St., Bar Harbor, ME 04609; (207) 288-3759. Rates are expensive. Visa, MasterCard and American Express are accepted. The Matters also offer a Spring Special (three nights for the price of two) including a complimentary bottle of wine, from April 15 through May 20. Children over 14 are welcome; no pets, please, and no smoking in the public rooms. Open April 15–Nov. 15.

Mira Monte Inn. Bar Harbor's oldest inn and one of the town's oldest existing houses, Mira Monte was built in 1864 by the son of an early settler. Its first guests were summer visitors who had "discovered" the island when they purchased paintings from artists of the Hudson River School. The inn acquired the name Mira Monte in 1892. Conveniently situated only a few blocks from downtown Bar Harbor, the Georgian-style house is set amidst spacious grounds and gardens. Your gracious hostess, Marian Burns, is in the process of restoring the Victorian gardens, where guests may picnic and play badminton, croquet and horseshoes; a second terrace has recently been added. Your hostess has completed restoration of the interior rooms of the house, and is continually adding interesting period furnishings,

Mira Monte Inn

which she finds at antique auctions. Her restoration efforts also include newly added bay windows and porches or balconies. Ask Miss Burns to tell you about Bar Harbor's fascinating early history; she is a native of the town and very knowledgeable.

Mira Monte offers eleven rooms for guests, all with private baths. Three of the rooms are on the ground floor. Guests are invited to enjoy the library with a piano, fireplace and games; the living room, also with a fireplace and books; broad porches and a terrace. Breakfast features homemade blueberry and some other flavor of muffins, and in the afternoon complimentary wine and cheese are offered. Refrigerators are available for keeping soft drinks or fruit, and guests may make their own coffee or tea at any time. Mira Monte guests are offered guest privileges at a prestigious country club nearby for a modest daily fee; the club has six clay tennis courts and an Olympic-size swimming pool.

The Mira Monte Inn, 69 Mt. Desert St. (Rte. 3), Bar Harbor, ME 04609; (207) 288-4263. Rates are moderately expensive to expensive. Visa, MasterCard and American Express are accepted. Children are welcome; no pets, please. Open May 1–Nov. 1.

Thornhedge. Victorian Thornhedge is owned by Alonzo and Elinor Geel, son Dana, and daughter-in-law Anne. The three-story yellow and white mansion was built around 1900 by Lewis A. Roberts, a retired Boston publisher, as his summer home. Roberts published Louisa May Alcott's *Little Women*. Many of the original furnishings are still in evidence, including Chinese tables and a gilt 1810 Phoenix mirror in the foyer. The dining room has leaded windows and mahogany period furniture including Chippendale chairs; the salon contains a satinwood tilt-top table, a Hepplewhite kettle bench and a pair of Hepplewhite chairs with their original exquisite coverings. Ten rooms, several with fireplaces, are available for guests; all have private baths. Four of the rooms are on the ground floor, and all of the guest quarters are named for mansions that were destroyed by the 1947 fire. Each room contains a photograph and write-up about the mansion and its owner. In addition to the three public rooms, there is a spacious front porch with wicker and old wrought-iron chairs for relaxing. A continental breakfast of homemade muffins and breads (blueberry and bran muffins, lemon and pumpkin breads are specialties of the house), juice and coffee is served in the dining room.

The Geels also operate another establishment directly behind Thornhedge, called 20 Roberts Guest House. Another Victorian turn-of-the-century home, 20 Roberts has six guest rooms; one has a private bath and the other rooms share baths. Continental breakfast is served daily.

Thornhedge and 20 Roberts, 47 Mt. Desert St., Bar Harbor, ME 04609; (207) 288-5398. Rates are moderately expensive to expensive. Visa, MasterCard and American Express are accepted. Children are welcome; no pets, please. Open April 15–Oct. 15.

Stratford House Inn. Norman and Barbara Moulton's handsome Bar Harbor "cottage" was built in 1900. Styled after William Shakespeare's sixteenth-century birthplace in Stratford-on-Avon, England, the English Tudor house contains beautiful antiques and furnishings from the Jacobean period. The first floor is paneled in ornately carved black oak. For guests, there are ten large upstairs rooms, appointed

with four-poster mahogany or brass bow-bottom beds; three of the rooms have working fireplaces. Seven of the guest rooms have private baths; three share a bath. The antique-filled library, where a cheerful blaze burns nightly in the fireplace in cool weather, is a charming place to relax and meet other guests. A continental breakfast is served in the elegant dining room each morning: juice, muffins, and coffee.

Stratford House Inn, 45 Mt. Desert St., Bar Harbor, ME 04609; (207) 288-5189. Rates range from moderately expensive to expensive; children under 5 free.

Visa, MasterCard and American Express are accepted. Children are welcome; no pets, please. Open May–Oct. 31.

Holbrook Inn. A twenty-room summer cottage built in 1876, Holbrook Inn has been restored to its former ambiance and furnished with a comfortable mixture of Colonial and Victorian pieces. Hosts Richard and Patricia Grant, and son Alan and his wife Violet, have twelve rooms for guests. There are eleven doubles and one triple; three have private baths. Five of the rooms are on the ground floor. Four-poster beds (some with canopies), mahogany chests, and Oriental and braided rugs are some of the inn's inviting features. Guests are welcome to share the living room, a large sun room and an open piazza. Your hosts' many interesting collections, including baskets, toys, glass, old kitchen utensils and an extensive collection of dolls, may be seen and enjoyed throughout the house. Breakfast, of homebaked coffee cake or blueberry muffins, juice, coffee, tea or milk is served in the sun room, as are late afternoon refreshments of wine, cheese and crackers.

Holbrook Inn, 74 Mt. Desert St., Bar Harbor, ME 04609; (207) 288-4970. Rates are moderately expensive, lower May 1–June 14 and Oct. 15–Oct. 31. Visa, MasterCard and American Express are accepted. Children are welcome; no pets, please. Open May 1–Oct. 31.

Hearthside Inn. This pleasantly appointed home, built in 1909, is decorated in the style of a pretty summer cottage, with a charming

blend of antiques and contemporary pieces. Flower-filled windowboxes add a colorful touch to the shingled exterior. Lois Gregg offers travelers nine inviting guest rooms. The house was originally owned by a doctor who conducted his practice from his home, and the first-floor guest bedroom—which once was his waiting room—is appropriately named "The Doctor's Room." It has a double and a twin bed, a fireplace, oak bookcases and a private bath. Four rooms, surrounding a large hall with access to a pleasant porch, are reached via a staircase from the entrance foyer. The "Blue Room" has a working fireplace and a private bath. The "Library Room," featuring book-lined shelves, a bay window with cozy window seat, and a private balcony, shares a bath with the intimate "Green Room." The grand "Master Bedroom," with private bath, can sleep four. Four more attractive guest rooms are on the third floor; all have private baths. A living room with books, comfortable chairs and a fireplace for chilly evenings is a pleasant place to read or socialize. There are also a music room with a grand piano and games, and a secluded porch and walled patio. Breakfast, of juice, homemade muffins, cold cereals, and coffee or tea, is served each morning; complimentary wine is offered in the evenings in the living room.

Hearthside Inn, 7 High St., Bar Harbor, ME 04609; (207) 288-4533. Rates are moderately expensive. Visa and MasterCard are accepted. Children over 10 are welcome; no pets, please. Open June 20–Oct. 18.

Cleftstone Manor. A rambling thirty-room mansion perched on a hill just outside Bar Harbor Village, Cleftstone Manor was built in 1894 as a summer home for James Blair, Secretary of the Navy under President Lincoln. (The Blair family also owned the Blair House, across from the White House in Washington, D.C.) The Manor was designed by Joseph Price, architect of the famed Chateau Frontenac in Quebec, and is just as impressive today as it was when the wealthy Blairs were in residence. Don and Phyllis Jackson and their two children, your present-day hosts, purchased the place in 1981 and opened its doors to guests the following year.

The mansion's eighteen guest chambers are decorated with Victorian antiques, hand-crocheted bedspreads, goosedown comforters, heavy lace curtains and Oriental rugs. Several of the spacious double rooms, thirteen with private baths, have fireplaces or balconies. Four of the guest rooms are on the ground floor. Guests are invited to enjoy three immense formal rooms and a quiet, second-floor library; on cool evenings fires blaze in two fireplaces. A lavish buffet breakfast

is served in the dining room, with juices, fruit salad, several varieties of homebaked muffins, poppyseed or fruit coffee cakes, popovers, coffee and imported tea. In the afternoon, from 4 to 5, a formal English tea features inn-baked Scottish shortbread, scones or "tassies," or perhaps Phyllis's prize-winning Apricot Strudel, and the tea is served from an elegant silver service in heirloom china cups. Each evening, your hosts hold a wine and cheese party from 8 to 10; all of these pleasant amenities are complimentary. A charming Victorian garden, with lawn games, is a nice place to roam outdoors. Guest privileges at the Bar Harbor Country Club are offered at a modest fee, and the Jacksons will arrange horseback rides for interested guests. Downtown Bar Harbor is a ten-minute walk or short drive. For travelers searching for a new experience, your hosts' son Barry and his wife Susan operate a hot-air balloon flight-service, called Omawki Balloon Adventures.

Cleftstone Manor, 92 Eden St. (Rte. 3), Bar Harbor, ME 04609; (207) 288-4951. Rates range from moderate to expensive. Visa, MasterCard and American Express are accepted. Well-behaved children over 12 are welcome; no pets, please, and smoking is limited to certain areas. Open May 15–Oct. 15.

Lindenwood Inn. Over on "the quiet side" of Mt. Desert Island in Southwest Harbor, Don Johnson's turn-of-the-century Lindenwood Inn offers a pleasant respite from the summertime crowds in Bar Harbor. Although built as a sea captain's home, the house is not a typical New England structure but was designed in the "Prairie Style"

more commonly seen in the Midwest. The captain called it "The Lindens" because of the stately trees that still line the front lawn. There are six double upstairs guest rooms (with down comforters for cool weather) in the main house, each decorated individually, and all but one have water views; three baths are shared. In addition, a cottage (accessible for the handicapped) with living room, a double bedroom and twin-bedded sleeping loft and private patio is available by the week. The inn's common rooms—a spacious, cypress-paneled entryway with TV and stereo, and the comfortable living room with plenty of reading material and an unusual corner fireplace—are open to guests at all times. Your host serves breakfast by the fire in the paneled dining room, offering one of the following each day: blueberry pancakes, French toast, baked scrambled eggs with blueberry muffins, or the house specialty, Cheddar and bacon quiche with baked tomato. Baked grapefruit, melon, or fruit salad start off the morning feast. On summer afternoons mint tea and sweets are offered on the porch; in the fall guests can enjoy apple crunch and tea or cider in front of a cheery fire. The harbor and lobster wharf are a short walk away; Acadia National Park is a few minutes' drive, as is Bar Harbor.

Lindenwood Inn, P.O. Box 1328, Southwest Harbor, Me 04679; (207) 244-5335. (Follow Rte. 102 south to the center of town, turn left on Clark Point Rd. and go ½ mile; Lindenwood is on the water side.) Rates are moderate, lower from Labor Day through June 15. Children 10 and older are welcome; no pets, please. Open year-round.

Penury Hall. Toby Strong, who with wife Gretchen operates Penury Hall in Southwest Harbor, replies thusly when asked about the house's name: "Penury—state of being without funds; broke; poor. Literal translation, 'The Poor House.' Confuses people sometimes." The rambling old house was built in 1830, added on to in 1865 and 1900, and has been remodeled by your hosts into a comfortable, informal guest house. Three upstairs rooms are available for guests; two baths are shared. The house reflects the Strongs' interests in art, antiques, books, gardening and sailing. (Guests who enjoy boating may hire a canoe, windsurfer or sloop.) Penury Hall offers a pleasantly relaxed ambiance and guests have complete freedom of the house. Gretchen is the Town Manager; while she accomplishes the job's duties, Toby handles the housekeeping and cooking, and his breakfast menu is impressive. Guests may choose juice, fruit compote, melon or other seasonal fruit, eggs Benedict, blueberry pancakes, "Penurious Omelet," date-walnut French toast, poached eggs and hash, or your favorite kind of eggs with muffins, accompanied by homemade jams and jellies, pure maple syrup and a variety of coffees and teas, or milk.

Penury Hall Bed 'n' Breakfast, Box 68, Main Street, Southwest Harbor, ME 04679; (207) 244-7102. (The gray house with red door and white porch trim on Main Street, 99 yards past blinker on right toward Manset.) Rates are moderate, lower Nov. 1–April 1. Mature children are welcome; no pets, please (two cats are in residence). Open year-round.

Island Bed & Breakfast. Sue Jones welcomes guests to her nice old house on Little Cranberry Island, a short ferry ride away from Mt. Desert Island. The turn-of-the-century house is furnished with Sue's collection of antiques of the period, many of which came from other houses on the island. There are three upstairs guest rooms: two doubles with a shared bath and one family bedroom. Antique quilts

Island Bed & Breakfast

cover the beds. The living room, with a wood stove to take the chill off cool mornings and evenings, contains a good selection of Maine books, puzzles and games. A side porch and ample lawn offer more space for sitting. Breakfast consists of juice, melon or other fruit in season, cereal, homemade bran and blueberry muffins, freshly ground coffee, or tea. Guests are invited to use the refrigerator for storing wine or snacks. Sue's house is located in the center of the small town of Islesboro, a minute's walk from the docks, restaurant, and shops, including a general store. It's a quiet town, ideal for travelers interested in nature, walks along the shore and a glimpse of Maine island life.

Island Bed & Breakfast, Box 275, Islesford (Little Cranberry Island), ME 04646; (207) 244-9283 or 244-5029. (Leave your car in ferry parking lot in Northeast Harbor; take the Beal & Bunker Ferry to the island. Walk up wharf, following road; bear right up the hill past the church; take the right fork. The house, with blue door and sign, is the 3rd on the right. Less than a 5-minute walk.) Rates are moderate, lower for longer stays. Children are welcome; pets may be allowed if prior arrangements are made. No smoking except on porch. Open June–Sept. 30.

Central and Western Maine

Augusta

Augusta, in central Maine, is the state capital. Situated on the Kennebec River, the city began as a trading post, established in 1628 by Pilgrims from Massachusetts. A fort was later constructed on the site of the post (opposite present-day City Hall) as a defense against the Indians. Today it houses the Fort Western Museum, with reconstructed stockades, barracks and blockhouses. Augusta visitors will also enjoy a visit to the impressive State House, partly designed by Charles Bulfinch, and Blaine House, a Colonial sea captain's home now serving as the governor's mansion.

Crosby's Bed and Breakfast. One of Augusta's most beautiful old houses, this white Italianate-style home with a cupola on its roof was built in 1904. David and Joyce Crosby have redecorated and refurbished the place and offer five spacious upstairs rooms for guests: one single, three doubles and one triple. One room has a private bath; the others share two and a half baths. The house's high-ceilinged rooms also include a large living room, a mahogany-paneled library with fireplace, and a formal breakfast-dining room

with a lovely crystal chandelier; antiques abound throughout. The complete breakfast includes juice, muffins or coffee cake, eggs and bacon or sausage, hot or cold cereals, and fruit. The Crosbys do not normally serve dinner, but will provide an evening meal by special request at extra charge. Laundry facilities, for a modest fee, are also available. The house is in a quiet, residential neighborhood; Augusta's downtown area, shopping malls and the State Capitol Complex are within a few minutes' walk.

Crosby's Bed and Breakfast, 51 Green St., Augusta, ME 04330; (207) 622-1861. (From Maine Turnpike, take Exit 15; from I-95 take Exit 30. Travel east on Western Avenue, Rte. 202, 1¼ miles; at 6th traffic light turn left onto Sewall Street and then right on Green Street. Crosby's is the second house on the left.) Rates are moderately expensive, lower for longer stays. Visa and MasterCard are accepted. Children are welcome; no pets, please. Open year-round.

Bridgton/Waterford

This scenic section of western Maine is a region of low mountains, winding country roads and many lakes. Most of the blue, fir-edged lakes are small, except for beautiful Sebago, a popular summer resort area. Second largest of the state's innumerable bodies of water (Moosehead is the biggest), Sebago is sixteen miles long and ten miles wide. Bridgton lies just northwest of Lake Sebago, near Long Lake, and Waterford is north of Bridgton. Each of these small Maine communities offers its own distinct charm: Bridgton is famed for its large collection of antique shops, and Waterford, one of New England's most enchanting villages, has been designated a National Historic Site. The town, with a pocket-sized village green, a brook running swiftly under the road and only a handful of buildings, does not appear to have changed much in the past two centuries.

The 1859 Guest House. Located in Bridgton, the 1859 Guest House is owned by Mary S. Zeller and her husband, Dr. William W. Zeller. The foundation of the house is actually circa 1820; the original structure, which burned in the late 1830s, was another of Maine's old taverns and stagecoach stops. Of Federal design, the present building on the site is appropriately furnished with Federal, Empire and Victorian pieces from Dr. Zeller's family. Your host is also a clock collector, and there are almost 100 clocks on view throughout the house. And Dr. Zeller very much enjoys talking about his treasures!

Two twin or double upstairs guest rooms are available, sharing a bath. Guests may also use the living room and spacious outside porch. Breakfast at The 1859 Guest House is a lavish affair ... Mary Zeller notes that she and her husband are of Pennsylvania German background and enjoy a large meal in the mornings! Served in the sun room in summer and in the kitchen by the fireplace in winter, breakfast consists of fruit (featuring local berries in season), hot or cold cereals, eggs any style, breakfast meat and homemade breads, cakes and rolls. Mrs. Zeller presents the feast beautifully, using her best china, crystal, silver and linens.

A public beach a block away offers a view of Mt. Washington; canoeing, boating and fishing are available nearby in summer. Pleasant Mountain Ski Area, five miles away, offers an Alpine slide in summer and fine skiing in winter. Antique and craft shops abound in the area and there are several fine restaurants not far away.

The 1859 Guest House, 60 S. High St., Bridgton, ME 04009; (207) 647-2508. (Corner of S. High and Rte. 302.) Rates are moderate. Children are welcome; no pets, please. Open year-round.

The Artemus Ward House. Situated on Keoka Lake in Waterford Village, this historic Federal house is owned by Lynn Baker. Built by Calvin Farrar in 1805, the house later became the home of his grandson, Charles Farrar Browne, the renowned nineteenth-century humorist known as Artemus Ward. Browne, born in 1834, spent his childhood years here. After his father's death, the young man was apprenticed to a printer in Lancaster, New Hampshire, but soon ran away to work on small newspapers around Maine. Eventually, Browne

moved West and worked himself up from printer's devil to journalist on the Cleveland *Plain Dealer.* There he invented Artemus Ward, and until his death in England at age 33 (he is buried in South Waterford, Maine), Browne wrote and lectured as his dryly humorous alter ego. Browne/Ward's satirical views of the world can be compared to those of his friend and contemporary, Mark Twain. In case you're not familiar with his work, the brochure for the Artemus Ward House includes this sample of his writings, taken from *Affairs Around the Village Green:*

> The village from which I write to you is small. It does not contain over forty houses, all told; but they are milk white, with the greenest of blinds, and for the most part are shaded with beautiful elms and willows. To the right of us is a mountain—to the left a lake. The village nestles between. Of course it does. I never read a novel in my life in which the villages didn't nestle. Villages invariably nestle. It is a kind of way they have.

The Artemus Ward House, which is (of course!) white with green trim, offers five spacious, airy rooms for guests. One of the rooms is on the ground floor. All of the sunny, comfortable accommodations are tastefully decorated and very appealing. Three have private baths and two connecting rooms share a bath. Guests are invited to use the informal lounge/sitting room with a wood stove and a more formal living room with a fireplace.

Wake-up morning coffee or tea, and a full country breakfast consisting of juice, fruit, cereal, pancakes, waffles or eggs, cinnamon or other kinds of rolls and coffee are included in the rates. Afternoon tea (except on Mondays and Tuesdays) is offered to house guests on request, for a modest fee. Both tea and breakfast are served in the charming tea room done in blue and white, with the original delicate stenciling on the walls. Your hostess lived for some years in England, and her tea fare is authentic—tea sandwiches, crumpets, scones and pastries, everything homemade and sinfully rich including tarts, buttery cakes and creamy trifles. In December, there are Christmas stories by the fire, followed by a special Christmas tea.

The house is situated on five acres of land, with flowers, woods and fields. A large meadow sweeps down to the lake where you can swim from the private sandy beach or go canoeing or fishing and—in winter—ice skating. Autumn visitors will enjoy a walk to the top of Mt. Tir'em to see colorful fall foliage reflected in five lakes, and may go apple picking or watch cider being pressed. Cross-country skiing starts right at the door of the house; downhill skiing, golf and tennis are available nearby. Lynn Baker's daughter India operates an equestrian center right on the premises, offering horseback riding and instruction. And special activity weekends are now being offered, for instruction in riding or crafts.

The Artemus Ward House, Rtes. 35/37, Waterford, ME 04088; (207) 583-4106. (Right in the village.) Rates are moderately expensive, lower for longer stays. Children are welcome; no pets, please. Open May 15–Jan. 15.

Bethel/Stratton

Bethel, north of Waterford and near the New Hampshire border, is a small mountain town on the banks of the Androscoggin River. Gould Academy—one of New England's fine prep schools—is in Bethel, a town known for its beautiful old houses, many of Greek Revival style. There are two covered bridges nearby, both constructed in the 1800s. A sixty-mile tour of scenic Evans Notch (part of the White Mountain National Forest) starts in Bethel, goes west on Route 2 to Route 113, through the notch to Fryeburg, then to Lovell, and back to Bethel. For skiers, Mt. Abrams, Sunday River and Evergreen Valley ski areas are all nearby.

Farther to the north, the wild and beautiful Rangeley Lakes area offers mountains, forests, more than 100 lakes and—quite possibly—a moose or two. The names of five of the six larger lakes that make up the Rangeley chain are tongue-twisting evidence that the region was once home of the Abenaki Indians. Besides Rangeley Lake itself, the others are Mooselookmeguntic, Umbagog, Mollechunkamunk, Welekennebacook and Cupsuptic. Once this region was popular only in summer; nowadays fall foliage tours, hunting, skiing and snowmobiling have opened it up year-round. Maine's largest ski resort, Sugarloaf/USA, is located near Stratton.

The Douglass Place. Barbara and Dana Douglass welcome guests year-round to their comfortable bed-and-breakfast house in Bethel. The oldest part of the house was built around 1790, the large Victorian addition a century later. Only two families have ever owned the place: well-to-do farmers named the Twitchells, and the Douglasses, who with their four daughters moved here from Portland in 1950.

Six upstairs bedrooms are available for guests, including one single and five doubles with twin beds. Two and a half baths are shared.

The attractively decorated accommodations include bureaus, boudoir chairs and fresh flowers in season. Guests are invited to share the living room, den and game room, with Ping-Pong, a pool table and piano, and a large screened gazebo. Five acres of land, with a row of 100-year-old pines as a backdrop, are a nice place to walk; behind the trees a skimobile trail runs over the mountains for five miles to a major skiway. Facing the highway is a 1500-square-foot flower garden. A continental breakfast of juice, homemade muffins or coffee cake, jams, and coffee, tea or milk is offered each morning. The village is one mile away, for restaurants and shops.

The Douglass Place, Rte. 2, Star Route, Box 90, Bethel, ME 04217; (207) 824-2229. Rates are moderate, lower for a week's or longer stay (not including holidays). Children and pets are welcome. Open year-round.

The Widow's Walk. When snow lies heavy on the ground, this guest house in Stratton is a cheerful haven for skiers. But it's also a great place to visit during the rest of the year. The gloriously turreted and multi-dormered late-Victorian structure, built around 1892 by the

The Widow's Walk

town's leading resident, is listed on the National Register of Historic Places. Hosts Mary and Jerry Hopson provide friendly, informal hospitality and six guest rooms, all with twin beds and semi-private baths. Breakfast and dinner are included in the rates during ski season; meals at other times may be arranged by advance reservation. Downhill skiing is excellent at Sugarloaf, only ten minutes away, and the beautiful Carrabassett Valley Touring Center offers superb cross-country skiing with sixty miles of trails. Spring, summer and fall activities include hiking, fishing, canoeing and foliage trips.

The Widow's Walk, Main Street, Box 150, Stratton, ME 04982; (207) 246-6901. (North end of Stratton, on Rte. 27, at intersection of Rangeley Road, Rte. 16.) Rates are moderate, lower from spring to fall. Sugarloaf Credit Card accepted. Children are welcome; no pets, please. Open year-round.

New Hampshire

Some people think of New Hampshire and Vermont as sister states, pretty much identical. They're not. New Hampshire has a rough-textured quality, quite different from the gentle, pastoral appeal of Vermont. It is a fiercer state . . . even its license plates carry the stern legend: "Live free or die." New Hampshire's mountains, many with barren peaks far above the timber line, are higher than Vermont's. Mt. Washington rises 6288 feet above sea level, and 182 other mountains in the state climb above 3000 feet. These ancient mountains were once taller than the Rockies, but vast white glaciers filed them down. When the glaciers had passed, less soil remained in New Hampshire than in Vermont and more rock was left exposed. It is called the Granite State with good reason.

Forests cover more than three-quarters of New Hampshire's land. The White Mountain National Forest alone extends for some 684,000 acres and includes about 47,000 acres more across the border in Maine. The state has more than 1300 lakes and even boasts a tiny seacoast, eighteen miles long. Portsmouth, a handsome old coastal city, lies at the mouth of the Piscataqua River, which separates New Hampshire from Maine. Out beyond Portsmouth in the cold waters of the Atlantic are the nine barren Isles of Shoals, once home base for a thriving fishing industry and the site of countless shipwrecks. Nowadays the islands are a popular destination for summer vacationers.

The French explorer Samuel de Champlain sailed along New Hampshire's coast in 1605 and discovered the Isles of Shoals. But Martin Pring, an Englishman, had already explored a bit of the Piscataqua River two years earlier. The first settlements in the region were grants from King James I; the area was later joined to the Massachusetts Bay Colony. In 1679 New Hampshire was named a separate royal province, but boundary disputes with Massachusetts continued until 1741. Possession of Vermont was also disputed, between New Hampshire and New York; in 1764 New Hampshire's western boundary was fixed at the Connecticut River. Two years later New Hampshire declared its independence and became the first American colony to adopt its own constitution.

New Hampshire is a year-round state for visitors. The summers offer countless things to do: exploring back-country roads, hiking, swimming, boating and fishing. Long hours can be spent beside a rushing mountain stream sniffing the exhilarating smell of sun-warmed firs and watching fish in the shallows. Natural wonders

55

NEW HAMPSHIRE

● Jefferson

Littleton ● ● Bethlehem

Sugar Hill ●

● Jackson

● Bath

●North Conway

● West Plymouth   ● Chocorua

● Plymouth

● Holderness

Lake
Winnepesaukee

●Wolfeboro

● Laconia

● Tilton

Sunapee ●

CONCORD ●

Goshen ●

● Bradford

●Portsmouth

● Alstead

●Rye

● Walpole

●Marlborough

●East Jaffrey

● Rindge

abound: caves, gorges, notches, waterfalls and rock formations. You can climb the mountains or ride to their tops via tramways, gondolas or even a cog railway. And you can collect covered bridges.

Covered bridges are a pleasing sight; photographers and artists love them. In summer the bridges are a cool haven from which to watch the water below or do some leisurely fishing. Many look like narrow barns, most likely because their builders were usually local carpenters who were used to that kind of construction. The bridges were covered, and sided, so they would last longer. New Hampshire still offers a fairly large number of these quaint structures. Vermont has more, about 100, but the other New England states have very few left. The ones that do remain are staunchly defended and protected against everything but fire and natural disaster.

In the fall New Hampshire attracts thousands of "leaf peepers" who come to admire the annual foliage display. The Indians called the spectacle "fire on the mountains," and a glorious sight it is. Steep hillsides flame with a riotous patchwork of color while high above the mountain peaks glisten beneath a blanket of early snow. In winter, the state's many ski resorts swarm with activity.

February in New Hampshire—in election years, and nowadays even in the preceding year—offers an unusual sport, that of politician watching. New Hampshire holds the country's earliest primary, and presidential hopefuls from all over the nation flock to the state, hoping to gain early exposure and approval. It's a bit like the swallows returning to San Juan Capistrano . . . or the buzzards returning to Hinckley, Ohio.

About the only season to avoid in New Hampshire is one that is not ordinarily included in the list—the fifth, or "mud" season. It usually arrives in March, which is not a particularly thrilling month anywhere. Dire tales are told of cars sinking deep into muddy ruts, needing a tow to get out. On the other hand, March and April are maple-sugaring months. So if you decide you want to see a sugar house in action, just keep to the main roads as much as possible—and wear boots. You can spot a working sugar shack way off in the distance by its plume of white smoke.

The major areas of scenic and historic interest in New Hampshire are the White Mountains and Mt. Washington Valley, the Lakes Region and the seacoast, the southwestern Monadnock region and the Connecticut River region bordering Vermont. Coastal beaches run along Route 1A. From the Massachusetts border, Route I-93 will take you swiftly north to the White Mountains. A jog eastward off I-93, south of the White Mountain National Forest, will get you to Lake Winnepesaukee. For a beautiful circle drive through the mountains, follow I-93 north through Franconia Notch, Route 302 east and south to Conway, and the Kancamagus Highway (Route 112) west back to I-93.

The New Hampshire Coast
Portsmouth/Rye

Historic Portsmouth, on the Piscataqua River, was founded in 1623. To see what this old settlement must have looked like in its early years, follow the strawberry signs to Strawbery Banke, ten acres of restored seventeenth- to nineteenth-century houses and shops. The first settlers discovered hillsides covered with wild strawberries here, hence the name. Restoration of the area began in the late 1950s and continues today. The attractive marketplace, with brick and stone sidewalks, offers an array of galleries and small stores displaying a host of items, including many with a strawberry motif. Modern-day artisans live in some of the restored houses, and visitors can watch demonstrations of all kinds of crafts.

In the city itself are more handsome old houses, built by ship captains and merchants. Many are open to the public. The Jackson House was built around 1664, the John Paul Jones House in 1758. Commander Jones didn't own the house; he was a boarder there while he waited for his ship, the *Ranger,* to be constructed at Kittery, across the river in Maine. The Portsmouth Navy Yard is located in Kittery, too. From the wharf off Portsmouth's Market Street you can sail on the *Viking Queen* out to the Isles of Shoals.

New Hampshire's brief seacoast, just south of Portsmouth, has several state parks, excellent beaches and a scenic shoreline drive. Hampton Beach is a lively family entertainment center in summer with amusements, band concerts, pageants and fireworks displays. North of Rye Beach you will find Rye Harbor State Park out on a rocky promontory, and then Wallis Sands and Odiorne Point state parks.

The Inn at Christian Shore. Of Federal architecture, this fine old Portsmouth house was built between 1790 and 1800. Your hosts, Louis

Sochia and Charles Litchfield—formerly proprietors of a Portsmouth antique shop—restored and decorated the place themselves. There are six pleasant rooms for guests, three with private baths and one with a half bath. Two of the rooms, with private baths, are on the ground floor. All of the accommodations have been recently repainted and papered, and are air conditioned and have color TV. A large, comfortable sitting room decorated in attractive country inn style, with a fireplace, is available for guests' use. The hearty New England breakfast, served in the dining room, includes eggs, meat, a vegetable and potatoes, and coffee or tea. Guests are offered homemade blueberry or cranberry bread while breakfast is being prepared.

In spring, summer and early fall, the grounds are green with shrubs and bright with flowers. Restaurants and shops are within easy walking distance of the house, and Portsmouth's historic seventeenth-century Jackson House is across the street. If you're wondering how this area of Portsmouth got its name, your hosts say that long ago the term "Christian captain" was given to civilian ships' captains to distinguish between them and Naval captains. Since many civilian captains lived in this part of town, the name Christian Shore was adopted.

The Inn at Christian Shore, corner of 335 Maplewood Ave. and 5 Northwest St., P.O. Box 1474, Portsmouth, NH 03801; (603) 431-6770. (From I-95 take Portsmouth Exit 5 to Portsmouth Rotary and go north on Rte. 1 a short distance to Abner's; take Portsmouth Business District Exit; at top of ramp bear right onto Maplewood Avenue.) Rates are moderately expensive. Children over 12 are welcome; no pets, please. Open year-round.

Rock Ledge Manor Bed and Breakfast. Over on the seacoast in Rye travelers will find Rock Ledge Manor, owned by Janice and Norman Marineau. Built between the 1840s and 1880s, the mansard gambrel-roofed structure overlooks the ocean at Concord Point. The Marineaus in their travels have stayed at many bed-and-breakfast houses, and when they decided to share their own home with guests they determined to include all the amenities they liked best. There are four attractive rooms for guests, all with private baths. Two of the rooms are on the ground floor. The house is furnished mainly with period pieces including brass and cast-iron beds and marble-topped sinks and dressers. The bedrooms also contain comfortable chairs and ceiling paddle fans. There is a library/music room with a white marble fireplace for guests' use, and the house's wide wraparound porch provides a fine view of the sea and Isles of Shoals. Breakfast at Rock Ledge Manor is served in the antique-furnished breakfast room with a handsome mahogany ceiling and ocean view. Your hosts offer a lavish meal of juice, fresh fruit, eggs, pancakes made from a cherished family recipe or variations of stuffed crepes, meat, homefries and vegetable, homemade sweet rolls, breads or muffins and toast, and coffee. The house is within easy walking distance of two beaches and several restaurants, a fifteen-minute drive from Hampton Beach, and a seven-minute drive from Portsmouth.

Rock Ledge Manor, 1413 Ocean Blvd. (Rte. 1A), Rye, NH 03870; (603) 431-1413. Rates are moderately expensive, lower from Columbus Day through Memorial Day and for longer stays. Advance reservations are requested. Children over 12 are welcome; no pets, please. Open year-round.

The Lakes Region
Wolfeboro/Holderness/ Chocorua/Laconia/Tilton

New Hampshire's scenic Lakes Region centers on beautiful Lake Winnepesaukee. The state's largest lake, Winnepesaukee is 28 miles long, dotted with almost 300 islands, and edged by green forests and innumerable little bays along its approximately 183 miles of ragged shoreline. Wolfeboro, on the southeastern edge of the lake, claims to be the oldest summer resort community in America. It's a peaceful little town with handsome old houses and nice shops. The Wolfeboro Railroad takes passengers from the old depot on a two-hour ride to Sanbornville and back. The route passes along a causeway over a small lake, then clackety-clacks its way through woods and fields.

Route 109 north from Wolfeboro will take you on a winding drive, with grand views of the lake and mountains, to the Castle in the Clouds. Seven miles beyond Melvin Village, turn right on Route 171 and go three miles to the entrance. The "Castle" was built in 1910 and perches high on a promontory, part of a 6000-acre estate with a panoramic view of Lake Winnepesaukee. Holderness and Squam Lake are just northwest of Winnepesaukee; Ossipee Lake is to the east, and tiny Lake Chocorua is reached by heading northeast toward Conway.

On the west side of Lake Winnepesaukee, the Weirs at Weirs Beach is a popular summer recreation area, with many amusements including waterskiing, a water slide and dancing. The excursion ship *Mount Washington* leaves Weirs Beach on three-hour lake cruises in season; the ship also stops in Wolfeboro to pick up passengers, and on alternate days at Center Harbor and Alton Bay. In winter, skiing is excellent at Gunstock, just south of Weirs Beach on Route 11A in Gilford.

Laconia, on Winnisquam Lake, is a short drive west from Lake Winnepesaukee; Tilton is just a few miles south of Laconia. In East Canterbury, about twenty miles south of Tilton, travelers can visit Shaker Village. The Shakers, who originated in England in 1747, practiced communal living and celibacy. Their name came from their custom of dancing during religious ceremonies, using a shaking movement. Shaker furniture, now avidly collected by museums, is renowned for its beauty and graceful simplicity. Only nine elderly Shaker Sisters survive today: three in Canterbury and the rest at Sabbathday Lake in Maine. New Hampshire's capital, Concord, lies a few miles south, and the old industrial city of Manchester—where bargains may be discovered at the **many** clothing and shoe outlets—is south of Concord.

The Tuc'Me Inn. Just two blocks from downtown Wolfeboro, the Tuc'Me Inn is a welcome addition to the bed-and-breakfast roster. A large, rambling old structure, the New England Colonial house—white clapboard with traditional green shutters—was built circa 1805. It sits on an acre of ground with lilac bushes, two apple trees, and flowers.

Owners Thomas and Ellen Quinn, with backgrounds in sales, marketing and management, had been trying for a number of years to come up with a way to "escape the rat race" and still make a living. One night, while watching the Bob Newhart show on television,

Ellen suggested that they search for a suitable house in which to operate a bed-and-breakfast inn. The Quinns discovered the Wolfeboro property was available, made settlement on April 24, 1985, unloaded the moving van on the 25th, and opened for business on Memorial Day weekend in May!

For guests, there are currently six double rooms on the second floor, three with private baths; two share a bath. The bright, cheerily decorated guest rooms are done in country style, with antiques including some pineapple beds and an old rope bed. A pleasant living room, which guests are encouraged to share, combines antiques and contemporary pieces. The carpeted and paneled room contains a fireplace, comfortable furniture, a TV, books and games. There are also two porches for guests to enjoy: one on the ground floor, glass enclosed in winter and screened in summer, and another on the second floor.

Breakfast, served in the cozy dining room on a large pine trestle table and a smaller maple table for four (or on the porch in warm weather) consists of juice, eggs and bacon, homefries and coffee or tea. In season there will be fresh fruit, and at the "cook's whim" perhaps Baked Alaska Grapefruit, pancakes or waffles.

The Tuc'Me Inn, 68 N. Main St. (Rte. 109 North), P.O. Box 657, Wolfeboro, NH 03894; (603) 569-5702. Rates are moderately expensive, lower off season; package rates are available. Visa and MasterCard are accepted. Well-behaved children over 14 are welcome; no pets, please. Open year-round.

The Inn on Golden Pond. For those readers who have seen the movie *On Golden Pond* starring Henry and Jane Fonda, no, the inn is not the cottage shown in the film. Squam Lake, however, directly across the road, *is* the renowned "Golden Pond" setting. Bill and Bonnie Webb, your cordial hosts, say that they so named the inn because they hope its ambiance reflects the warm, sharing feelings portrayed in the movie. The only other connection with the film was Jane Fonda's one-time use of the upstairs bathroom!

The inn, a traditional Colonial house, was built in 1879, replacing a smaller eighteenth-century Cape Cod–style home. Part of the original structure still stands, attached to the back of the house. Eight spacious, individually decorated upstairs bedrooms are available for guests. Six have private baths, two share a bath. Downstairs, there is a large living room with a fireplace, comfortable chairs and couches, books and magazines, a TV, and a picture-window wall looking out on the back yard and surrounding woods. A screened-in porch runs along the entire front of the house. Your hosts' collection of handcarved wooden objects and Bonnie's handmade needlepoint may be noted throughout the inn.

A complete breakfast is served each morning, with freshly baked breads or muffins (including apple, blueberry and pecan), eggs and bacon or apple pancakes, or perhaps sausage/egg/cheese casserole, and coffee or tea. Bonnie is the skilled cook; recipes for many of her specialties appear in a cookbook she authored. Coffee, tea, hot chocolate and a variety of soft drinks and mixers are also available for a small extra charge during the day and evening hours. Picnic lunches, too, will be packed on request.

The inn stands on fifty-five acres, with huge catalpa trees, maples, evergreens, flowering bushes and wildflowers. Front and back yards are enclosed by century-old split-rail fences; farther afield are numerous walking and cross-country ski trails. Swimming, golfing, horseback riding, boating and skiing are all easily accessible, as are several excellent restaurants.

The Inn on Golden Pond, Rte. 3, Box 126, Holderness, NH 03245; (603) 968-7269. (Four miles from Exit 24, I-93.) Rates are moderately expensive, lower for a week's stay. Visa and MasterCard are accepted. Children over 12 are welcome. No pets, please; there is a resident cat named Brandy. Non-smokers are preferred; no smoking allowed in the guest rooms. Open year-round.

The Farmhouse . . . Bed and Breakfast. Situated in the picturesque New England village of Chocorua, the Farmhouse is a wonderful old place with a great deal of country charm. Your hostess, Katherine Dyrenforth, says: "It's like coming to Grandma's for a visit!" The handsome homestead, with barn and outbuildings, is surrounded by giant maples. Cross-country skiing starts right at the doorstep, and the White Mountain National Forest nearby offers facilities for hiking, canoeing, picnicking and swimming. Chocorua Lake, one of New Hampshire's most scenic, lies at the foot of much-photographed Mt. Chocorua.

The original part of the old farmhouse was moved to its present site by a young man for his bride, back before the Civil War. The building had previously been a blacksmith shop on a nearby river bank. During World War II, a former owner—having sent six sons off to war—found that she had lots of time and plenty of space for guests so opened the house to travelers. Thirty years later the Dyrenforths discovered her sign in the woodshed, put it up once more, and—says Kathie—"It worked!"

There are four double upstairs rooms for guests, sharing two baths. The sunny bedrooms, with mountain views, are attractively decorated with antiques and period pieces, papered or stenciled walls, and handmade quilts. A comfortable living room with TV, books and table games is a pleasant place to relax after sightseeing, hiking or skiing. The Dyrenforths pride themselves on their leisurely country breakfasts, including fresh fruits in season, fresh eggs from their own hens, bacon, ham or sausage, pancakes with maple syrup made by John at the Farmhouse Sugarbush, and Kathie's homemade muffins and

The Farmhouse . . . Bed and Breakfast

breads. Afternoon tea is also served, on the flower-filled porch in summer and by the wood stove in winter. There are several good restaurants not far away, and Chocorua Village's shops are within walking distance.

The Farmhouse . . . Bed and Breakfast, Page Hill Road, P.O. Box 14, Chocorua, NH 03817; (603) 323-8707. (At junction of rtes. 16 and 113.) Rates are moderate; special weekly rates are available. Children are accepted but not encouraged; no pets, please. Open year-round.

The Cartway House. A 1791 renovated Colonial farmhouse, Cartway House sits at the top of a hill in Laconia. Every room offers a view of mountains, fields or lake. Owned by the Shortway family, the house has ten spacious upstairs rooms for guests: two singles, four doubles and four triples. One of the bedrooms has a private bath; each two of the others shares a bath. Guests are invited to use the living room, game room and TV room for socializing, quiet reading or just sitting by the fire. A complete breakfast is served each morning with fresh eggs and bacon, pancakes topped with real maple syrup, or perhaps eggs Benedict or waffles. Afternoon tea is also offered. Your hostess,

Gretchen Shortway, sets the pace at Cartway House—one of "laidback" relaxation and casual comfort. A beach nearby offers good swimming, and all of the area's many attractions are easily accessible including skiing, shopping and restaurants.

The Cartway House, Old Lakeshore Road, Box 575, RFD 5, Laconia, NH 03246; (603) 528-1172. (Take Exit 20 off I-93 to Rte. 3 north to the Laconia Bypass, rtes. 3 and 11. Follow Bypass to the end, take a left at the traffic light, then your first right. The house is approximately ¾ mile up the hill.) Rates are moderate; group rates are available. Visa and MasterCard are accepted. Children are very welcome; no pets, please. Open year-round.

The Country Place. Claire and Edmond Tousignant are the owners of the well-named Country Place, in Tilton. The house, a typical New England farmhouse, nicely maintained, is almost a century old. The six-acre property includes spacious lawns and stately old maples; the views of the mountains are lovely. The Tousignants, who speak fluent French, have four double rooms for guests, sharing baths, all on the second floor. Rollaway beds are available for an extra person in the room. All of the guest accommodations are corner rooms; three have three windows and one has two. One bedroom contains a king-size bed, another has twin beds, and two have double beds. Downstairs there are a family room with TV and a charming country parlor for guests to enjoy, and an open porch runs along two sides of the house. Breakfast is served in the large country kitchen and the meal is a lavish one. The menu varies but always includes fruit juices and fresh

fruit in season, toast, muffins, and plenty of good hot coffee or tea, or fresh milk. Depending on the day your hosts also offer eggs with bacon or sausage, quiche, French crepes with their own maple syrup, or whatever other new and interesting breakfast treat they happen to discover.

Things to do at the Country Place include following a path around the grounds, relaxing under the trees and contemplating the views, or—in winter—going cross-country skiing starting outside the kitchen door. All manner of other sports activities are easily accessible as are antique shops, summer theater and a variety of restaurants. The intriguing Shaker Village is only a short drive away.

The Country Place, RFD 2, Box 342, Tilton, NH 03276; (603) 286-8551. (Take Exit 20 off I-93, turn left, then take first left if coming from the south or second left if coming from the north onto Rte. 132 north. The house is .9 mile up the road, on the right.) Rates are moderate. Children over 6 are welcome; no pets, please. Open year-round.

The White Mountains
Plymouth/Sugar Hill/Bethlehem/Littleton/ Bath/Jefferson/Jackson/North Conway

Tucked into and around the edges of the beautiful White Mountains region of New Hampshire are a number of nice small towns. Some, like North Conway and Jackson, are busy tourist centers year-round. Others are sleepy hamlets where the only activities (other than skiing or mountain climbing) might be watching the seasons pass or a rushing stream race under a covered bridge. Within an easy drive, however, will be a host of interesting places to explore.

The hilly town of Plymouth, not far from Squam Lake to the east and lovely Newfound Lake to the south, is located at the southernmost tip of the White Mountain National Forest. Plymouth is called "The Gateway to the White Mountains," and from just outside the town if you look straight ahead, you can see Franconia Notch far off in the distance—a narrow cut between the mountains. Five miles west of Plymouth are the Polar Caves, ancient glacial caverns which may be toured. Heading north, you will come to North Woodstock; from there, Route 112 west leads to Lost River, in Kinsman Notch. Running through a series of glacial caverns and giant potholes, the river derives its name from its habit of disappearing under the surface here and there before finally emerging in a stunning waterfall. Youngsters love to crawl through the gorge; adults may use pathways above the caves if they prefer.

Route 112 also goes east from North Woodstock as the Kancamagus Highway, ending at Conway, thirty-four miles away. The Kancamagus, considered to be one of the most scenic stretches of road in the country, climbs high on the flank of Kancamagus Mountain, crossing a 3000-foot-high pass. All along the way are swift, rocky streams, and there are numerous outlooks where you may stop and photograph the mountains and forests beyond. It is wild and uninhabited country, and travelers in the very early hours of the morning might even see a moose tranquilly grazing beside the river road.

Although New Hampshire has some 1500 bears nowadays, it's not likely that you will ever spot one, even here. If you do, be reassured:

according to the state's Fish and Game Department nobody has been known to have been killed by a bear in New Hampshire since the Revolutionary War. Tame bears, sleepily passive creatures, may be admired at Clark's Trading Post one mile north of North Woodstock. In summer, the animals perch atop platformed posts and wait for travelers to place bear food in small cups which are then hauled up on a pulley—by the bears.

Heading north from North Woodstock you will come to spectacular Franconia Notch, an eight-mile pass between the Franconia and Kinsman ranges of the White Mountains. Just before entering the Notch look to your left and see Indian Head, the rock profile of an Indian and his feathered headdress of trees. Once in the Notch you will come almost directly to the entrance gate to the Flume, on the right.

The Flume is a deep, narrow gorge carved out by the force of the Pemigewasset River; a walkway leads visitors through its 800-foot length along the flank of 4460-foot Mt. Liberty. Steep granite walls, formed long before the Ice Age, rise 60 to 70 feet on each side, and the icy mountain stream tumbles headlong through the gorge from a lacy waterfall at its top. The Flume is deliciously cool; ferns grow from the ancient boulders and the air smells refreshingly damp and woodsy. At the top, continue on around the path to the Pool and Sentinel Pine Bridge.

The Pool, a deep basin in the river at the foot of another waterfall, has emerald-green water so clear you can see pebbles on the bottom. The Sentinel Pine, which fell in the 1938 hurricane, stood on a cliff 150 feet above the Pool. The tree, a white pine, was 175 feet tall with a girth of 16 feet. The late Tom Bodwell, long-time manager of the Flume Reservation, Lost River and Echo Lake facilities, decided that the fallen pine should be made into a miniature covered bridge—which now spans the river just above the Pool. Bodwell and several other men counted the tree's rings and discovered that it was almost 300 years old. They cut a 60-foot section of its trunk; a team of horses on the other side of the river pulled it across, using a steel cable. Timbers for the top and sides of the bridge were adz-cut, and only hand-carved pine pins were used to secure it.

Continuing on through Franconia Notch watch for the old road going off to the left, leading to the Basin, a large glacial granite pothole at the foot of a small waterfall. Back on the highway again keep your eyes open for the Old Man of the Mountains. You'll see a remarkably detailed stone profile high up on the left, 1200 feet above tiny Profile Lake. The sculpture is a natural phenomenon formed an estimated 500 million years ago, made up of five separate granite ledges.

Just before reaching Echo Lake you will arrive at the base station of the Cannon Mountain Aerial Tramway. The first aerial tramway in North America, it was built during the winter of 1937-38. In 1980, the old cars—each of which carried twenty-seven people—were replaced by new ones carrying eighty passengers. The cars, suspended by cables, take you swiftly up the mountain (weather permitting) to the 4200-foot summit. Route 18, or I-93, will bring you next to Franconia Village. The Gale River burbles along through the middle of this quiet little mountain town, a popular resort year-round. Route 117 out of the village leads to the small town of Sugar Hill. Bethlehem is reached via Route 302 northeast of Franconia, Littleton via Route 302 to the west. Tiny Bath is southwest of Littleton on Route 302, and Jefferson lies northeast via routes 116 and 2.

Mt. Washington, New England's tallest peak, is east of Littleton and Bethlehem. Follow Route 302; as you drive you will catch occasional glimpses of the 6288-foot mountain. If it's the right season of the year you may want to ascend its summit. You can walk up, but unless you are a skilled climber it is not recommended. There are two other, easier ways of getting to the peak: the Cog Railway and the Auto Road. In either case, plan a full day for the venture and be sure to take along a sweater or jacket. The base station for the Cog Railway is six miles from Fabyan, reached by a marked road off Route 302. The railway, first of its kind in the world, has been running almost continuously since 1869. The cars are pushed by specially built steam locomotives; their horizontal boilers are tilted lower in front, so that the water level remains even while on the mountain. And they're cute, all spiffily painted in bright colors. When the train reaches Jacob's Ladder, where the grade is 37.41 percent, the soot-grimed conductor may come walking through the cars seemingly at an odd angle. That's the moment to try to stand upright; you will be fighting gravity and it won't be easy. When it is time to descend, the engine *backs* down the mountain, the cars joggling along behind it.

Don't let the steepness of the grades or the quaint appearance of the train stop you from making the trip. The Cog Railway is a very safe mode of travel. Not so was the method of descending the mountain used by some local folk in the old days. They simply whizzed down on slide boards, pieces of wood that fitted onto the cograil. The boards were called Devil's Shingles, and a few may be seen on display at the summit. These brave (foolhardy?) souls would climb aboard and let her rip, covering the three-mile descent in two minutes and forty-five seconds. (The train takes over an hour to make the same trip.)

If you would like to try driving up the mountain, the eight-mile Auto Road is on the eastern side. The base station there is off Route 16 north of Jackson. The road is a good one, but it's a shade scary for those not used to mountain driving. You might prefer to be driven up in comfort by driver-guides in special van stages. Mobile campers and trucks are not permitted on the road, by the way. And both the Auto Road and Cog Railway are closed in winter.

Mt. Washington has a nasty temperament. The weather at its summit can be unspeakably rotten—such as on April 12, 1934, when the wind velocity was measured at 231 miles per hour, the highest ever recorded in the world. Its average snowfall is 177 inches. And it is cloud-covered more often than not. Washington is not a mountain to be taken lightly; even experienced climbers have met their death on its slopes. Still, ascending it on foot, by car or via cog railway is a marvelous experience. The view from the summit is sensational—on a clear day you can see as far as Canada.

Continuing on Route 302, turn south and pass through Crawford Notch, another of New Hampshire's magnificent mountain gaps, and one of the most impressive. The roadway curves up and around and down through wondrously wild and awesome scenery, the mountains looming thousands of feet above. At the northern end of the notch, stop and look up at lovely Silver Cascade, a narrow waterfall crashing down a 1000-foot drop. Crawford Notch State Park is the site of the Samuel Willy House. In 1826, an avalanche crashed down the mountainside. Willy, his family and two hired men heard it coming. Trying to save themselves, they rushed out of the house. The avalanche killed them all—but left the house untouched.

At the town of Glen, turn left (north) onto Route 16 and then right on 16B over a red covered bridge to Jackson, a charming little village at the southern end of Pinkham Notch. Several of New Hampshire's best ski resorts are in this region, including Wildcat, Intervale and Black Mountain. North Conway is farther down the Mt. Washington Valley from Jackson. The town, known for its array of fine shops and excellent restaurants, is also famous for its delightfully eccentric railway station—a Victorian edifice with a whimsical touch of Old Russia.

Crab-Apple Inn. Bed and breakfast in the English tradition is offered at the delightful Crab Apple Inn, just outside Plymouth. The inn, an 1835 red brick Colonial situated beside a bubbling brook at the foot of Tenney Mountain, is owned by Janene and Ed Davis. Ed, originally

from Massachusetts, has lived all over the world in his career as pilot for a number of airlines. Janene is a native of Brisbane, Australia, where her family operated a bed-and-breakfast motel. The two met in Rhodesia and together have traveled extensively in Europe.

The Davises purchased their unusually elegant old New Hampshire farmhouse in 1983. They added a deck off their own newer section in the back, put up a white picket fence and installed brick courtyards in front and back. The inn's very attractive interior boasts wide pine floors, and most of the windows have the original glass. There are four double rooms for guests, two with private baths; the others share a bath. Two of the spacious bedrooms, each with a fireplace, are on the second floor; the other two bedrooms, on the third floor, offer panoramic views of the mountains. All of the accommodations are individually decorated and tastefully furnished with appropriate period pieces. Guests will find a host of gracious added amenities, too, such as comfortable new mattresses, lace-trimmed sheets, colorful handmade quilts and sherry-filled decanters. One of the bathrooms has the original clawfoot tub, and a fireplace!

On the inn's ground level are a den/library with a fireplace and a large selection of books and magazines, and the breakfast/sitting room with an antique wood stove and French doors that lead to a brick patio and garden. Guests are also invited to enjoy the passive solar room with glass cathedral ceilings; one of the glass walls opens onto the deck, the other onto the brick courtyard. A typical breakfast at Crab Apple Inn—served out on the brick patio in warm weather—will include fresh fruit salad, orange juice, Brie cheese and an almond omelet with ham or perhaps an herb and cheese omelet, blueberry or zucchini nut muffins, English jams and coffee. Several excellent restaurants are nearby, and the inn is a ten-minute drive from downtown Plymouth.

Crab Apple Inn, RFD 2, Box 200B, West Plymouth, NH 03264; (603) 536-4476. (Four miles west of I-93, Exit 26, Rte. 25.) Rates are moderately expensive, lower for longer stays. Visa and MasterCard are accepted. Children over 8 are welcome; no pets, please. Open year-round.

Northway House. Micheline and Norman McWilliams own Northway House, a white two-story Colonial built around 1840, just north of Plymouth. They have two double upstairs bedrooms for guests, sharing a bath. One room features antique single beds, and an antique bureau and chest; the other bedroom has a double bed, comfortable chairs and a desk. Two landscaped acres surround the house, with gardens and fields, and there is a secluded patio for warm weather relaxing. Indoors guests may share the living room with color cable TV. Breakfast at Northway House is hearty English style, served in the country kitchen, dining room, or out on the patio. Your hosts offer juice or fruit cup, a house specialty such as stuffed crepes or eggs Benedict, fruit streusel or other homemade breakfast pastry, and coffee, tea or milk. Downtown Plymouth, Plymouth State College and Holderness School are minutes away, as are shops, restaurants and a variety of sightseeing and sports attractions.

Northway House, RFD 1, Plymouth, NH 03264; (603) 536-2838. (Two miles north of Plymouth on Rte. 3.) Rates are moderate, lower for longer stays and for children. Children are welcome; dogs are allowed with advance notice. Open year-round.

Southworth's Bed & Breakfast. Travelers will enjoy this nice bed-and-breakfast house in tiny Sugar Hill, a few miles outside of Franconia. David and Amy Southworth currently manage the place; when David's parents, Judy and Bruce Southworth, retire they will take over. The younger Southworths moved to the area in 1981 from

Pittsburgh, Pennsylvania. Their old, typically New England house—white with green shutters—is furnished with a variety of antiques and country-style pieces. Some of the items were already in the family; others were purchased at Pennsylvania auctions. There are three double upstairs guest rooms, sharing a bath. All have been newly painted and papered; two of the rooms have double brass beds and the other has a double poster bed. Guests are invited to share the large living room and a TV room with board games. A continental breakfast is served daily, with coffee and doughnuts. Polly's Pancake Parlor, renowned for its pancakes, waffles and maple syrup, is within walking distance as are the Sunset Hill House and Harman's Cheese Store, which ships its excellent cheeses nationwide. The Robert Frost Museum is not far away, and year-round activities including skiing, hiking, golf, glider rides, swimming and antiquing are all easily accessible.

Southworth's Bed & Breakfast, Main Street (Rte. 117), Sugar Hill, NH 03585; (603) 823-5344. (Across the street from the Sugar Hill Meeting House.) Rates are moderate. Children and pets are not encouraged, and only two persons per room. Open year-round.

The Highlands Inn. Back around the turn of the century, Bethlehem, New Hampshire, was a bustling summer resort town with some thirty large hotels. In those days, horse-drawn carriages met incoming guests at the railroad station, and guests who came to spend the summer whiled away the time with lavish meals, dancing, and rocking on the wide porches. Today, most of the old hostelries are long gone, but the sleepy little mountain town still attracts its share of visitors. Nowadays people come year-round: in summer for the mountain views, golf, hiking and sightseeing, and in winter for skiing.

The Highlands Inn, operated by Grace Newman and Judith Hall, was built almost 200 years ago as a farmhouse and has been welcoming guests since the early 1900s. There are fourteen individually decorated upstairs guest rooms. Ten of the comfortable rooms, all furnished with antiques, have private baths; the others share a bath. A

The Highlands Inn

TV room and a living room with a fireplace and extensive library are pleasant places to sit, chat or read, and the broad porch provides superb sunset views. The inn is situated on a hill at the end of a country lane and overlooks its own 100 acres of land with miles of trails for walking, bird watching or cross-country skiing. There is a swimming pool with a gazebo, and a newly added hot tub. Wintertime activities at the inn also include ice skating and snowshoeing. Clay tennis courts and two 18-hole championship golf courses are close by. Breakfast at the Highlands consists of juice, homemade muffins and coffee, and in the afternoon guests are offered tea and cookies. Other meals are available for groups only, by prior arrangement and at extra cost. You will need a car to reach the many fine restaurants in the area.

The Highlands Inn, Valley View Lane, P.O. Box 118Z, Bethlehem, NH 03574; (603) 869-3978. (From I-93 take Exit 40, then Rte. 302 east for 2 miles.) Rates are moderate, lower in April, May and November and for stays of three nights or longer (except during foliage and holidays weekends). Visa and MasterCard are accepted. Children are welcome; no pets, please. Open year-round.

Beal House Inn. Built in 1833, this delightful guest house with its relaxing, old-timey atmosphere was once a farmhouse and barn on the outskirts of town. Since those early days Littleton has grown

considerably, and now the house, a handsome white Federal-style structure with green roof and shutters, is only a minute's walk from downtown shops and restaurants. Despite its proximity to the center of town, Beal House is wonderfully quiet and peaceful, set on four acres of lawns and woods.

The Beal family purchased the place in the 1930s; when Mr. Beal died a few years later, Mrs. Beal began taking in guests. She later remarried, and as Mrs. Grady, continued to operate the establishment as a guest house while adding an antique business. The present owners, Doug and Brenda Clickenger, bought Beal House in 1980. Since taking possession they have completely refurbished the house and now offer fourteen very comfortable, tastefully decorated rooms for guests, ten with private baths. Three of the guest rooms, with private baths, are on the ground floor.

Some of the rooms are located in the main house; others are in "The Annex," an addition connecting the house to the old barn. Furnished with antiques, such as canopy beds and wingback chairs, the rooms also boast handmade quilts and period wallpapers. A shop on the premises offers antiques for sale—and visitors will be delighted to discover that many of the marvelous old pieces in the rooms may be purchased as well! Guests are welcome to enjoy the pleasant parlor with wing chairs, piano and fireplace, an upstairs sitting room, and a deck and gazebo overlooking the wooded hillside. A glassed-in front porch with wicker rockers offers a grand view of the mountains.

Breakfast at Beal House is locally renowned, served by the fireplace in an attractive breakfast room on long, candlelit tables set with Blue Willow plates. Brenda Clickenger, attired in an old-fashioned cap and long dress, serves the meal, prepared by husband Doug. His specialties are delectable hot popovers and homemade toast, along with fresh fruit, creamy scrambled eggs (offered in charming servers called "hens on nests"), waffles, ham, bacon and sausage. A light breakfast of juice, popovers or toast and beverage is included in the rates; a full country breakfast is extra. Afternoon tea and hot mulled cider are also included. Ordinarily no other meals are served, although dinners may occasionally be arranged for groups at extra charge. Your hosts do provide menus from local restaurants for guests to peruse.

Beal House Inn, 247 W. Main St., Littleton, NH 03561; (603) 444-2661. (Junction of rtes. 18 and 302, 1 mile east of Exit 42 off I-93.) Rates range from moderate to moderately expensive; group rates are available. All major credit cards are accepted. Children are welcome and portable cribs are available. No pets, please, and no smoking during meals in the dining room. Open year-round.

1895 House Bed & Breakfast. Zucchini muffins, homemade raspberry jam, cinnamon butter and freshly ground Amaretto coffee are only some of the delicious breakfast offerings at the 1895 House in Littleton. Owner Susanne Watkins rounds out the glorious meal with a variety of egg dishes, fluffy buttermilk pancakes with maple syrup and maple-smoked bacon, or perhaps *Apfelpfannkuchen*, a baked apple pancake.

Her large, striking Queen Anne Victorian house—painted white with green shutters—is fronted by a wide porch and surrounded by sugar maples and old lilac bushes. From an elegant entry hall a handsome staircase leads to six nicely appointed guest bedrooms on the second and third floors. One has a private bath; the others share two baths. Oak furniture, colorful Oriental or braided rugs and handmade quilts decorate the high-ceilinged guest quarters. Downstairs there's a living room for guests to enjoy, with antiques, Oriental prints, stereo (with a fine selection of classical music), books and bay windows. Breakfast is served in the formal, bay-windowed dining room just beyond, which has a fireplace with an unusual carved oak

mantel portraying Old Man Winter in bas relief. Downtown Littleton, for restaurants and shops, is three blocks away, and all of the region's many sites of interest are within a short drive.

1895 House Bed & Breakfast, 74 Pleasant St., Littleton, NH 03561; (603) 444-5200 or (800) 237-3809. (Off Main Street.) Rates are moderate to moderately expensive, lower for longer stays except during foliage season. Visa, MasterCard and American Express are accepted. Children are welcome; pets may be accepted by prior arrangement with a deposit. Open July 15–Oct. 24.

Bridgehouse Bed & Breakfast. Helene Hymoff and Mark Guerin welcome guests to Bridgehouse, a restored 1860 clapboard farmhouse in Bath. Although on a main state road, the white two-story structure with black shutters offers rural peace and quiet, and overlooks ninety acres of field, a river, farms and rolling hills. The property was a working dairy farm until 1970. Four double upstairs rooms are available for travelers, all leading off the central hallway. Two baths are shared. A cot may be added for a third person in the room, at a small extra charge. The decor is cheerful, with a romantic touch; all of the bedrooms, furnished with antiques, have period wallpapers and wall-to-wall carpeting. There are a spacious library/TV lounge on the first floor for guests to enjoy and an outdoor shaded sitting area where summer barbecues are permitted. The field adjacent to the property offers cross-country skiing in winter. Breakfast at Bridgehouse consists of orange juice, toasted French croissant stuffed with locally smoked ham, cheese, eggs, and coffee or other hot beverage, or milk. Your hosts will be delighted to suggest places to see and things to do in the area. Antique hunters will want to visit Mark's and Helene's own antique shop in a nearby town. Mark is also a licensed auctioneer. Helene is a linguist, and has traveled extensively.

Bridgehouse Bed & Breakfast, Rte. 302, Bath, NH (mailing address: RFD 2-Box 7B, Lisbon, NH 03585); (603) 838-6370. (2.2 miles west of Lisbon center, 3.2 miles east of Bath center.) Rates are moderate, lower for longer stays and for singles. Advance reservations are required. Well-behaved children and pets are welcome. Open year-round.

The Country Inn on Jefferson Hill. Offering marvelous views of New Hampshire's Presidential Range, Greg Brown's rambling 1896 Victorian inn is located in Jefferson. In addition to a porch for sitting and admiring the view, the property includes several acres of fields for roaming. Swimming and golf are within walking distance, and all manner of other outdoor activities are easily accessible. Host Greg, and wife Anne, have six rooms for guests, two on the ground floor. Four of the rooms are doubles and two are triples; two full baths are shared. Each guest room has been decorated individually; all are furnished with antiques and a firm bed. Polished hardwood floors and woodwork add to the warmth of the rooms, and the baths are distinctly Victorian in flavor. Your hosts, former residents of England,

own numerous English furnishings such as foot/bed warmers which they distribute during evening tea! The complimentary tea, consisting of tea or hot chocolate, banana or coconut nut bread or perhaps a dessert, is one of the many pleasant amenities provided by the inn. A hearty breakfast is served each morning, at a small extra charge. The filling meal often includes the house specialty, baked apple cinnamon pancake. Guests will need a car to reach a restaurant for other meals.

The Country Inn on Jefferson Hill, Rte. 2, RFD 1-Box 68A, Jefferson, NH 03583; (603) 586-7998. (In the village center on Rte. 2.) Rates are moderate, lower for longer stays. Quiet, well-behaved children are welcome; no pets, please. Open year-round.

Nestlenook Inn. If you've been cherishing a wish to gather your own eggs for breakfast, and perhaps help slop the hogs, the Nestle-nook Inn in Jackson will fulfill your dream! A nicely refurbished old farmhouse set on sixty-five acres of fields and woods on the banks of the Ellis River, Nestlenook is owned by Tom and Patti Burns and

their son Cullen. Horses, chickens, pigs and other farm animals are also in residence, and the general air is one of casual relaxation and fun. The bed-and-breakfast inn, a Colonial structure, has two sections: one is the oldest house in Jackson, circa 1830, and the other dates to around 1880. There are ten guest rooms in the inn, most with private baths and all furnished with period antiques. One bedroom, with private bath, is on the ground floor. In addition, there are three cottages on the grounds and five more bedrooms, with shared baths, in the Manger, a converted carriage house. Each of the inn's bedrooms has been decorated with a theme: antique cameras or muffs, dolls, whirligigs and other whimsical collections of country folk art. Cozy quilts and quaint country wallpapers add to the cheery ambiance.

Each morning guests may choose either a deluxe continental breakfast with homemade breads, fresh fruit, juice, cheese and freshly brewed coffee, or a full country breakfast. The latter may include farm-raised eggs and bacon, or Tom's specialty of French toast with walnuts, raisins, and cinnamon and apple slices, along with his hot-out-of-the-oven beer bread with pumpkin butter. Breakfast is served, family style, in the dining room where a large collection of old hats is fun to see (and try on). For other meals, the towns of Jackson and North Conway offer a wide choice of restaurants.

For indoor relaxing, guests are invited to use the reception area, the spacious dining room and a living room with large-screen TV. There are many books and magazines, and the Burnses offer the use of a video disk player and their film library of more than 150 movies. Out of doors, the Nestlenook Inn provides guests with an amazing variety of activities. There are a large outdoor pool and the river for swimming; the kitchen and flower gardens offer an opportunity to munch or sniff while learning about organic gardening; there are the farm animals to admire, and hay rides. Your hosts also operate a complete equestrian program on the property with jumps, dressage rings and more than sixteen miles of wooded trails. In winter, their ski touring center offers miles of groomed trails, a ski school and rentals. Best of all delights are the old-fashioned sleigh rides, in a specially built copy of an old logging sleigh drawn by two Belgian draft horses. Evening rides along the banks of the river and through the woods are lighted by kerosene lanterns along the trail, and passengers are snuggled under warm blankets. A mug of hot spiced cider greets guests on return to the inn.

Nestlenook Inn, Dinsmore Road, P.O. Box Q, Jackson Village, NH 03846; (603) 383-9443. (Rte. 16 to the Jackson Covered Bridge, go over the bridge and after 50 feet turn right onto Dinsmore Road.) Rates are moderately expensive, lower off season; package rates are available. Visa and MasterCard are accepted. Well-behaved children and small pets are welcome. Open year-round.

Sunny Side Lodge. Located in a quiet residential section of North Conway, Sunny Side Lodge is owned by Tracy Minnix and Anthony Tulip. The main part of the lodge, a New England farmhouse; was built around 1850 and added onto in later years "in every possible

way," according to your hosts. Eleven pleasant bedrooms are available for guests: five doubles, one triple and five that can accommodate one to four persons. Three of the rooms, all with private baths, are on the ground floor; the other rooms share baths. A guest living room with a fireplace and TV offers a comfortable, homey atmosphere, and there is a reading nook by the wood stove for quiet times. Porches trimmed with flower boxes are also available for summer relaxation.

A full breakfast is served in the dining room, with a pitcher of orange juice or cider, fresh fruit, and a choice of two or three main dishes: homemade whole wheat buttermilk blueberry pancakes, Cheese Strata, your hosts' special French toast or perhaps scrambled eggs with bacon or sausage, and hot cereal. There will also be homebaked goodies such as poppyseed cakes, and coffee or tea. The house is within easy walking distance of the town with its wealth of fine shops and restaurants, and Mt. Cranmore for skiing.

Sunny Side Lodge, Seavey Street, North Conway, NH 03860; (603) 356-6239. (Heading north on Rte. 16, turn right at traffic light on Kearsarge Street and at hilltop turn right again; the house is ½ block on the left.) Rates are moderate, lower off season; package rates are available. Visa and MasterCard are accepted. Children are welcome; no pets, please. Open year-round.

The Monadnock and Lake Sunapee Regions
E. Jaffrey/Rindge/Marlborough/Walpole/ Alstead/Bradford/Goshen/Sunapee

Mt. Monadnock is the star of the gently rolling Monadnock region down in the southwest corner of New Hampshire. About 60,000 people climb the mountain each year, following its reasonably easy trails. Mt. Monadnock isn't all that tall—only 3165 feet—but it does command the entire area. "Monadnock," the regional Indians' name for the peak, is now also a geological term for any mountain that stands alone. In the early 1800s wolves in fairly large numbers lived on the summit of the mountain, dining happily on local farmers' sheep. The outraged farmers eventually dislodged the critters by setting fire to the dead timber where the wolves lurked, reducing the top to bare rock. Monadnock may not be as attractive as when it was tree covered, but it is wolfless.

Several excellent ski area are nearby, including Crotched Mountain, Temple Mountain and Bobcat, and the region is criss-crossed with scenic back roads for leisurely meandering. In Rindge, off Route 124, a visit to the Cathedral of the Pines is an experience not to be missed. The nondenominational shrine is set on a ridge, with wooden pews resting on a deep bed of pine needles under a cathedral roof of trees. Mt. Monadnock can be seen beyond the simple stone altar; in the fall the view is particularly grand.

The nearby towns of Peterborough and Jaffrey are both attractively nineteenth-century in mood and offer an array of antique, craft and gift shops and art galleries. In July the Rhododendron State Park in Fitzwilliam, south of Mt. Monadnock, is a gorgeous mass of red, pink and white flowers. The town of Marlborough is just northeast of Mt.

Monadnock, outside of Keene, a central shopping town. Walpole lies northwest of Keene on the Connecticut River, and Alstead is a short distance to the north.

Pretty Lake Sunapee to the northeast has a fine, mile-long beach for swimming and Mt. Sunapee, altitude 2700 feet, may be ascended via a gondola in summer and early fall. In winter the mountain offers good skiing. An enormous crafts fair, sponsored by the League of New Hampshire Craftsmen, is held annually at Sunapee State Park; the fair begins on the first Tuesday in August and lasts for six days. Goshen and Bradford are a short drive south and southeast of Sunapee, respectively.

Over in Cornish, on the Connecticut River, travelers can visit the fascinating Saint-Gaudens National Historic Site. Containing the largest collection anywhere of works of the great sculptor August Saint-Gaudens, it is the only national historic site in the country devoted to an artist. The 149-acre estate encompasses handsomely landscaped grounds and gardens, and the artist's studios. Among the many pieces of sculpture to be seen are a copy of the artist's magnificent Lincoln (the original is in Washington, D.C.) and the working plaster casts for Boston's Shaw Memorial. The site is open to the public daily from May 15 to October 15, weekdays only the rest of the year. On summer Sundays, informal outdoor concerts are held in the gardens.

Hanover, home of Dartmouth College, is about eighteen miles to the north. A very attractive community, Hanover offers a number of fine shops and restaurants. You may walk around Dartmouth's campus by yourself or take a guided tour. New Hampshire's oldest educational institution, Dartmouth was chartered under a grant from King George III in 1769. Concerts, theatrical performances, art exhibits and other events take place throughout the year. In early February the college holds its famous Winter Carnival, when students compete to create the most unusual ice sculpture.

The Benjamin Prescott Inn. In 1775 Benjamin Prescott erected a house on Old Turnpike Road in Jaffrey, and in 1802 Prescott and his son Oliver built an inn adjoining the homestead. The present inn, located on the site of the original house, is owned by Richard L. Rettig, who continues an almost 200-year-old tradition of innkeeping. As does the present-day Benjamin Prescott, the Inn Cat.

Antique furniture, handmade quilts and a comfortable, relaxed ambiance are only a few of the bed-and-breakfast inn's many lures for travelers. There are eight double guest rooms, six with private baths; two rooms share a bath. One of the bedrooms, with private bath, is on the ground floor. All are attractively decorated in country style. There is a living room with a fireplace for relaxing, and in summer the screened porch offers a cool spot for reading or chatting with other guests. Breakfast is served by the fire, on the porch in warm weather, or—if you like—brought to your room to be enjoyed in bed. Your host provides juice, fresh melon or other fruit in season, homemade bread and/or muffins, and often, French toast with an apple-cranberry compote. Local farm eggs or griddle cakes with maple syrup are other possibilities. Afternoon tea and perhaps an evening snack are sometimes offered, and there is always an old-fashioned cookie jar brimming with "Tasty Teddies."

Activities at the inn are many and year-round. Mt. Monadnock, the Cathedral of the Pines, and the Colony Mill Market Place are minutes away. Hiking, swimming, cross-country and downhill skiing, sleigh rides and ice skating are all easily accessible. Cultural pleasures abound, too, and antique hunting in the region is renowned. You may even purchase some of the inn's own antiques; many pieces are for sale!

The Benjamin Prescott Inn, Rte. 124, East Jaffrey, NH 03452; (603) 532-6637. (2.3 miles east of Jaffrey on Rte. 124 heading toward New Ipswich.) Rates are moderately expensive, lower for a week's stay off season. Visa and MasterCard are accepted. Children over 5 are welcome; pets may be accepted with prior consultation with innkeeper. Open year-round.

Tokfarm Inn. Once a stagecoach inn on the Boston to Keene King's Highway, 100-acre Tokfarm Inn in Rindge is more than 120 years old. Mrs. W. B. Nottingham is your delightful hostess and has a fascinating tale to tell about the bed-and-breakfast inn's name, and how she came to own it. Her name is Ev, and her late husband (a professor of physics at the Massachusetts Institute of Technology in Cambridge, Massachusetts) was Wayne, but long ago the two acquired the nicknames of Tik and Tok. Mrs. Nottingham, Tik, explains that her husband was "the kind of genius who couldn't spell, so the 'c' in the names was left out." During World War II Professor Nottingham was working on the development of radar at M.I.T., which, along with several other American universities and colleges, had set up special laboratories to assist with the war effort. Tok's specialty was vacuum pumps, and creating a vacuum—using glass tubes—was integral to radar research. In those days glass tubes were handblown and very fragile. As it was feared that the Germans might be able to bombard Boston from U-boats, and M.I.T. on the Charles River was vulnerable to attack, the scientists worried that the precious glass tubes could be broken. So the professor purchased the farm in New Hampshire, a safe haven from enemy submarines.

Today, Mrs. Nottingham grows Christmas trees on twelve acres of the land; also on the property are an old barn, a stream, and a clear, cool swimming hole. Views of Mt. Monadnock abound, birds galore offer sport for bird-watching enthusiasts, and the Cathedral of the Pines is just a short distance away. The inn contains six pleasant bedrooms for guests, including singles, doubles and triples, sharing baths. Two of the rooms are on the ground floor. All are simply furnished, have good beds, and are carpeted. For indoor relaxing guests are invited to enjoy the living room with a fireplace, wood stove and TV. There are couches and a comfortable loveseat, a "two-passenger" beanbag chair Tik made for her cat and herself, and a carpet purchased by your hostess in an Istanbul bazaar. The pillows on the couches are covered with cloth brought home from her extensive travels. Breakfast, served in the large farm kitchen, consists of juice, toast with Vermont honey, marmalade or jams and jellies, and coffee or tea.

Tokfarm Inn, Box 229, Rindge, NH 03461; (603) 899-6646. (Off Rte. 119, just over the Massachusetts/New Hampshire line, on Wood Avenue.) Rates are moderate. No children or pets, please, and no smoking. Open July 1–Nov. 1.

Peep-Willow Farm. A twenty-acre breeding and training farm for thoroughbred sport horses, Peep-Willow in Marlborough is owned by Noel Aderer. The Skidmore College graduate, before taking on the farm and opening her Colonial-style house to bed-and-breakfast guests, led a distinctly unusual life. Deciding to work her way around the world after college, Ms. Aderer taught Chinese students in north Borneo, helped build a kibbutz in Israel, trained polo ponies for the Maharajah of Jaipur, and tutored two children aboard a Volkswagen bus while traveling slowly from Western Europe to India. In 1970, upon return to her native Connecticut, she ran (but lost) as a Democrat for the State Senate—galloping on horseback from town to town in an effort to draw attention to the transportation and environmental issues symbolized by the horse. Your hostess also holds a black belt in judo.

Guests at Peep-Willow Farm are invited to help with the chores or simply admire the beautiful animals. When winter snow conditions are right guests may be offered a ride on a sled or toboggan towed by one of the farm's pampered horses, but they are *not* for riding. Horseback riding is available nearby, however, as are swimming, boating, cross-country skiing, fishing and hunting, and climbing Mt. Monadnock. In addition to the horses, resident animals on the farm include Marigold, the cat, and Music and Strider, two dogs whose major occupation is harassing the cat and chasing her up a tree whenever they think they can get away with the sport.

Ms. Aderer has three double bedrooms available for guests, one on the ground floor with a private bath. The other two share a bath. Quilts keep sleeping bodies warm during cold weather. A den and a living room are available for relaxing, and use of the kitchen is allowed for long-staying guests. Breakfast at Peep-Willow Farm offers your hostess's special French toast with maple syrup from her own trees, locally smoked bacon and good bread or toast, or, as she says, "anything guests want."

Peep-Willow Farm, Bixby Street, Marlborough, NH 03455; (603) 876-3807.

(Rte. 101 to 124, 1st left up Pleasant Street to stop at top of hill, right onto Bixby; the house is the 2nd drive on left.) Rates are moderate. Children are welcome; no pets, please. Open year-round.

Bed & Breakfast/The Whites. Dr. Walter T. White and his wife Margaret Ann welcome guests to their contemporary home in Walpole over near the Connecticut River. The house, built in 1970 on 110 acres of land, offers magnificent views of meadows, woods and hills. There are a brook and a pond on the property, too. Two double upstairs rooms are available for guests, sharing a bath. Guests are welcome to enjoy the Whites' living room and TV room, and there is an extensive library. Breakfast consists of juice, fruit, a choice of cereals and/or eggs, and coffee or tea. The house is two miles from the village, so you will need a car to reach restaurants for other meals.

Nearby activities include a country club with golf and tennis and a recreation area with swimming pool, tennis courts, jogging paths and picnic tables. Local trails offer hiking, cross-country skiing and snowmobiling fun, and Alpine skiing is accessible thirty to forty minutes away. The Connecticut River and nearby lakes are excellent for canoeing. In summer, the village of Walpole holds band concerts on the green, and in the fall the entire region is splendidly arrayed in colorful foliage.

Bed & Breakfast/The Whites, Thompson Road, Walpole, NH 03608; (603) 756-4721. (In Walpole, go up Prospect Hill; continue straight ahead to big red barn on the right. Turn left onto Thompson Road; the house is the first on the right, 2 miles from center of town.) Rates are inexpensive, lower for longer stays and free for children in the same room as parents. Children are welcome. No pets, please, and non-smokers are preferred. Open year-round.

Darby Brook Farm. Antique house enthusiasts will love this charming old house in a rural setting among rolling hills in Alstead. Of typical eighteenth-century saltbox design, the house is notable for its fine architectural details including raised panels, wainscots, wide floor boards and exposed beams. The center hall is decorated with distinctive stenciling. There are several fireplaces, and most of the furnishings are of period design or of native origin. The earliest record of a birth in the venerable home, according to owner Howard C. Weeks, is dated 1798.

The grounds, landscaped with lawns, terraces, old-fashioned flower beds and blooming shrubs, are lovely; in May the old lilacs bloom in profusion. And there is, of course, a brook. Mr. Weeks engages in small fruit production of strawberries, raspberries and apples on the farm. For guests, he has three upstairs rooms including one single and two doubles, sharing a bath. Guests are invited to

enjoy the living room, parlor and dining room, as well as the surrounding grounds and fields. For breakfast, your host offers fruit, juice, cereal, eggs any style, toast or muffins with locally made preserves, or pancakes with New Hampshire maple syrup, and coffee or tea. You'll need a car to reach restaurants for other meals; the town of Keene is not far away and has a good choice of dining establishments, and shops. Golf, tennis, and river and lake swimming are easily accessible, as well as a host of cultural events.

Darby Brook Farm, Hill Road, Box 249, Alstead, NH 03602; (603) 835-6624. (From Alstead on Rte. 123, 2 miles south on Hill Road.) Rates are moderate. Children are welcome; no pets, please. Open May 1–Oct. 31.

Massasecum Lodge. After twelve years and two prior inns, Mary Jo Shipe and her husband Jim finally found the place they were looking for—a wonderful old house on a knoll overlooking a pretty lake, surrounded by 167 acres of rolling New Hampshire countryside. Your hosts' favorite place on the property—understandably—is by their

own waterfall, which drops some forty feet through a cleft in the granite streambed and over a series of wide, step-like rock terraces.

The house, just outside of Bradford, was built about fifteen years before the American Revolution by Isaac North, believed to be Bradford's first settler. The property was a working farm for about a century; in 1850, Isaac's descendants opened the house to travelers. Today, continuing the tradition, the Shipes have nine guest rooms, all upstairs and all doubles, some in the original house and others in the wing, which was added in this century. Seven of the rooms have private baths; two share a bath. All are furnished and decorated in typical New England farmhouse style and have views of either Lake Massasecum or the mountainside that lies to the rear of the lodge.

Two cozy sitting rooms are available for guests' enjoyment, one with TV and a wood stove, and a "gathering room" with games and an old Brunswick pool table, and a wealth of books. The public rooms are comfortably and casually furnished with period American and English antiques along with contemporary pieces. Breakfast can be either continental or a hearty country meal. The latter consists of a choice of juices, hot or cold cereals, eggs with bacon, ham or sausage, homemade warm muffins and rolls, and coffee or tea. The Shipes make their own maple syrup on the grounds, in an authentic old sugar house. Often, afternoon tea will be offered, and cheese and chips before dinner. The Shipes do serve dinner, too, upon request and by reservation only, for an extra fee.

For outdoor activities, there is a sandy swimming beach on the lake, a canoe, a small skiff for fishermen, and bikes for discovering back-country roads. Trails and paths lead through the wooded grounds. Within a few miles are golf, tennis, horseback riding and a wide variety of "country stuff" such as hay rides, fairs and barn sales. Lake Sunapee, about eight miles north, offers seaplane rides, water sports and dinner cruises. In winter there's excellent skiing nearby, and all manner of other winter sports.

Massasecum Lodge, Rte. 114, RFD 1-Box 494, Bradford, NH 03221; (603) 938-2136. (West side of Rte. 114, 5 miles north of Henniker or 2 miles south of Bradford, on Lake Massasecum.) Rates are moderate. Properly behaved children are welcome; no pets, please. Open year-round.

Cutter's Loft. Bryant and Karen Winterholer's home in Goshen was built in the 1790s by John Cutter, a glassmaker from Jaffrey, New Hampshire. The large Colonial house has an attached ell and barn, and the barn's loft contains two rooms for bed-and-breakfast guests—hence the name Cutter's Loft. Both guest bedrooms have private baths and are reached either by a stairway from the sun room or by a private outside stairway. The rooms are decorated in country style with mostly handmade furnishings and accessories, including the two double beds in each room, quilts, pillow shams, curtains and lamps. Each very spacious guest room, with a sitting area, has been coordinated around the stenciled walls.

A three-sided fireplace in the center of the kitchen, dining area and parlor is a popular spot for sitting and enjoying a cup of coffee in cool weather. More stenciled walls may be seen in this area of the house, as well as the original old beams, now exposed. Note the eight-foot kitchen/dining table and Shaker-style benches; they are all handmade. Breakfast consists of juice or fresh fruit in season and a varied menu that might include omelets or scrambled eggs with sausage, pancakes with your hosts' own maple syrup or French toast, homemade granola, homebaked muffins, breads and pastries, and tea or freshly ground coffee. Karen and Bryant also provide snacks at other times of the day of cheese and crackers or pretzels, or perhaps homemade goodies. They love living in their comfortable old house, and want their guests to appreciate it and the area—and feel just as much at home—as they do.

In addition to using the parlor and sun room/greenhouse, guests are welcome to roam about the property, five acres of woods and fields with lovely views. There are an old apple orchard and a newly established fruit orchard, a pleasant path through the woods, a picnic area with a view of the mountains, and an enclosed herb and flower garden where hummingbirds come to feast. The garden offers outdoor chairs and a small table for relaxing, reading or sipping a cool beverage. Swimming is available at Gunnison Lake, a short walk down a country lane, and a broad range of year-round sports activities and interesting things to do and see are easily accessible. You will need a car; Cutter's Loft is deep in the countryside. For travelers intrigued by legends, it is said that John Cutter hanged himself in 1829 and is buried in a small cemetery a short walk from the house. Karen Winterholer also reports that some say a "presence" has been felt in the house, and several unexplained incidents have occurred, possibly at the hands of a "helpful" or "fun-loving" spirit!

Cutter's Loft, Rte. 31, Goshen, NH 03752; (603) 863-5306. Rates are moderate, lower for stays longer than 3 days. Children over 6 are welcome; no pets, please. Open year-round.

Times Ten Inn. Located in the small town of Sunapee, the Times Ten Inn is an 1820 farmhouse overlooking a twenty-five-acre wildlife preserve. The appealing bed-and-breakfast inn, owned by Audrey and Dick Kelly, is a fine place to stay while exploring the region. There are three double upstairs rooms for guests, sharing a bath; handmade quilts grace the beds. Guests may also share the large living room and TV room. Breakfast at the inn features Swedish pancakes served with homemade jams and jellies or maple syrup. And the Kellys offer complimentary wine in the evenings. In warm

weather, a deck is available for sunning or enjoying a cocktail (BYOB) before dinner. Nature walks or snowshoeing in the adjacent wildlife preserve are only two of the many activities available nearby. There's a town beach one and a half miles away and the large state beach on Lake Sunapee is two miles away—as is the ski area. Golf, sailing and fishing are easily accessible; there are excellent restaurants to choose from, and the antiquing is great. Over in the delightful hilltop town of New London to the east you'll find the renowned Barn Playhouse and—close by—several more ski areas.

Times Ten Inn, Rte. 103B, Box 572, Sunapee, NH 03782; (603) 763-5120. Rates are moderate, lower for longer stays and for children. Children are welcome; small pets may be accepted upon request. Open year-round.

Vermont

A trip through Vermont can give you the feeling that you've some-how strayed into the pages of a book, a picture book portraying everyone's idea of quintessential New England. Curving roads both broad and narrow lead the traveler through lovely valleys and stretches of dark forest, and over breathtaking mountain passes called "gaps." Friendly, crystal-clear streams follow alongside almost every road, appearing first on one side and then on the other. The state's small, pristine villages, each with its spiky church steeple and cluster of white frame houses, look exactly like paintings come to life—almost too perfect to be real. To complete the picture, there are farms—almost 4000 of them—with their traditional (and photo-genic) red barns and neat farmhouses.

Most of Vermont's farms are in the dairy business, and although cows no longer outnumber humans in the state, it sometimes appears that way. In summer, the cows seem to be everywhere, grazing placidly in valleys and on rock-strewn upland pastures. They are a peaceful sight, exceedingly soothing to observe as they munch daisies and contemplate passers-by with their large, gentle, brown eyes. Other major industries in the state include manufacturing, forestry, and granite and marble quarrying. Vermont boasts some 100 varieties of marble; some towns even have marble sidewalks.

And there is maple sugaring. In most years, Vermont is the nation's leading producer of maple syrup. From March until early April travelers are welcome to watch the operators at work collecting buckets from the trees and boiling down the sap in sugar shacks over hardwood fires. The sugar-makers often hold sugar-on-the-snow par-ties for visitors. Hot, fresh syrup is poured into a pan full of packed clean snow. The sticky concoction, called a "leather apron," is tradi-tionally eaten along with doughnuts and sour pickles, the latter to cut the sweetness.

The Green Mountains, part of the Appalachian chain, run all the way down the center of the state; Mt. Mansfield is the highest peak, rising 4393 feet above sea level. Vast chunks of Vermont are wild: 262,000 acres belong to the Green Mountain National Forest. A sturdy hiker can walk the length of the state on the 260-mile Long Trail, which took twenty years to cut. Enormous Lake Champlain, 125 miles long, forms the boundary between New York State and northwestern Vermont. Samuel de Champlain was the first European to explore the region, in 1609, and later in the seventeenth century a number of French and English settlements and forts were established. In the mid- to late-1700s, Vermont was claimed by both New York and New Hampshire, causing some hot and heavy arguments.

The settlers who were caught in the middle were not pleased. They were told by New York that they had to pay a new fee for every acre they had already purchased. Some of them resisted with force and were arrested as rioters. A militia called the Green Mountain Boys, led by Ethan Allen, was formed to protect the settlers. That feisty band later carried out the first aggressive act of the American Revolution. Virtually waging their own private war, Ethan Allen and his men captured Fort Ticonderoga, over on the New York side of Lake Champlain, from the British in May, 1775. Vermont then declared itself an independent republic, with its own coinage and postal system and a clause in its constitution prohibiting slavery. In 1791, Vermont joined the Union, the first state admitted after the original thirteen colonies.

The best way to enjoy the state is to choose any appealing route and mosey along, visiting historical sites or other points of interest on the way. Route 7 is a good choice, beginning at the northwest border of Massachusetts and heading north along the western side of Vermont. Another scenic road running the length of the state is Route 100. But don't feel you have to restrict yourself to any specific area; winding side roads are everywhere, leading to other routes and regions, so explore with abandon. The only time you will find the roads really heavy with traffic is during the spectacular fall foliage season (which is mispronounced "foilage" by many people who ought to know better).

Vermont's mountainous terrain offers superb winter sports, too, and no matter where you travel in the state there will be at least one ski resort nearby. Winters here are long and very cold, with a great deal of snow most years, so please remember to put snow tires on your car before you go. Vermonters are usually well-mannered about pushing or pulling people out of drifts, but it's wise not to test their patience too far. Sinclair Lewis once described the natives of Vermont as "a complicated, reticent, slyly humorous lot." Calvin Coolidge has often been held up as the perfect example of a typical Vermonter. The native humor *is* dry, but nowadays most Vermonters seem to be as loquacious as any other New Englander. And many still speak with the unique, vowel-twisting accent of old Vermont; President Coolidge, it is said, excelled in this. Even other Vermonters were impressed with his pronunciation of "cow"—drawling the word out to four syllables.

Southern Vermont

The Brattleboro Area/Guilford and Wilmington/West Dover

Brattleboro, down at Vermont's southeastern tip, was the site of the state's first permanent settlement, established in 1724. The town, now a popular resort and home of a number of industries, offers an interesting museum and art center and, each February, a winter carnival. Marlboro, a few miles west, is internationally known for its summer music festival. Held each July and August, the festival presents a series of chamber music concerts performed by renowned musicians from all over the world. Several miles farther along, you'll come to the attractive town of Wilmington and the Mt. Snow Valley. The valley, which stretches alongside the southern ridge of the Green Mountains, offers superb sport at a number of ski areas.

The Capt. Henry Chase House. In Guilford, just a few miles outside of Brattleboro, Patrick and Lorraine Ryan cordially welcome guests to their beautifully restored 1798 Colonial farmhouse. The house was built by Jonathan Chase, a carpenter and dairy farmer who served as an army captain in the War of 1812, and named after his son, Henry

S. Chase. Henry was born in 1811; he became a farmer and educator, teaching school for fifty-five terms and serving as superintendent of schools for ten years. He also served for several years as captain of the Guilford Rifle Guards.

Set in a lovely rural valley, the house is only a short walk from the tiny village of Green River where you will find handsome old homes, a covered bridge and a wooden dam believed to be the last of its kind still in use. On hot summer days a large swimming hole offers a cool respite. Hiking, foliage drives and cross-country skiing are only a few of the other attractions in season. The farmhouse itself is a joy to explore, with four fireplaces, wide-board floors, original wainscoting and twelve-over-twelve windows. The Ryans have three double upstairs rooms for guests, sharing two baths. For relaxing, there is a spacious living room with the original massive fireplace and beehive oven, an upstairs living room, and—for warm weather—a screened summer room.

Breakfast at the Capt. Henry Chase House features pancakes served with maple syrup made at the farm. Afternoon tea is also offered, perhaps with a freshly baked pie from Lorraine's oven. For other meals there are restaurants within a fifteen-minute drive; your hosts will be delighted to recommend a few.

The Capt. Henry Chase House, West Guilford Road, Guilford, VT (mailing address: RFD 4, Box 788, W. Brattleboro, VT 05301); (802) 254-4114. (The Ryans will give you precise directions when you call or write for reservations.) Rates are moderate, lower for children. Children are welcome; no pets, please. Open year-round, but please make reservations in advance.

The Nutmeg Inn. A charming 200-year-old Vermont farmhouse in Wilmington, the Nutmeg Inn is now operated by Del and Charlotte Lawrence and their children. The nicely restored and remodeled house, situated at a bend in the road across from the river, is painted a cheerful red with white shutters. In summer, colorful flowers bloom

all around the inn. Nine comfortably furnished rooms are available for guests; four are on the ground floor. Seven of the rooms have private baths; the others share a bath. A pleasant living room with fireplace, piano, TV, games and a library is located in the old carriage house. There is also a BYOB bar, for evening cocktails.

The Lawrences have completely redecorated the inn, maintaining its appealing country flavor, with new carpeting, curtains and fresh paint or wallpaper, and they have added attractive quilts and comforters to the beds, along with antique dressers and other nice touches. Many of the rooms have new beds and mattresses, too. Your hosts serve a hearty country breakfast daily with a variety of juices, eggs any style, French toast or pancakes, bacon or sausage, blueberry muffins, English muffins or toast, homemade preserves and coffee, tea, milk or hot chocolate. In winter the rates also include dinner, featuring delicious country-style cooking; during the summer and fall seasons dinner is available on Friday and Saturday evenings at extra charge.

The Nutmeg Inn, Box 818, Rte. 9 West (Molly Stark Trail), Wilmington, VT 05363; (802) 464-3351. (One mile west of Wilmington's traffic light.) Rates range from moderate to expensive; midweek ski packages are available. American Express is accepted. Children over 9 are welcome; no pets, please. Open year-round.

Snow Den Inn. Snow Den, owned by Milt and Jean Cummings, is in West Dover, six miles north of Wilmington. The comfortable century-old Vermont farmhouse has eight double rooms for guests, all with private baths. Two of the rooms are on the ground floor. Antiques abound including brass, sleigh, canopy and poster beds, covered with colorful handmade quilts. Extra feather pillows are offered in each room for guests' comfort, and five of the bedrooms have working fireplaces and TV. A cozy den provides a library, TV, and a marvelous view of the mountains. Each morning a full country

breakfast with juice, eggs, French toast or pancakes with bacon or sausage is served for a modest fee; in winter, breakfast and dinner are included in the rates. Your hosts also provide an extra refrigerator for guests' use. Restaurants and shops are within walking distance and several excellent ski resorts are nearby. In summer, activities in the area include a gondola ride to the top of Mt. Snow, swimming, boating, golfing and tennis.

Snow Den Inn, Rte. 100, P.O. Box 615, West Dover, VT 05356; (802) 464-9355. Rates are moderately expensive. Visa, MasterCard and American Express are accepted. Children are welcome; no pets, please. Open year-round.

Weathervane Lodge. This attractive Swiss-style lodge in West Dover, on a hill a mile off Route 100, offers quiet relaxation and a panoramic view of the mountains. Liz and Ernie Chabot have ten rooms for

guests (seven on the ground floor), plus a suite and a two-bedroom apartment. Two of the rooms have private baths; the others share six baths. For reading or conversation there is a pleasant living room with a fieldstone fireplace, and a game room contains another fireplace, a piano and TV, video and card games, Ping-Pong and a set-up bar (BYOB). In winter, the Chabots provide free cross-country ski equipment, a toboggan, sleds and snowshoes. In the summer, a wealth of activities include badminton, volleyball, water sports of all kinds and horseback riding. A full breakfast is served daily, consisting of a selection of four juices, eggs any style, French toast or pancakes (blueberry or plain) with bacon or sausage, and coffee or tea.

Weathervane Lodge, Rte. 100, West Dover, VT 05356; (802) 464-5426. (About 6 miles north of Wilmington; 1 mile off Rte. 100 on Dorr Fitch Road.) Rates are moderate to expensive, lower for children under 10. Special holiday weekend and ski week packages are available. Children are welcome; no pets, please. Open year-round.

Bennington

Route 9, the Molly Stark Trail, leads westward across southern Vermont all the way from Brattleboro to Bennington. The home of

Bennington College, Bennington is also known for its fine pottery. In historic Old Bennington, two miles west of town, visitors can explore a superb museum and an old church, and take an elevator to the top of the 306-foot Bennington Battle Monument.

The Battle of Bennington took place on August 16, 1777. The British general, John Burgoyne, desperately needed to capture American ammunition that was stored nearby, to help his troops cut New England off from the other colonies. Burgoyne sent an impressive army of 800 Hessians and Indians to capture the storehouse. To the general's astonished disbelief, the Americans, led by Gen. John Stark of New Hampshire, soundly trounced the British forces, including later reinforcements. British casualties were 207 killed or wounded, 600 taken prisoner. The Americans lost only 14 men, and 42 were wounded. The battle was a turning point in the American Revolution. Burgoyne's command was weakened; two months later he and his battered army surrendered at Saratoga.

Our oldest Stars and Stripes flag, which flew in the Battle of Bennington, may be seen in the Bennington Museum. The museum also contains collections of early American glass, Bennington pottery and Grandma Moses paintings. Nearby is the Old First Church, Vermont's Colonial Shrine; the poet Robert Frost is buried in the ancient graveyard.

The Colonial Guest House. Charles and Josephine Reis welcome travelers to their 100-year-old restored Colonial home situated on a hill just outside of Bennington. The tastefully furnished house has seven upstairs rooms for guests, all cheery, comfortable and impeccably clean. All but one of the rooms has its own sink; the bathroom is shared. Air conditioning and black-and-white cable TV are available in some of the guest chambers. There are two parlors with comfortable chairs and love seats, and your hosts' own library provides an extensive selection of books and magazines. A hearty, homecooked breakfast is served each day, for a moderate fee. Family-style dinners are also available at extra charge if ordered in advance. The meals are served in two large dining rooms, one with a fireplace made of bricks from an old schoolhouse. Outdoors, guests may relax on the sunny patio or under shady trees and enjoy a panoramic view of the mountains. The Bennington Monument is clearly visible in the distance. Nearby activities include browsing through Bennington's art galleries and craft and antique shops and visiting woolen mills and fabric shops. All manner of sports are available in summer; in winter several fine ski areas are easily accessible.

The Colonial Guest House, Historic Rte. 7A (North), Bennington, VT; (802) 442-2263. (Mailing address: Orchard Road, RR 1-Box 0163, Bennington, VT 05201-9702.) (On Harwood Hill just past the junction with Rte. 67A.) Rates are inexpensive. Children are welcome; no pets, please. Open year-round.

Manchester/Dorset

The Manchester/Dorset area, a short drive north from Bennington, has been drawing summer visitors for more than a century. Now, with some of Vermont's best skiing nearby, the lovely, mountain-ringed region is a year-round attraction. Manchester Village offers an array of interesting shops, several excellent restaurants, and the Southern Vermont Art Center. In Manchester Center just beyond, collectors of miniatures will find the Enchanted Doll House a special delight; the 1812 farmhouse contains room after room of dolls, dollhouses and dollhouse furniture. Five miles south of Manchester, the Equinox Sky Line Drive leads to a 3861-foot summit with magnificent views. The pretty little mountain village of Dorset is just northwest of Manchester Center, on Route 30. The town's sidewalks are marble, and as you drive in the area you may catch glimpses of old, abandoned marble quarries by the road, sheer-walled with jade green water below.

1811 House. To quote innkeepers Mary and Jack Hirst, "The 1811 House is *not* just another early American inn." And as guests who are fortunate enough to enjoy a stay in the large, handsome house in the center of Manchester Village will discover, the Hirsts are quite correct. Your hosts have created an exceptionally elegant home, in a beautiful setting, with a delightfully relaxed and informal atmosphere.

Built in the 1770s, the historic structure has been operated as an inn since 1811, except for a brief period when it was the private residence of Mary Lincoln Isham, the granddaughter of President Lincoln. The Hirsts purchased the inn in 1982, and since then have painstakingly restored the exterior to the Federal style of the early 1800s. Eight men burned off old paint for ten weeks before applying new colors in authentic earthtones. Shutters and porches were removed, Colonial twelve-over-twelve windows with authentic old glass were installed and a new main entrance was created.

The back two acres of land were cleared of over 200 trees, so that the house now has a spectacular view of the mountains beyond lawns, flower gardens and an adjacent golf course. Mary Hirst, a dedicated gardener, is in the process of transforming the grounds into a typically English garden. Eventually there will be charming rock, rose and herb gardens, among others.

The inside of the house has also been completely renovated and redecorated in Colonial style with the Hirsts' own collection of exquisite Early American and English antiques, paintings, antique Oriental rugs, china, crystal and silver. There are ten tastefully appointed rooms for guests, three with fireplaces. All have private baths, and one of the rooms is on the ground floor. A living room and library, both with fireplaces, are comfortable areas for reading or chatting, and there is a full bar with a fireplace.

Your hostess is English, and breakfast at the 1811 House is in the hearty British tradition. You'll be offered freshly squeezed orange juice and fresh fruit in season, followed by several of the house specialties, which might include eggs or pancakes; bacon or sausage; fried bread; sauteed apples, mushrooms and tomatoes; homefries; and English muffins, coffee or tea. There may even be eggs Benedict, kidneys in cream, chicken livers on toast or kippered herring!

1811 House, Box 39 (Rte. 7A), Manchester Village, VT 05254; (802) 362-1811. Rates are expensive. Visa, MasterCard and American Express are accepted. Children over 16 are welcome; no pets, please. Open year-round.

Maplewoods Colonial House. Marge and Leon Edgerton are your hosts at Maplewoods, a large, traditional old New England farmhouse one mile north of Dorset village. The twenty-room, 250-year-old house with green shutters contains five comfortable upstairs guest rooms, sharing three baths. The corner bedrooms offer a grand view of mountains and valley. All of the antique-filled rooms, and the baths, too, are carpeted. A spacious living room and a family room with TV and book-lined shelves are available for quiet relaxation; in winter a cheerful blaze crackles in the fireplace. Guests are invited to explore the entire house, and enjoy the Edgertons' lovely antiques, fascinating collections of magnificent Chinese screens, jade and crystal, carvings from Oberammergau, and Eskimo carvings from Alaska. Plants bloom year-round in a greenhouse and acres of pasture

and woods, with meandering brooks and a pond for fishing or canoeing, surround the house. For skiers, Bromley and Stratton are only a half-hour drive; a fine cross-country skiing center is just three miles away. Breakfast, served daily on a handsome pre-Civil War table in the dining room, features French toast, pancakes or waffles with your hosts' own prize-winning maple syrup made in their own sugar woods. Guests are also offered afternoon tea or hot chocolate.

Maplewoods Colonial House, Rte. 30, Box 1019, Dorset, VT 05251; (802) 867-4470. Rates are moderate, lower for longer stays. Well-mannered children are welcome; occasionally pets may be allowed. Open year-round.

The Little Lodge at Dorset. This delightful guest house offers just about everything a visitor to Vermont could ask for. The setting is ideal—on a hillside overlooking a trout pond and surrounded by wildflowers, white birch and pine trees, with a mountain beyond. Behind the lodge is a forest laced with trails for strolling, bird watching or cross-country skiing. According to owners Allan and Nancy Norris, the old Colonial house was an antique when it was moved to its present site more than fifty years ago. Several additions have been made to the original structure, each in keeping with its architectural style. Foot-wide floorboards and fine old paneling grace the house, along with charming period wallpaper and some lovely antiques.

There are four double rooms and one triple room for guests. Three of the rooms have private baths; two share a bath and one of these also contains a basin for washing. One of the rooms, with private bath, is on the ground floor. The bedrooms, done in a colorful "country look," are bright with calico, patchwork and hand-crocheted bedspreads and fluffy quilts. Guests are invited to enjoy the barnboard-walled den with TV, fireplace, wet bar and refrigerator for storing drinks or picnic lunch "fixings." The den also has a dartboard, puzzles, games and a well-stocked library. There is a living room, too, with a wood stove and comfortable seating area.

A light breakfast with a choice of juices and cereals and Nancy's delicious toasted Vermont Honey Loaf or other out-of-the-ordinary homemade breads is served each morning, in warm weather out on the hexagonal sun porch. Coffee and hot chocolate are always available and at cocktail time (BYOB), crackers and Vermont cheese or fondue are offered. Three excellent restaurants are within easy walking distance, and the area offers a wide choice of interesting shops. Hiking, fishing, tennis, golf, boating and swimming, and skiing, are all available nearby.

The Little Lodge at Dorset, Rte. 30, Box 673, Dorset, VT 05251; (802) 867-4040. (About 1 block north of Dorset village green.) Rates are moderately expensive, 10 percent off for stay of one week or more. American Express is accepted. Children are welcome; no pets, please. Open year-round except for part of April or May, and November.

Bondville/Weston/Grafton/Chester

Bondville, east of the Manchester area, is reached via routes 11 and 30. Stratton Mountain Ski Area is just to the south. The Stratton Arts Festival, displaying works by Vermont craftspeople and artists, takes place each year from mid-September to mid-October at the

Stratton Mountain Base Lodge. Follow Route 100 north, past the tiny, hilly town of Londonderry, to Weston where you will find a number of fine craft shops, a renowned summer theater and the intriguing Weston Priory. Here, too, are the old-fashioned and famous Vermont Country Store and the Weston Bowl Mill; the latter has been turning out bowls and other wooden items for more than seventy-five years.

Picturesque Grafton is east of Londonderry, via Route 11 and then a ten-mile, mostly unpaved stretch of Route 121. An alternate—but less interesting—way is to take Route 11 to Route 35 south. A drowsy little town, Grafton is noted for its collection of handsome white and brick houses. Chester, eight miles north of Grafton via Route 35, offers some unusual old stone houses and a red-and-green Victorian train station.

Bromley View Inn. Amy and Bick Atherton, owners of Bromley View in Bondville, offer weary travelers an unusual amenity called a *calidarium*. A modern-day version of the ancient Roman baths, the Calidarium consists of three uniquely designed tub rooms with two Jacuzzi spas and a six-foot redwood tub. Each of the tub rooms has a private shower, and towels, hair dryers and music are provided.

The inn, of contemporary wood frame design built in 1960, has twelve bedrooms for guests including one single and eleven doubles.

All have private baths and are furnished simply but comfortably. Five of the bedrooms are on the ground floor. A spacious lounge area with a marvelous view of the mountains contains both a wood stove and an open fireplace, books, and darts, ring toss and video games. There's also a small bar in the lounge, which boasts the largest selection of imported and domestic beers in Vermont. Bick Atherton's beer list currently offers more than sixty brews for the connoisseur to try.

A full breakfast is served at Bromley View, with eggs, French toast, or the house specialty, sourdough pancakes. The menu also includes bacon or sausage, homemade muffins and breads, and coffee or tea. During ski season guests are offered homemade soups and sandwiches, for an extra fee. Several restaurants are within a short drive, as are numerous year-round activities including superb skiing at Bromley, Stratton and Magic Mountain.

Bromley View Inn, Rte. 30, Bondville, VT 05340; (802) 297-1459. (The inn is 2.2 miles from intersection of rtes. 11 and 30.) Rates range from moderately expensive in ski season to moderate the rest of the year; 2-, 3- and 5-day ski packages are available. Visa, MasterCard and American Express are accepted. Children are welcome; no pets, please. Open year-round.

1830 Inn on the Green. Located on scenic Route 100 in Weston, across the road from the village green, this nineteenth-century Vermont structure was originally a blacksmith-wheelwright shop with living quarters above. Over the years the building was used for a number of other purposes, including serving as the town hall, before evolving into the elegant bed-and-breakfast inn it is today, with its handsome circular staircase that once graced one of Hetty Green's homes.

New owners Susan and Arthur Burke have furnished the house with a blend of traditional and family antiques, complemented by lots of pillows in front of the fireplace, snuggly afghans, books, games, music, flowers, and bowls of fruit and nuts for guests to snack on.

There are four upstairs guest rooms, each with its own character; all contain rocking chairs and fluffy comforters that match the color-coordinated bed and bath linens. Two of the rooms have private baths; the other two share a bath.

Breakfast at the inn is ample, featuring a daily "surprise" entree, fresh fruit, juice and homemade hot breads. In the early evening, Vermont cheese and crackers are offered, and at bedtime guests are treated to tea or cider and homemade cookies. The Weston Playhouse is just across the green, the town's interesting shops and country store are within two blocks, and the Weston Priory is four miles away. Winter and summer sports of all kinds are easily accessible as are a number of excellent restaurants.

1830 Inn on the Green, Rte. 100, P.O. Box 104, Weston, VT 05161; (802) 824-6789. Rates are moderately expensive, lower for 4 or more days' stay.

Children 14 or over are welcome; no pets, please. Open Memorial Day-Oct. 31 and Dec. 1-Easter.

The Darling Family Inn. Chapin and Joan Darling's 150-year-old restored farmhouse, just outside Weston village, offers a splendid view of the mountains. Inn guests can fish 100 yards from the house, and there is a pool for swimming or sun bathing. Hikers will find excellent trails nearby, both downhill and cross-country skiing are easily accessible, and the famed Weston Priory is three miles away.

Wide floorboards, American and English country antiques and glowing touches of copper, brass and pewter are visible throughout the Darlings' old Colonial home. There are five double rooms for guests, decorated with period furniture and accessories, and colorful, locally crafted quilts. Two of the rooms have private baths; the others share a bath. One of the guest bedrooms, with private bath, is on the ground floor. Two completely furnished housekeeping cottages on the grounds are also available for rental, year-round.

The inn's pleasant living room, with a fireplace, is a comfortable place for indoor relaxing or socializing with other travelers. Guests staying in the inn are provided with a full country breakfast, with eggs, French toast, omelets, or perhaps the house specialty, Chapin's secret-recipe pancakes served with Vermont maple syrup. There will also be bacon, ham or sausage, hot cereal, and homefries. Afternoon tea is offered, and packed lunches and dinner—at extra cost—are available upon request for both room and cottage guests.

The Darling Family Inn, Rte. 100, Weston, VT 05161; (802) 824-3223. (Half a mile from Weston village.) Rates are moderately expensive, lower for longer stays. Children 8 or over are welcome in the inn, but no pets. Children of any age, and pets, are welcome in the cottages. Open year-round.

The Hayes House. Margery Hayes Heindel is your energetic hostess at Hayes House in the small, pretty village of Grafton. In addition to welcoming guests and caring for her two dogs and two cats, Mrs. Heindel is a dedicated gardener, growing vegetables and flowers and

maintaining smooth green lawns. She's also chairman of the Grafton Board of Selectmen. Her comfortably furnished home, a seventeenth-century farmhouse, contains four rooms for guests. There are one double with a private bath and fireplace, and two doubles and a single that share baths. One of the guest rooms is on the ground floor. Guests may also use the family room with fireplace and color TV. A continental breakfast of juice, homemade muffins and jam or jelly (such as chokecherry, elderberry or blackberry) and coffee or tea is served each morning. In wintertime, your hostess welcomes skiers back from a day's run on the slopes with hot, homemade soup. Grafton village offers some good places to eat, historic buildings to tour and several shops.

The Hayes House, Grafton, VT 05146; (802) 843-2461. (A 3-minute walk from the village, on Bear Hill Road where the north and south branches of Saxton's River meet and the road crosses a covered bridge to climb Bear Mountain.) Rates are moderate. Children and pets are welcome, but must stay with parents or owner. Open year-round.

Woodchuck Hill Farm Inn. One of the oldest structures in Grafton, Woodchuck Hill is a white Colonial farmhouse surrounded by 200 acres of farmland. The circa 1790 house sits on a hilltop and commands a spectacular view all the way to Mt. Monadnock in New Hampshire, seventy-five miles away. Hosts Anne and Frank Gabriel describe their nice old home as being "at the end of the road, perfect for those who love the peace and quiet of rural New England." Guests may walk through the fields and woods, swim in the pond, or spend a restful summer afternoon reading or dozing on the broad porch that overlooks the countryside. There is also a charming gazebo for similar pursuits. Browsers will enjoy investigating the Gabriels'

antique shop, located in the old barn, and chock full of country furniture, stoneware pottery, baskets, copper, pewter and brass items, and lots more. Inside the house a spacious lounge offers TV and a large fireplace, where a cheery blaze is lit on cool evenings.

Ten pleasant rooms, decorated with antiques, are available for guests; five have private baths. One of the bedrooms, with private bath, is on the ground floor. The fully restored barn, wood paneled with the old beams, containing a loft bedroom, living-dining area and kitchen and bath, and the fully equipped housekeeping studio apartment which adjoins the main house, are also available for rental. Breakfast at Woodchuck Hill, served to guests staying at the inn, consists of juice, croissants or sticky buns, jam, and coffee or tea. Your hosts also provide guests with fine Grafton cheese and crackers each day at 5 p.m. Afternoon tea may be ordered, complete with fancy sandwiches, cookies or cake and hot scones and jam, for an extra fee and by prior reservation. Dinners, too, are offered at extra cost and by reservation.

Woodchuck Hill Farm Inn, Middletown Road, Grafton, VT 05146; (802) 843-2398. (Two miles west of Grafton village.) Rates are moderately expensive to expensive, lower for longer stays. Children over 8 are welcome; no pets, please. Open May 1–Oct. 31.

The Hugging Bear Inn & Shoppe. Teddy bear admirers—and their numbers are legion—will find perfect happiness at the Hugging Bear Inn in Chester. Bears are everywhere—staring out the first and second floor windows, on much of the furniture, playing the piano, in cribs, in cradles, and on every bed. The shop in the attached barn behind the kitchen offers more, hundreds of the huggable creatures!

How did it come about, you may ask, this wealth of bears deep in the heart of rural Vermont? Paul Thomas, who with his wife, Georgette, purchased the 1850 Victorian home in 1982, explains. First of all, the couple worked with architects and contractors to modernize the structure, carefully maintaining its nineteenth-century ambiance. But Georgette, when all was completed, felt that the house was now a touch too elegant, too formal, and the idea of inhabiting it with teddy bears came to pass. The Thomases also have an entertaining dog named Bear. Bears in the inn led to bears in a shop, and—says Paul—the combination has proven to be a felicitous one. All visitors, no matter of what age, are encouraged to hug any and all of the bears. Children staying at the inn may take as many bears as they wish from the shop to sleep with, as long as they promise to return them by 9 a.m. the next day, so that, the Thomases tell them, "the bears will be on time for work." Adult guests, of course, already have a bear on their beds for security.

The house, with its classic Victorian tower and wide porch, boasts oak trim throughout, a black cherry stairway railing with carved posts, and oak and hickory steps. The furnishings are mostly antiques from various periods, including Oriental rugs. For guests, there are six spacious upstairs rooms, all with private baths. Occasionally, when the house is full, the downstairs den is also used as a guest room, sharing a bath. Guests are invited to enjoy the living room, and—when it is not being occupied—the den, with a fireplace and library. Breakfast at the inn offers eggs any style with bacon or sausage, French toast, whole wheat or buckwheat pancakes with sunflower seeds or apple slices, pitchers of orange, cranberry or grapefruit juice, serve-yourself coffee and a variety of herbal or other teas. Coffee and tea are available all day, as is a well-filled fruit bowl; late afternoon snacks of hot or cold cider, local cheese and crackers are also provided. And on Thanksgiving Day and Christmas, your hosts provide complimentary dinner for guests.

The inn, situated on the village green, backs on to open fields which border a creek, with wooded hills beyond. Several good restaurants and shops are within walking distance, and there are many pleasant walks and drives to be taken in the area. Your hosts will be happy to suggest a variety of sightseeing or sports activities.

The Hugging Bear Inn & Shoppe, Main Street, Chester, VT 05143; (802) 875-2412. (Exit 6 off I-91, 10 miles northwest on Rte. 103. The inn is on the right 1 block after Rte. 103 joins Rte. 11.) Rates are moderately expensive, lower off season except for major holidays and fall foliage weekends, and for longer stays. Visa and MasterCard are accepted. Children are welcome; pets may be allowed by prearrangement. No smoking within the inn; upstairs and downstairs porches have ashtrays. Open year-round.

Central Vermont

Cuttingsville/Killington/Windsor/ Woodstock/West Hartford

The small community of Cuttingsville is on Route 103, northwest of Chester past Ludlow, and a few miles southeast of Rutland. An intriguing stained-glass studio and the Haunted Mansion Bookshop are fun to explore in the Cuttingsville area, and nearby—in Healdville—you can tour a renowned Vermont cheese-making enterprise. The Crowley Cheese Factory, located in an old barn, has been making delicious Colby cheese since 1824.

Killington, one of Vermont's most famous ski areas, lies east of Rutland and northeast of Cuttingsville. Legend has it that Vermont was named from the top of Mt. Killington, in 1763, by a pioneer preacher named Samuel Peters. Reverend Peters, inspired by the panorama of green spreading in every direction, christened the land "Verd-mont," or "green mountains."

Historic Windsor to the southeast on the Vermont/New Hampshire border, boasts America's longest covered bridge. The 462-foot span was built in 1866 and crosses over the Connecticut River to Cornish, New Hampshire. Vermont's constitution was drawn up and signed in Windsor, in 1777. While the delegates were in session, postriders raced into town to warn of trouble at Ticonderoga. Although the representatives wanted to adjourn immediately to defend their homes, a terrific thunderstorm held them captive. So they used the time in typically thrifty Yankee fashion by speedily voting to adopt the new constitution, and then, when the storm had ended, they went off to fight the enemy. The Constitution House on Main Street where the document was signed is now a museum.

Woodstock, one of Vermont's most visited villages, is northwest of Windsor via routes 12 and 4, and West Hartford lies a few miles beyond, to the north. An exceptionally attractive town set in the foothills of the Green Mountains, Woodstock offers lovely old houses, many fine shops, good restaurants, a village green and several covered bridges. Founded in 1765, Woodstock became the Shire Town, or seat of Windsor County, and for a time was a thriving business and political center with five weekly newspapers. In 1934, the first rope tow up a mountain was constructed for skiers on a Woodstock hill, an unassuming start for a giant industry.

Maple Crest Farm. Shaded by sugar maple trees and offering a beautiful view of the mountains, this brick Colonial structure was built in 1808 as a tavern. Located in historic Shrewsbury, a part of Cuttingsville, the farm is owned by William and Donna Smith. They have four spacious rooms for guests, including one on the ground

floor. Two rooms have private baths; the others share a bath. The bedrooms, decorated with antiques and colorful quilts, are large; each contains one double and one single bed. There's a comfortable living room for relaxing and meeting other guests, and a full country breakfast is served each morning. Maple Crest, an operating dairy farm, also has its own sugar house where sap collected from the old maple trees each spring is boiled down into delicious syrup—which guests will be able to sample on their breakfast pancakes. You will need a car to reach restaurants and shops; several ski areas are accessible in the area as well as historic sites including Calvin Coolidge's birthplace in Plymouth. If you come at the right season, you can watch the Smiths at work maple sugaring.

Maple Crest Farm, Box 120, Cuttingsville, VT 05738; (802) 492-3367. (South of Rutland, 2½ miles off Rte. 103 in Shrewsbury Center.) Rates are moderate, lower for longer stays. Children are welcome; no pets, please. Open year-round.

Mountain Morgans. At Mountain Morgans in Killington, guests may gather their own eggs for breakfast! Many of the farm animals, including horses, donkeys, sheep, rabbits and other friendly creatures, roam freely in the yard and are pleased to be admired. A great place for children, the farm also offers a swing and a sandpile. Jeffrey and Susan Hiers are your hosts; they live on one side of their 1975 rustic-style duplex, and bed-and-breakfast guests share the other side. There are three double guest rooms, all with private baths. One of the rooms is on the ground floor. There is a living room with fireplace and TV for relaxing, and a fully equipped kitchen where guests make their own breakfasts. Your hosts provide the food: farm-fresh eggs from the barn, orange juice, English muffins, and coffee, tea or milk. Outdoors are a barbecue grill and picnic table for guests to use. Things to do in the area include skiing at Killington, winter sleigh rides or summer horse-drawn carriage rides and lots more. Ask Jeff Hiers to suggest some activities; he was previously an official tour guide and knows all of the interesting sites in the region.

Mountain Morgans, Box 138-A, RD 1, Killington, VT 05751; (802) 422-3096. (Ask for directions when you call or write for reservations.) Rates are inexpensive. Children are welcome; no pets, please. Open year-round.

Juniper Hill Inn. Jim and Krisha Pennino are the new owners of Juniper Hill, a strikingly handsome and historic mansion in Windsor. The house was built between 1901 and 1903 by Maxwell Evarts, a descendant of Roger Sherman, one of the signers of the Declaration of Independence. Evarts was the chief lawyer and general counsel for the E.H. Harriman Railroad, forerunner of the Southern Pacific, and often entertained Mr. Harriman at Juniper Hill. President Theodore Roosevelt, a personal friend, was another of the many notables who visited the mansion. The Evarts family occupied the house until 1935; in subsequent years it has served as a private school, a Catholic retreat center, and an inn.

Jim and Krisha purchased Juniper Hill in 1984 and have furnished it with their own collection of European and American antiques. There are fourteen upstairs rooms for guests, tastefully furnished in period decor with antique beds and accessories. Nine of the rooms have private baths; the others share three baths. Downstairs, guests are welcome to enjoy the baronial, oak-paneled, thirty-foot by forty-foot entrance hall with its massive fireplace, the cozy sitting rooms, and the library, decorated with your hosts' collection of copper and country pieces.

A full breakfast is served each morning in the dining room; breakfast in bed can be arranged upon request. Offered are juice, eggs, French toast or pancakes with bacon or sausage, and coffee or tea. Krisha puts up her own preserves, and the maple syrup is collected from

trees on the property. Dinner is also available, upon reservation and at extra cost.

The beautifully restored mansion, fronted by stately white columns, stands high on a hill with views of landscaped grounds and a pond, and Mt. Ascutney in the distance. A wide variety of year-round sports are available nearby, as are shops and restaurants.

Juniper Hill Inn, Juniper Hill Road, RR 1, Box 79, NEB Windsor, VT 05089; (802) 674-5273. (One-quarter mile off Rte. 5.) Rates are moderate to expensive, lower for longer stays. Visa and MasterCard are accepted. Children over 12 are welcome; no pets, please. Open year-round.

Three Church Street, Bed and Breakfast. Conveniently located in the center of Woodstock, this spacious house—listed in the National Register of Historic Places—is owned by Eleanor C. Paine. The original, brick portion of the structure was built in the 1820s; later additions brought the total number of rooms to twenty-five, and the house is now, as your hostess puts it, "a mish-mash of Federal, New Orleans and two new contemporary rooms."

For guests there are ten comfortable double bedrooms, five with private baths. Two of the rooms, with private baths, are on the ground floor. (The accommodations can be arranged to include one two-room suite, with a small kitchen, and two three-room suites, one with a kitchen and the other with toaster oven, refrigerator and hot plate. The suites, ideal for families or couples traveling together, are available only by the week or on weekends.) No two of the rooms are

Three Church Street, Bed and Breakfast

alike; most are decorated in Early American style, and three have four-poster canopied beds.

The ambiance at Three Church Street is relaxed and friendly. Guests are invited to enjoy the sitting room with fireplace and TV, and the cozy library with a wood stove, TV and a fine collection of books. A gallery overlooks the Ottauquechee River and Mt. Tom. Outdoors are a swimming pool and a clay tennis court.

Breakfast at Three Church Street is not simply a meal, it's an occasion! Your hostess quotes Nathaniel Hawthorne's thoughts on the subject: "Life, within doors, has few pleasanter prospects than a neatly arranged and well provisioned breakfast table." Mrs. Paine obviously agrees, offering her guests a selection of juices, hot cereals, sausage, bacon or ham, corned beef hash, chicken livers, homefries and grits. There will also be eggs cooked in a variety of ways, omelets, pancakes or French toast, pastries and coffee or tea. On Sundays your hostess outdoes herself with eggs Benedict or blueberry pancakes. Additional specialties include a platter of seasonal fruits and fruited pancakes in summer, baked apples and apple pancakes in winter. Complimentary coffee, tea, hot chocolate and soups are available throughout the day, and snacks of popcorn or cheese and crackers are offered in the evening.

Several excellent restaurants are within walking distance of the house. Boutiques, antique shops and historic homes are also close by, and horseback riding, fishing and hiking trails are easily accessible. Silver Lake, six miles away, offers a fine beach; the Country Club (open to the public) with golf, tennis and cross-country skiing, is a half mile away. For downhill skiers Killington is a forty-minute drive, and five other major ski areas may be reached within an hour's drive.

Three Church Street, 3 Church St., Woodstock, VT 05091; (802) 457-1925. (In the village on Rte. 4 immediately west of the Town Hall/Movie Theater.) Rates range from moderate to moderately expensive, with a 10 percent discount for a week's or longer stay; no charge for cribs. Visa and MasterCard are accepted. Children are welcome and extra cots and cribs are available; youngsters using the pool must be accompanied by adults. Well-mannered pets are also accepted but must be attended at all times. Open May 1–April 1.

Clifford's Guest House. Mrs. Maude Clifford welcomes travelers to her nice old farmhouse in West Hartford, ten miles northwest of Woodstock. The century-old house, surrounded by lovely wooded grounds, includes six spanking clean, comfortable rooms for guests, sharing three baths. There are one single and five double rooms, and three of the latter will accommodate three persons if needed. One of the rooms is on the ground floor. In summer, a small cabin on the grounds is also available for two people. Guests are invited to share Mrs. Clifford's living room with TV, and a small room with a wood stove which opens up like a fireplace so that everyone can enjoy the cheerful blaze in the wintertime. Outdoors there's a charming little screen house for sitting and relaxing in warm weather. Your hostess serves breakfast daily, offering whatever guests would like and often including delicious homebaked blueberry muffins. Restaurants are available within a short drive, as are a variety of activities including sightseeing, shopping and skiing. For youngsters there is a pleasant playground near the house.

Clifford's Guest House, West Hartford, VT 05084; (802) 295-3554. (On North Pomfret Road, 3 miles off Rte. 14. The house is 10 miles from Woodstock and 10 miles from White River Junction, and your hostess will give you specific directions when you call to make a reservation.) Rates are very inexpensive, lower for children under 12, and a crib is available free for babies. Children are welcome; no pets, please. Open year-round.

Bethel/Chelsea/Middlebury/Vergennes

Route 12 north from Woodstock will bring you to Bethel. Chelsea— well off the beaten path—lies to the northeast at the junction of routes 110 and 113. The entire town (a very small one) is listed on the National Register of Historic Places and has a rare double common, or village green. Middlebury is northwest of Woodstock, on Route 7, and Vergennes is just a few miles farther north, on Route 22A off Route 7. Home of Middlebury College, the photogenic town of Middlebury has a group of nicely renovated Victorian buildings that now house a variety of fine shops and restaurants. The Vermont State Craft Center, in an old mill beside a rushing stream, displays a changing array of handsome handmade crafts and pottery.

The famous Morgan Horse Farm, two and one half miles northwest of town just off Route 7, is another interesting site to explore in the region. Some sixty horses can be seen; they're bred and trained on the farm. In 1795, a singing master named Justin Morgan brought a colt from Massachusetts to Randolph, Vermont. That horse—named

Justin Morgan after its owner—turned out to be an amazing creature. A distinct new breed of horses descended from him, all sturdy legged, deep chested, swift, graceful, courageous and intelligent. These may sound like a great many adjectives for a horse, but the Morgan lives up to all of them and more. It became America's war horse: General Custer rode a Morgan, and an entire regiment was mounted on Morgans during the Civil War. Mounted police prefer Morgans, and the beautiful animals are also superb trotting horses.

Poplar Manor. Bob and Carmen Jaynes searched for several years before finding just the house they wanted in Vermont: a home large enough to be turned into a "bed and breakfast," located well off the road but still visible, and with old lilac bushes. This nineteenth-century Colonial farmhouse in Bethel fulfilled all their requirements, and more. Set back from the road at the end of a long driveway, the white clapboard house with black shutters is surrounded by a meadow and cornfields backing up to the White River. Inside are wide floorboards and exposed beams. There's an unusual barn on the property: originally a schoolhouse in Bethel, the building was dismantled, floated up the river and rebuilt here. In addition, the property boasts a delightful small swimming hole, with a waterfall. And there are rows of poplars, both native and Lombardy.

Ebenezer Putnam, one of Bethel's earliest settlers and a general in the Revolutionary War, owned the land originally and lived there in a log cabin. Putnam's son built the present house around 1810. The Jayneses, who moved here from Tarrytown, New York, purchased Poplar Manor in 1980 and have furnished it with antiques, collectibles, art, and many plants. One notable antique is a striking old wagon bed that now serves as a coffee table in the spacious living room. Carmen, a native of Puerto Rico, enjoys showing her collection of early island folk art, and prints, paintings and sculptures created by her father, a sculptor and professor emeritus at the University of Puerto Rico.

For guests there are five upstairs rooms, sharing baths. A light breakfast is served each morning, with juice, cereals, a variety of homebaked breads or muffins, and coffee or tea. At other times your cordial hosts may offer tea, wine, or cold or hot mulled cider, depending on the season. Restaurants and shops are within an easy drive and things to do in the area are many, including year-round sports activities, scenic drives and walks, and antiquing.

Poplar Manor, RD 2, Bethel, VT 05032; (802) 234-5426. (On Rte. 107 west, about 4 miles from Exit 3, I-89 north.) Rates are inexpensive, lower for small children and for longer stays. Children are welcome. Pets are occasionally accepted, but the Jayneses have two Chesapeake Bay retrievers so the animals must be kept separated. Open year-round.

Shire Inn. Chelsea, shiretown of Vermont's rural Orange County, is

a diminutive country village that might easily go undiscovered by
travelers. That would be a mistake, for Chelsea contains one of the
nicest bed-and-breakfast inns in the state. Owned by De and Ingeborg
("Tilli") Davis, the Shire Inn is an exceptionally handsome fourteen-
room brick mansion, built in 1832 and listed on the National Register
of Historic Places. The Federal-style house has six attractive rooms,
four with working fireplaces, for guests. Two of the bedrooms,
including one on the ground floor, have private baths. The other
rooms share baths; two also contain washbowls and all are distinctively decorated with period antiques. A spacious living room, with
a fireplace and an extensive library, offers a pleasant place for
conversation or reading.

Outdoors, guests can relax on the broad porch or explore the inn's
seventeen acres of land, through which runs a fine—and scenic—
trout stream. Huge old sugar maples grow on the grounds, and a
brick path leads to lovely gardens. Throughout the spring and summer the gardens provide a variety of flowers and herbs. A bridge over
the stream leads to rolling hills and forest, ideal for winter cross-
country skiing or summertime hiking. Downhill skiing is easily
accessible, too, as are swimming, boating, antiquing and other enjoyable country pursuits.

A complete breakfast is served at the inn, with some unusual
delicacies prepared by Tilli such as grapefruit Alaska, hot buttered
plums, baked apples, *eierkuchen* (German oven-baked egg pancakes), and homemade pastries. Full five-course candlelit dinners
are also available, at extra charge. Tiny Chelsea is a good half-hour's
drive from the nearest restaurant, so taking advantage of your hostess's
culinary skills is a worthwhile and thoroughly pleasurable idea.

Shire Inn, S. Main Street (Rte. 110), Chelsea, VT 05038; (802) 685-3031. (In
the village, off the town green.) Rates are moderately expensive. Visa and
MasterCard are accepted. Children over 10 are welcome; no pets, and no
smoking, please. Open year-round except for April.

Breadloaf Farm. Rene and Paul Saenger's farm near Middlebury was once part of the original Morgan Horse Farm, which is now owned and managed by the University of Vermont. Breadloaf is a working farm; the Saengers raise sheep, beef, turkeys and hay. The farmhouse, built in the early 1900s, has four rooms up and four down. Three of the upstairs bedrooms, all doubles, are available for guests. All are furnished with antiques and handmade quilts; the rooms share a bath. Guests may also share the family/living area and dining room. A country breakfast with yeast waffles, omelets or pancakes is served, with real Vermont maple syrup and other locally grown or made products. Coffee and tea are available at all times. Guests are welcome to enjoy the farm animals and perhaps help with some of the farm chores. The nearby Morgan Horse Farm may be toured, too, and all of the region's multitude of year-round activities are easily accessible, as are restaurants and shops.

Breadloaf Farm, RD 1, Box 195, Middlebury, VT 05753; (802) 545-2101. (From Rte. 7 take Rte. 125W through town; turn right on Rte. 23 and right again on Pulp Mill Road. Take left fork on Horse Farm Road; the house is 1.8 miles on left.) Rates are moderate, lower for children and for longer stays. Children are welcome; pets are accepted but must remain outside. Open year-round.

Samuel Paddock Strong House. Standing on a slight ridge with views of the Green Mountains to the east and the Adirondacks to the west, this beautiful old house is just outside historic Vergennes in the Champlain Valley. Samuel Paddock Strong, the third generation of a family locally renowned for their grand homes, built the Federal-style house in 1834. Its many fine architectural details have been carefully preserved, including the free-standing main staircase with

curly maple railings, a formal carved marble fireplace in the parlor, and elegant, intricate moldings and doors throughout.

Hosts Laura and Liam Murphy have six distinctively different rooms for guests. The master bedroom is furnished with an Empire period mahogany sleigh bed and unusual carved gooseneck chairs; it also has a working fireplace and its own half bath. Bedroom 2, a bright, cheerful room, offers an antique iron-and-brass double bed covered with a handmade quilt. Bedroom 3, the "Victorian Room," has a rare double butternut bed with carved, arched headboard, and Bedroom 4 has two brass-and-iron beds, one single and one double, and one of the few closets in the house. Cozy Bedroom 5, with sloped ceilings, is in the south wing of the house and offers both a double bed and a fold-out couch, suitable for a child. Rooms 2 through 5 share two full baths. Bedroom 6 is on the first floor of the north wing, has its own private full bath and contains antique mahogany furniture including a four-poster bed with carved finials.

The spacious living room with a fireplace and the dining room are both available for guests to enjoy. In the summer, a charming court-yard offers mountain views and lovely sunsets. Liam and Laura have filled the house with an interesting mix of antiques and collections of whimsical and modern art, including works by renowned Vermont artists. A full breakfast is served each morning with fruit, meat, an entree, and tea or freshly ground coffee. Your hosts' specialties include colorful fresh fruit salads, French bread French toast, and a variety of homebaked treats such as tangy apricot bread or lemon blueberry muffins. Afternoon tea or cold drinks are also offered, and dinner is available—at extra cost—by reservation.

The small town of Vergennes is a ten-minute walk away, Middlebury is a twelve-mile drive, and the famous Shelburne Museum is fifteen miles away. Lake Champlain—for summer activities and winter ice fishing—is a six-mile drive; skiing and hiking are easily accessible. *Samuel Paddock Strong House, RD 1, Box 9, Vergennes, VT 05491; (802) 877-3337. (From Rte. 7 take Rte. 22A south through Vergennes. The house is on Rte. 22A, ¾ mile south of stoplight in center of Vergennes.) Rates are moderately expensive, lower Dec. 26–March 15. Visa, MasterCard and American Express are accepted. Children are welcome; no pets, please. Open May 15–Nov. 15 and Dec. 26–March 15.*

Northern Vermont
Burlington/Lake Champlain Islands

Burlington, high above the shores of beautiful Lake Champlain, is Vermont's largest city. Its commanding views of the lake were helpful in the War of 1812, when guns at Battery Park fought off British warships. Hilly Burlington is the home of the University of Vermont, and at the university's Robert Hull Fleming Museum visitors can enjoy an outstanding collection of European and Oriental art. In summer, a one-hour ferry ride takes passengers from the city across the lake to Port Kent, New York. During July and August, Mozart and Shakespeare festivals are held at various sites in and around Burlington.

The fascinating Shelburne Museum, seven miles to the south, is a treat not to be missed. The museum, which now sprawls over forty-five acres, was created in 1947 by Mr. and Mrs. J. Watson Webb, originally as a place to display their family carriages and sleighs. Today thirty-five eighteenth- and nineteenth-century buildings transported from all over the state are arranged in a rural village setting. Three centuries of Americana are on view ranging from a blacksmith/wheelright's shop, an old apothecary shop and a schoolhouse to a steam locomotive and the 1906 Lake Champlain sidewheeler steamer *Ticonderoga*. Six restored Colonial homes are also on view, and galleries and museums house superb collections of antique folk art, sculpture, carriages, farm tools and countless other items. The museum is open daily from mid-May through late October.

Route 2 northwest from Burlington leads to a string of islands out in Lake Champlain. There are several excellent state parks, and in Grand Isle, an interesting log cabin to visit. Thought to be the oldest structure of its kind in the country, the cabin was built in 1783 by Jedediah Hyde, Jr. Fishing enthusiasts will find the waters off the south end of North Hero Island a bountiful source of sport. For historians, Isle La Motte is the site of Vermont's first white settlement—Fort St. Ann—constructed by the French in 1666.

The Yellow House. The charming bed-and-breakfast Yellow House is located on the hill in Burlington, conveniently near four college campuses: the University of Vermont, Champlain College, Trinity and St. Michael's. A classic Colonial with a handsome center staircase

and a view of Lake Champlain, the house contains many heirloom furnishings. Your hostess, Mrs. Robert Bensen, has two upstairs bedrooms for guests, one single and one double. The bathroom is shared. Rooms and bath are sparkling clean and tastefully decorated, with good comfortable beds and reading lamps. Guests are invited to use the family living room and library, and to enjoy the splendid deck which overlooks the garden and offers a fine vantage point for watching birds and having afternoon tea. A full Vermont-style breakfast is served, with juice, a choice of hot or cold cereal, toasted homemade bread with jam (sometimes homemade marmalade), a variety of egg dishes, and coffee or tea. For other meals, Burlington offers a wide choice of excellent restaurants.

The Yellow House, P.O. Box 118, Burlington, VT 05402; (802) 864-4002. (When you phone or write for reservations, Mrs. Bensen will provide directions to her house.) Rates are moderate. Children over 12 are welcome; no pets, please, and no smoking. Open year-round.

Proctor Avenue Bed and Breakfast. Elaine Greenfield, a professional musician, welcomes guests to her comfortable home in Burlington. She is a concert pianist, and sometimes guests will have the pleasure of hearing music! The house, built circa 1950, is cozy and traditional in appearance—almost a Cape style. Two pleasant rooms are available for guests. One, containing a double bed and a single bed, is in the basement and is connected to a den/sitting room with TV. The other guest room is a double on the second floor. A small cot is also available. Both of the traditionally furnished rooms are removed from the center of activity and are peaceful and quiet. A bath on the main floor is shared. Ms. Greenfield offers a gourmet continental breakfast of juice, warm Danish, croissants or bagels, or toasted homebaked bread with homemade jam, Yogurt Parfait (yogurt, granola, nuts, honey and fruit) or cold cereals, and freshly ground coffee, tea or homemade cocoa. Your hostess will be delighted to recommend some of the city's fine restaurants for other meals, and offer suggestions for things to do and see in the area.

Proctor Avenue Bed and Breakfast, 47 Proctor Ave., South Burlington, VT 05401; (802) 864-9209. (Ask for specific directions when you call or write for reservations. Best times to call are before 9 a.m. and after 6 p.m.) Rates are moderate; special rates can be arranged for longer stays, holiday periods, and children. Children are welcome. No pets, please, and no smoking. Please park in driveway at side of house, on Orchard Road. Open year-round.

Charlie's Northland Lodge. You'll find Charlie and Dorice Clark's pleasant guest house out on North Hero, one of the Lake Champlain islands north of Burlington. The restored Colonial house, circa 1800–1850, is in the center of North Hero Village. There are four double rooms for guests, two with double beds and two with twin beds. Two baths are shared. One of the rooms is on the ground floor. Separate guest cottages, fully furnished and electrically heated, are also available. Breakfast at the lodge features rhubarb cake, blueberry or other kinds of muffins or sweet buns, orange juice and coffee.

A comfortable lounge/reading room in the main house is a nice place to relax indoors. On the grounds are two excellent tennis courts for guests' pleasure, and in wintertime, thirty wooded acres offer fine cross-country skiing. Skis are available for renting. And if you enjoy fishing, Charlie's Northland Lodge is the place to come, even in fall or winter. The lake abounds with fish: bass, walleye and great northern pike, and there is a sport and tackle shop right at the lodge. All baits are available in season; boats and motors may be rented.

The lodge offers unparalleled views of both lake and mountains; the adjoining islands of South Hero and Isle la Motte are great fun to explore, and their level terrain makes them ideal for bicycling. Other activities include pleasure boating and sailing, swimming and hiking. Restaurants and shops are within walking distance of the lodge.

Charlie's Northland Lodge, Rte. 2, North Hero, VT 05474; (802) 372-8822. (On North Hero Island, 30 miles north of Burlington, 60 miles south of Montreal.) Rates are moderate. Children are welcome, but there are no rollaway beds available. No pets, please; no bare feet in the house or food kept in rooms. Open year-round.

The Montpelier Area: Barre/Waterbury/Stowe

Situated on the Winooski River in northcentral Vermont, Montpelier is our nation's smallest state capital. Somehow the city, nestled in the midst of Vermont's Green Mountains, is always a surprising sight. Perhaps it is just that one doesn't expect a city here, and the gold-leafed dome of the State House appears charmingly incongruous, gleaming brightly against the tree-covered hills. A classic small example of Greek Revival architecture, the State House is constructed of Vermont granite, with soaring Doric columns; a fourteen-foot statue of Ceres, goddess of agriculture, stands atop the dome. In the adjacent Vermont Historical Society Museum and Library are a number of interesting exhibits, including a display covering the fourteen-year period (1777–1791) when Vermont was an independent republic.

Barre, a few miles southeast of Montpelier, has long been renowned for its granite quarries, the world's largest. From May through October the awesome Rock of Ages Quarry offers free guided tours; visitors peer down into the depths of 350- to 400-foot-deep canyons and observe the activity below. At the Craftsman Center you can watch skilled stonecutters at work as they create finished monuments from the rough stone.

Waterbury is northeast of Montpelier, via either Route 2 west or I-89. The famed year-round resort of Stowe lies at the junction of routes 10 and 108, about ten miles north of Waterbury. Nestled in a valley below Mt. Mansfield, Stowe is beloved by skiers for the great abundance of snow that falls almost every year. The town also offers a wealth of shops, galleries and interesting restaurants. If you follow Route 108 northwest, you'll come to the toll road that leads to Mt. Mansfield's summit; at 4393 feet the mountain is Vermont's highest.

The road, offering impressive vistas at every turn, is open only in summer. Another way to reach the summit is to ride a gondola, ascending from the Spruce Peak Ski Area.

Continuing along Route 108 will bring you to Smuggler's Notch, a marvelously sinister mountain pass so named because goods were smuggled into Canada via the route during the War of 1812. Black forest encroaches on either side as you creep along the narrow, twisting road; rock walls tower ominously above. If you are at all romantic, you may have the prickly sensation that a highwayman lurks behind every one of the immense boulders that lie tumbled along the way.

Woodruff House. An 1893 Queen Anne Victorian situated on a quiet park in the center of Barre, Woodruff House offers informal hospitality and a good breakfast. The house was built by a local quarry owner, John E. Smith, and purchased by the Woodruff family in the 1920s. Present owners Robert and Terry Somaini bought the place in 1977, and since then have completely renovated the house, restoring it as much as possible to its original Victorian appearance and charm.

Two double rooms and one with twin beds, sharing two baths, are available for guests. Two are on the ground floor. The tastefully decorated accommodations, done in cheerfully eclectic style, contain a host of interesting antiques and memorabilia. The friendly Somainis encourage their guests to explore and enjoy the entire house, and to become part of their family. Two comfortable living rooms on the first floor, with TV and a piano, are pleasant places to gather and chat. Breakfast, served upstairs in one of two dining rooms, can be light or gourmet. There will always be homemade bread and plenty of good Vermont cheese in the eggs. Robert and Terry promise: "You'll never go away hungry!" Afternoon tea is almost always offered, too, presented on a lovely silver service, and in cool weather guests are served an evening dessert of some sort.

Restaurants and shopping are available nearby, and the region offers a wealth of activities including visits to the granite quarries and museums, skiing in winter and foliage tours in the fall. Montpelier, the state capital, is seven miles away.

Woodruff House, 13 East St., Barre, VT 05641; (802) 476-7745. (In center of town; from Rte. 302 east take Academy Street on your left; the house is on the park.) Rates are moderate; advance reservations are requested. Children are negotiable; no pets, please, and no smoking. Open year-round.

Schneider Haus. This attractive guest house, in a quiet country setting just south of Waterbury, is a picturesque Tyrolean-style chalet. George and Irene Ballschneider built the house—which stands high on a hillside far from the road—after falling in love with similar structures in Austria. The exterior is authentically Austrian, with sharply pitched roofs and railed balconies. Inside, a cozy lounge features an enormous stone fireplace. There's also a game room with Ping-Pong and TV.

Present-day hosts Aaron, Sandy, Brett and Allison Hill have twelve guest rooms, furnished with antiques and handmade quilts. The rooms share six baths. Two of the rooms are on the ground floor. A full breakfast, served in the wood-paneled dining room, includes eggs or French toast with bacon, croissants topped with strawberries and whipped cream, and coffee, tea or hot chocolate. Other meals can be arranged for groups, with advance notice and at an extra charge. A refrigerator is available for guests' use, as are outdoor barbecue grills for summer cookouts. There is also a heated outdoor spa, with a hot tub for summer and fall, and a sauna for winter use. Restaurants and shops are five to fifteen minutes away; Sugarbush Ski Area is fifteen miles south.

Schneider Haus, Rte. 100, Duxbury, VT; (802) 244-7726. Mailing address: Box 283A, Waterbury, VT 05676. (Four miles south of Waterbury Village, 5 miles south of Exit 10 off I-89.) Rates are moderately expensive, lower for longer stays. Visa, MasterCard and American Express are accepted. Children over 4 are welcome; no pets, please. Open June–Oct. 15 and Dec. 15–mid-April.

The 1860 House. A very attractive structure in the center of Stowe village, the historic 1860 House is a popular subject for artists and photographers. A two-story clapboard building with interesting gables, the house is painted dark brown with white trim. Architecturally, it is a good example of the Italianate domestic style. All of the windows are topped by thin, peaked lintel boards supported by brackets; over the door is a similar, more projecting hood, and paired scroll brackets decorate the roof cornice on the main block, side ell and connecting gable front.

Hosts Rick Hubbard and his wife, Rose Marie Matulionis, offer five spacious upstairs bedrooms for guests, suitable for singles or doubles. Three have private baths; the others share a bath. For conversation or quiet relaxation there is a large, plant-filled living room with a

cozy reading nook, a small antique writing or game table, an upright piano, a stereo and an open wood stove. In summer, a deck and terraces are pleasant places to sit and sun, overlooking lovely flower gardens. A continental breakfast is served each morning with fresh fruit, orange juice, freshly baked breads and brewed coffee or tea. Coffee and tea are available throughout the day, and guests may, if they wish, prepare dinner for themselves and dine by candlelight accompanied by Vivaldi.

The 1860 House, School Street, P. O. Box 276, Stowe, VT 05672; (802) 253-7351 or 253-8544. (Near the post office.) Rates are moderate, lower May 1–June 30 and Oct. 20–Nov. 17, and for longer stays. Visa and MasterCard are accepted. Children are welcome; pets may be accepted with advance permission. Non-smokers only, please. Open year-round.

Guest House Christel Horman. Christel Horman is a native of Hamburg, West Germany; her husband Jim was born in Australia. An ex-ski instructor, Jim formerly managed a hotel in Stowe where Christel worked as housekeeper. The two decided to use their knowledge of innkeeping and start a small business of their own—which,

Christel says, has worked beautifully and has provided them with a lot of fun. Their guest house is typically European in style, resembling a large Swiss chalet. There is a spacious living room with a fieldstone fireplace, color TV and many books and magazines for relaxing. Eight comfortable double guest bedrooms offer two double beds each, with firm new mattresses, wall-to-wall carpeting, individual thermostats and private baths. Four of the rooms are on the ground floor. A hearty breakfast includes orange juice, eggs any style, bacon or sausage, sweet rolls and toast, marmalade, and coffee or tea. Coffee and tea are also available in the afternoon. Activities offered are walks in the woods, swimming in the Hormans' outdoor pool and trout fishing in the brook behind the house. Nearby, guests will find tennis, horseback riding, golf, and—of course—superb skiing. Cross-country skiing can start right outside the house and an excellent cross-country ski center is within walking distance. The Trapp Family Lodge is close by, and Mt. Mansfield is one and a half miles away.

Guest House Christel Horman, Mountain Road, RR 1, Box 1635, Stowe, VT 05672; (802) 253-4846. Rates are moderately expensive, lower from end of April to mid-June and from Oct. 20 to mid-December. Special rates are available in summer for a three-night or longer stay and for winter five-night ski weeks. Visa and MasterCard are accepted. Children are welcome but must be accompanied by parents; no pets, please. Open year-round.

Fiddlers Green Inn. A Colonial farmhouse built in 1820, Fiddlers Green in Stowe is owned by Bud and Carol McKeon. Seven double bedrooms are available for guests; one contains four twin beds and another has two twins and two sets of bunks. Four of the rooms have private baths; the others share a bath. Two of the rooms are on the ground floor. Breakfast at Fiddlers Green features blueberry, raspberry or juneberry pancakes; dinner is also available by reservation for groups in summer and for all guests in winter. Meals are extra in summer; breakfast and dinner are included in the winter rates. Complimentary afternoon tea or coffee, and hors d'oeuvres at cocktail

time (BYOB) are provided. A comfortable living room with stereo and a fieldstone fireplace is a pleasant place for indoor relaxing. Outdoors a brook just beyond the back door offers trout fishing; walking paths and hiking trails also lead from the door. Wintertime activities include skiing, snowmobiling and skating; in summer there are tennis, theater and antique-hunting.

Fiddlers Green Inn, Mountain Road (Rte. 108), Stowe, VT 05672; (802) 253-8124. Rates are moderate. All major credit cards are accepted. Children are welcome; no pets, please. Open year-round.

The St. Johnsbury Area and East Burke/Craftsbury Common

Northeastern Vermont, sometimes known as the Northeast Kingdom, is a relatively unknown section of the state to many travelers. Although much of the region is wild, and sparsely settled, there are also many attractive small villages to see, streams and mountains, and one of Vermont's most beautiful lakes. Visitors heading in this direction should begin with a stop in the small city of St. Johnsbury, on Route 2 just off I-91. Several excellent museums may be toured here including the Athenaeum, a handsome old public library and art gallery, and the classic old Fairbanks Museum and Planetarium— one of the most interesting and eccentric museums you will ever see. The Maple Grove Museum at the eastern edge of the city is another appealing place to visit, with an authentic sugar house and free maple sugar samples to taste.

From St. Johnsbury follow I-91 north and then Route 114 to East Burke, a wee northern village. Lake Willoughby, a stunningly scenic body of water, lies just beyond. Mt. Pisgah, a sheer, stark, glacier-cut cliff, towers 2600 feet above one side of the 500-foot-deep lake; Mt. Hor looms on the other side. The hamlet of Craftsbury Common is northwest of St. Johnsbury, via Route 2 west, then Route 15 west and Route 14 north.

Burke Green Guest House. A friendly welcome for weary travelers is assured at Burke Green, owned by Harland and Beverly Lewin. The Lewins like to travel, and during three trips to Scotland they stayed at many bed-and-breakfast houses, giving them the idea of having one of their own. They've been taking in guests since 1982, and thoroughly enjoy it, meeting people from all over the country, Canada and even from England. Their circa 1840 farmhouse, in a peaceful country setting, has been remodeled to include all modern conveniences while still retaining the original wooden beams and all the warmth and charm of an old house. Beverly says that they have always called their decor "Old New England Attic," but she thinks it is now termed "Country"!

Four comfortable rooms, (two doubles, one triple and a large room

Burke Green Guest House

for four to six persons) are available for guests. Two baths are shared; if the house is not full, a private bath may be available. Two of the bedrooms are on the ground floor. Antiques abound, including an old brass bed, Grandmother's four-poster, and a round oak table where breakfast is served. Your hostess makes all the drapes and slipcovers herself, and cut-and-pierced lamp shades. You will also note her collection of early irons, prompted, Beverly claims, by her dislike of ironing. Guests are invited to enjoy conversation or quiet reading in the attractive, paneled family room, once the old carriage shed. A 15-foot-wide wall of old brick surrounds the fireplace with its raised hearth, and braided rugs brighten the old wide-board flooring.

Typical breakfast offerings at Burke Green are orange juice, eggs, muffins, popovers or homebaked bread served with homemade crabapple jelly, Melitta coffee or Twinings tea. Other days there will be French toast or pancakes with wild blueberries and Vermont maple syrup. Tea, coffee and milk are available anytime—hot spiced tea during the winter ski season—and there's an open cookie jar to dip into. A guest refrigerator is handy for keeping snacks, and there is a big picnic table outside. Swimming, fishing, hiking, biking, canoeing and skiing (downhill and cross-country) are all available within a fifteen-mile radius. You will need a car to reach restaurants and shops. *Burke Green Guest House, RR 1, Box 81, East Burke, VT 05832; (802) 467-3472. (From I-91 take Route 5 to Route 114; as you enter East Burke Village, turn left at Mobil station, cross the bridge and immediately turn right. Take the next two rights; the house is the first one on the left and there is a sign.) Rates are moderate. Children are welcome; no pets, please. Open year-round.*

One Aker Farm. Dale and Ed Leary are your hosts at One Aker Farm, a restored 1830 farmhouse near Craftsbury Common. The Learys' one acre of land (until 1973 part of a working farm) has—in addition to the house—a barn and an old milking shed, horses, chickens, turkeys, a sheep (and sometimes a newborn lamb) and four dogs! The spelling of the farm's name, "Aker" for "Acre," is in honor of Dale's grandparents in Arizona.

Two comfortably furnished upstairs rooms are available for guests: one double and one single. Two baths are shared. Guests are encouraged to make themselves completely at home, and they do, say the Learys. There is a pleasant living room, but most guests prefer to gather in the large old kitchen around the always-lit wood-burning cookstove. Breakfast, prepared by chef Ed, offers juice, a choice of

cereals, farm-fresh eggs or pancakes, muffins or toast, and coffee, tea or hot chocolate. In addition to observing and spoiling the farm animals, guests can partake in a wide variety of activities nearby including hiking, horseback riding, fishing, biking and skiing. Your hosts also have a sleigh, and offer old-fashioned winter sleigh rides at $15 a half hour.

One Aker Farm, Craftsbury Common, VT 05827; (802) 755-6705. (Just outside the village of South Albany on the E. Craftsbury Road.) Rates are moderate, lower for children under 16. Children and pets are welcome; but pets must be leashed in case they don't get along with the resident dogs. Open year-round.

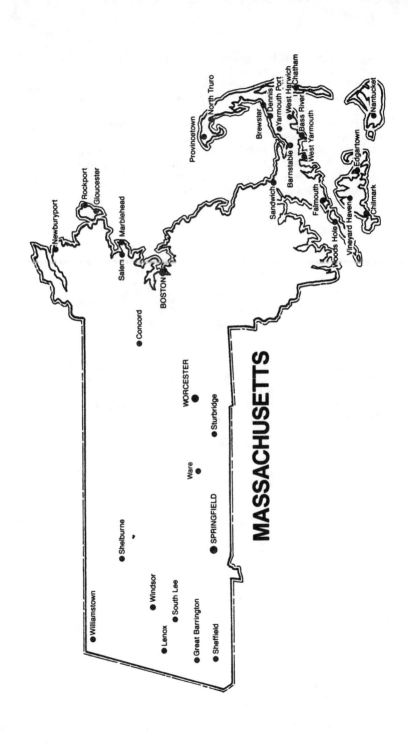

MASSACHUSETTS

Williamstown
Shelburne
Windsor
Lenox
South Lee
Great Barrington
Sheffield
SPRINGFIELD
Ware
Sturbridge
WORCESTER
Concord
Newburyport
Rockport
Gloucester
Marblehead
Salem
BOSTON
Sandwich
Provincetown
North Truro
Brewster
Dennis
Yarmouth Port
West Harwich
Chatham
Bass River
West Yarmouth
Barnstable
Falmouth
Woods Hole
Vineyard Haven
Edgartown
Chilmark
Nantucket

Massachusetts

It's an oddly shaped state, Massachusetts—roughly resembling a rectangular elephant without legs. Cape Cod is the trunk, curving out and upwards. Leif Ericson, the Norwegian explorer, may have sailed along the Massachusetts coastline around the year 1000, and John Cabot (actually Giovanni Caboto) briefly visited the region in 1498. The first permanent settlement was established in 1620, when the Pilgrims landed at Plymouth. Boston was founded ten years later by a band of English Puritans led by John Winthrop. In the following century, during the 1760s, the colonists began to rebel against England's harsh taxation policies. The infamous Boston Massacre and the Boston Tea Party took place in the early 1770s, and in 1775 confrontations with the British at Concord and Lexington set off the Revolutionary War.

Although relatively small in size, Massachusetts contains enough scenic and historic areas to keep a visitor busy for a lifetime. In the western part of the state the low, rolling hills of the Berkshires have long lured summer vacationers and winter skiers. Central Massachusetts offers a host of attractions including Old Sturbridge Village and the vast Quabbin Reservoir. In the east are historic Boston, Concord and Lexington, picturesque seacoast villages, Cape Cod and the enchanting islands of Martha's Vineyard and Nantucket.

The state's coastal areas usually enjoy mild winters with little snow. Inland the temperatures rise higher in summer and drop lower in winter. Apple blossoms froth in countless orchards each spring, and in autumn the scent of ripe apples, Concord grapes and wood smoke fills the air. Farmstands along the roadsides offer fresh apple cider, squash and great mounds of orange pumpkins. Even on rainy days the brilliant foliage seems to light up the countryside as though the sun were shining. In December, small towns everywhere turn into live Christmas cards. Balsam wreaths hang on almost every door, candles glow from windows, and Christmas trees twinkle brightly.

Western and Central Massachusetts

The beautiful Berkshires region of western Massachusetts offers gentle mountain scenery, small villages and nineteenth-century mill towns, excellent antiquing and a variety of year-round sports activities. In summer, the entire area becomes a gigantic cultural festival, presenting a fabulous array of art, music, dance and theater.

Great Barrington, in the southern Berkshires, puts on a real country fair every September; the fair has been held each year for more than a century. Not far away are Bartholomew's Cobble, a natural rock garden, and scenic Bash Bish Falls. Stockbridge, a short drive north on Route 7, was the home of the late Norman Rockwell. Many of the beloved artist's delightfully nostalgic paintings can be seen at the Old Corner House on Main Street.

In Becket to the east, the Jacob's Pillow Dance Festival offers everything from ballet to folk dancing each summer. Fabled Tanglewood, the summer home of the Boston Symphony Orchestra, is in Lenox, north of Stockbridge. The Music Shed and other buildings are situated on a magnificent 210-acre estate; the program of concerts begins in late June and runs through August. Visitors can listen to the music inside the Shed or recline lazily on the grass outside, sipping wine, gazing at the stars, and, at times, swatting mosquitoes. (Few things are perfect.)

North of Lenox, visit the Hancock Shaker Village (on Route 20, five miles west of Pittsfield) where some of the celibate Shakers settled in the late 1700s. The round stone barn and other restored buildings may be toured. Way up in the northern Berkshires is the attractive community of Williamstown, home of Williams College and the Sterling and Francine Clark Art Institute. A remarkably fine museum, the Clark displays more than thirty Renoirs as well as the works of other famous Impressionists; paintings by Rembrandt, Rubens, Fragonard, Gainsborough and Winslow Homer; superb collections of old silver, and prints and drawings from the fifteenth to the twentieth century. The town also hosts a renowned summer theater festival; presented from late June to August, it is considered one of the country's finest.

Four routes are available for travelers heading east from the Berkshires; all lead eventually to Boston at the other end of the state. Toward the south are the Massachusetts Turnpike, I-90, and Route 9; in the middle is Route 20 and to the north, Route 2. For a grand view of the Berkshires, follow Route 2 east from Williamstown to the road leading up Mt. Greylock. At 3491 feet the mountain is the state's highest. Farther on, Route 2 becomes the scenic Mohawk Trail, part of the old route used by the Indians of the Five Nations to pass between the Connecticut and Hudson River valleys. At the Hairpin Turn—which is exactly as it sounds—an observation tower provides sweeping views of northwestern Massachusetts and southern Vermont.

In Shelburne Falls, a small mountain village just off the Mohawk Trail before Greenfield, travelers can observe glacial potholes along the Deerfield River and visit the Bridge of Flowers, a 400-foot-long old trolley crossing now bedecked with colorful gardens. Just beyond Greenfield, take Route 5 south to Old Deerfield. The historic town, settled in the 1600s and twice destroyed in Indian massacres, has a number of restored buildings that may be toured. Amherst, a short drive south, is the home of the University of Massachusetts, Amherst College and Hampshire College. The famed poet Emily Dickinson lived much of her life here. Smith and Mount Holyoke colleges are in nearby Northampton.

To the east, in central Massachusetts, lies the enormous Quabbin Reservoir, a lure for birdwatchers (the rare bald eagle nests here) and fishermen. Formed by flooding five towns, the 128-square-mile Quabbin is a strikingly beautiful body of water dotted with islands and surrounded by pine forests. This region has been described as a cross between the English Lake Country and the Scandinavian fjords. Southeast of Quabbin, just beyond the Massachusetts Turnpike on Route 20, you will come to Old Sturbridge Village. If possible, plan to spend a full day exploring. A re-created village of the 1800s, Sturbridge includes a working farm with animals, a blacksmith's shop, pewterer and pottery, a tavern, several historic houses and much more. One shop offers delicious cookies, freshly baked. Guides in period dress demonstrate old-time crafts and work the farm where, in season, visitors can watch such traditional activities as sheep shearing, fence building and maple sugaring.

Sheffield/Great Barrington

Ivanhoe Country House. Travelers will find the Ivanhoe on Route 41 near Sheffield, just south of Great Barrington in the southern Berkshires. A handsome white Colonial built in 1780, the house is

situated at the foot of Mt. Race and surrounded by twenty-five acres of woods and lawns. For guests, hosts Carole and Dick Maghery have four rooms with private baths, three rooms sharing one bath, and a two-bedroom unit with private bath. Several of the quiet, comfortable, country-style rooms have working fireplaces; some offer fully equipped kitchenettes. Guests are invited to use the pleasant Chestnut Room with a fireplace, library, TV, piano and game tables. Refrigerators are available for keeping perishables, wine, beer or soft drinks.

Outdoors, guests may roam the extensive grounds and—in season—enjoy a refreshing dip in the pool. Dog fanciers will undoubtedly make friends with the Magherys' beautiful golden retrievers, which your hosts raise on the premises. In winter, after a day's downhill or cross-country skiing nearby, you can whiz down your hosts' lighted slope on a sled. All of the region's famed summer musical and theatrical events are accessible within a reasonable drive; other nearby activities include golf, tennis, hiking, bicycling and antiquing.

A continental breakfast of muffins, coffee, tea or cocoa is brought to your door each morning. For other meals there are a number of excellent restaurants not far away, and the Magherys provide sample menus to help you decide.

Ivanhoe Country House, Rte. 41, Undermountain Road, Sheffield, MA 01257; (413) 229-2143. Rates range from moderate to moderately expensive, lower off season. A 2-day minimum weekend stay and 3-day holiday minimum stay are required. Children are welcome. Because of the golden retrievers, your hosts suggest you don't bring a pet of your own. If you do, the dog must be leashed and accompanied whenever away from your room and walked away from lawns and pool. Open year-round.

Elling's Guest House. Tall shade trees surround this charming establishment in Great Barrington. The town's second oldest still-inhabited house, the large white Colonial was built in 1746 by Stephen King, a wealthy woolen mill owner. Hosts Josephine (Jo) and Ray Elling have six comfortable upstairs rooms for guests, two with private baths and four sharing two full baths. There's also a separate guest cottage on the grounds. A parlor with a fireplace and a porch that offers marvelous views of the countryside and mountains are pleasant places to relax. Each morning a continental breakfast of fruit, hot biscuits, jelly and jam and coffee or tea is served.

Elling's Guest House, 250 Maple Ave., RD 3, Box 6, Great Barrington, MA 01230; (413) 528-4103. (One mile west of Rte. 7.) Rates are moderate. Children are welcome; no pets, please. Open year-round.

Seekonk Pines. Originally a large working farm dating back to the 1830s and then a country estate, Seekonk Pines in Great Barrington is set on four acres of lawns, gardens and wildflower meadows. Long ago, the native Indians called the area "The Place of the Seekonk," or "wild goose." The rambling old Colonial, once the estate's main house, is owned by Linda and Christian Best. Upstairs are five guest bedrooms and a large suite, with private bath. One of the bedrooms has a newly added private half bath, with handsome wide-board floors and stenciling. The other rooms share two baths. Downstairs there is another guest room, with a private bath. The attractively decorated accommodations contain colorful old handmade quilts, family heirlooms and antiques. One of the rooms, recently redecorated, features stenciling on the walls and matching stenciling on the drapes.

For relaxing, there is an exceptionally spacious L-shaped living room with a raised fireplace, TV and game tables. Outdoors, guests will find a pool for summer fun. Host Linda is a watercolorist, and

many of her paintings are displayed in the house. Both Linda and Chris sing, and guests occasionally are treated to surprise recitals! A continental breakfast of homebaked bread or muffins and coffee or tea is included in the rates. For a modest extra charge you can indulge in a full breakfast of juice, eggs any style or pancakes (the latter are made from scratch, with fresh fruit mixed in), bacon or sausage, and Linda's delicious muffins and breads.

Guests are encouraged to picnic on the lawn and roam through the meadow; bicycles may be rented at Seekonk Pines for exploring nearby country roads. In late summer and fall, fresh produce from the Bests' garden is available for purchase. The area offers excellent restaurants, distinctive shops and year-round sports activities; all of the region's summer festival events are easily accessible.

Seekonk Pines, 142 Seekonk Cross Rd., Great Barrington, MA 01230; (413) 528-4192. (Two miles west of Great Barrington at corner of Seekonk Cross Road and Rte. 23.) Rates are moderate to moderately expensive, 10 percent discount on 7-day or longer stays. There's a small charge for a child or extra person in room. Children are welcome but must be supervised by an adult; no pets, please. Open year-round.

South Lee/Lenox/Windsor

Merrell Tavern Inn. This historic structure, in South Lee about a mile east of Stockbridge, was built around 1795 for Joseph Whitton. Whitton, who served as a general in the War of 1812, also operated an iron foundry and brick works and—as a surveyor—worked on the Boston-Albany Pike. In 1817, William Merrell purchased the property and opened the building to the public as a stagecoach inn. General Whitton's old living room became the tavern room; the circular Colonial bar installed by Merrell still stands today, one of the few in America that survive intact. The double-decker front porch and a third floor were added to the inn in 1837, the latter providing space for a high-ceilinged ballroom and rooms for stagecoach drovers.

In 1947, a later owner turned the building over to the Society for the Preservation of New England Antiquities. Under the Society's stewardship program, Merrell Tavern Inn was sold to Charles and Faith Reynolds in 1980. Their restoration work on the inn, which was one of the first properties in Berkshire County to be listed in the National Register of Historic Places, won them a Preservation Award presented in 1982 by the Massachusetts Historical Commission.

Authentic details abound throughout the quaint old inn: the pewter gray used in the hallways reproduces the original color, and the entrance hall contains a handsome case clock made in Scotland in the 1790s. The original "smoke painting," an imitation of marble, can be seen on the stairway leading to the third floor. Most of the inn's furnishings, which date from the late 1700s to the early 1800s, have been collected by the Reynolds over the past twenty-five years.

There are nine spacious guest rooms, one on the ground floor; all have private baths. Four of the upstairs rooms were once the grand ballroom, and the four nineteenth-century drovers' quarters have been converted into baths. All of the guest chambers are tastefully decorated in appropriate period style and contain canopy or four-poster beds; some have working fireplaces. Downstairs, the old tavern room is a pleasant place to meet other guests, read, or play games. In cold weather there will be a cozy blaze in the fireplace. Outdoors, guests can enjoy a stroll on the grounds, with their rambling stone walls and old foundations. The property extends to the banks of the Housatonic River.

Breakfast at the inn consists of juice, cereal with fresh fruit, omelets or perhaps French toast or griddle cakes and ham, homebaked pastries or breads, and a hot beverage. Two restaurants are within walking distance; downhill and cross-country skiing facilities are accessible within minutes as are Tanglewood, Jacob's Pillow Dance Theater and many more of the region's attractions.

Merrell Tavern Inn, Main Street (Rte. 102), South Lee, MA 01260; (413) 243-1794. (From Massachusetts Turnpike, I-90, take Exit 2 at Lee and continue toward Stockbridge for 3 miles.) Rates range from moderately expensive to expensive, lower for weekdays and from Oct. 24 to June 30. Visa, MasterCard and American Express are accepted. Children are welcome; no pets, please. Open year-round except Dec. 24 and 25.

Whistler's Inn. A combination of French Manor and English Tudor architecture, Whistler's Inn in Lenox was built in 1820. The mansion originally belonged to the uncle of famed artist James McNeill Whistler. Today, Mr. and Mrs. Richard C. Mears are the owners. Richard Mears, a Baltimore native who divides his time between the Berkshires and northern California, is the author of the acclaimed novel

Ebb of the River. The inn has eleven guest rooms of varying sizes, each individually decorated and two with fireplaces. All have private baths, and two of the rooms are on the ground floor. An extensive library, a living room, music room, sun porches and large deck are available for guests' use. Six acres of grounds offer flowers, a sunken garden and peaceful seclusion. Cross-country ski and horseback riding trails start 100 yards from the house; seven downhill ski areas are within a twenty-mile radius; lake beaches are nearby, and Tanglewood is only one and a half miles away. Guests are provided with a continental breakfast of fruit, blueberry muffins or special cakes, cream sherry, coffee or tea, served on the sun porch or terrace.

Whistler's Inn, 5 Greenwood St., Lenox, MA 01240; (413) 637-0975. Rates are expensive, lower off season. A 3-night minimum stay is required in season. Visa and MasterCard are accepted. Well-supervised children are welcome; no pets, please. Open June 1–Jan. 4.

Brook Farm Inn. A fine collection of art, spanning five centuries, and a period library are only two of the many attractions to be found in Brook Farm, an 1889 Queen Anne Victorian house in Lenox. Hosts Mary and Frank Newton have eleven upstairs bedrooms for guests, four with fireplaces. Six have private baths; the other rooms share six baths. All of the guest quarters are graciously decorated in period style, with handsome old hand-rubbed furniture and elegant linens. Downstairs, the reception hall and library, both with fireplaces, provide comfortable places for guests to relax, read and meet other travelers. A full breakfast, including fresh fruit in season or baked apples, is served—accompanied by Mozart—in the sunny dining room overlooking the garden. Other meals are available only for groups of twelve or more, at extra charge. In summer, guests are invited to stroll through two acres of gardens or enjoy a swim in the pool. Lenox Village, a minute's walk, offers excellent dining and shopping, and Tanglewood is two miles away. Wintertime guests will find cross-country and downhill skiing, indoor-outdoor ice skating and ice fishing nearby.

Brook Farm Inn, 15 Hawthorne St., Lenox, MA 01240; (413) 637-3013. (One block from center of town.) Rates are moderately expensive, lower from November to May, and there is a 10 percent discount for weekly or monthly stays. Visa and MasterCard are accepted. Children over 16 are welcome; no pets, please. Open year-round.

Windfields Farm. Windfields Farm, situated on a quiet, traffic-free road and surrounded by 300 acres of woodland and fields, is just outside of Windsor in the scenic Hampshire Hills of western Massachusetts. Hosts Carolyn and Arnold Westwood operate a thriving maple syrup, egg and vegetable business on the property, which offers lovely country views, summer swimming in a pond, picnicking, cross-country ski trails and hiking, and highbush blueberries for picking. The farmhouse, built in the 1790s and nicely restored, is of post-and-beam construction with an active solar addition. The Westwoods have furnished their home with a blend of antique and Danish modern furniture, and many original paintings.

Two attractive upstairs corner bedrooms are available for guests. One of the double rooms features an antique four-poster bed with rebuilt hair mattress; the bed in the other room has a firm, queen-size

mattress. One bath is shared. For relaxing, there is a large living room with a fireplace, piano, stereo, and an extensive library. A full New England farm breakfast is served, consisting of muffins with homemade jams and jellies, pancakes, fresh eggs, and berries in season. And there will be maple syrup, made on the property; your hostess regularly wins prizes for her syrup and garden produce. Home-cooked dinners are also available, by advance arrangement only, for a moderate extra fee.

You will need a car to reach restaurants and shops. Windsor Jambs waterfall in Windsor State Forest is a mile's walk or drive; Cummington, a short drive away, offers the William Cullen Bryant Homestead and Kingman Tavern Museum, and Tanglewood and Williamstown are about forty minutes away.

Windfields Farm, Windsor Bush Road, Windsor; (413) 684-3766. Mailing address; RR 1, Box 170, Cummington, MA 01026. (Northeast of Pittsfield off Rte. 9; directions will be provided when you call or write for reservations.) Rates are moderate. Children are welcome; no pets, please. Open May–February.

Williamstown

River Bend Farm. Col. Benjamin Simonds, one of Williamstown's thirteen original settlers and leader of the victorious Massachusetts forces at the Revolutionary War Battle of Bennington, built this delightful Georgian farmhouse in 1770. Judy and Dave Loomis purchased the place in 1977. Dave, a retired schooner captain, decided to "take to the hills" and let others bring the world to his doorstep!

Now beautifully restored, their home—which is included in the National Register of Historic Places—still boasts a central chimney with five fireplaces and two baking ovens. Also notable are an attic

smoking chamber and a large ashpit in the cellar. Five nicely decorated rooms, furnished with Early American antiques and sharing
two baths, are available for guests. Two offer fireplaces, and one of
the rooms is on the ground floor. A charming Colonial keeping room
with a fireplace is a pleasant spot for relaxing. Breakfast, of freshly
baked muffins and bread with the Loomis's homemade jams and
honey from their own bees, and coffee or tea is served daily.

River Bend Farm is surrounded by three landscaped acres of land,
and your hosts have a large vegetable garden, an herb garden, an
asparagus bed and berry bushes. Restaurants and shops are close by,
as are Williams College, the Clark Art Institute and Williamstown
Summer Theater. Summer festivals and other Berkshire attractions
are within an easy drive.

River Bend Farm, 643 Simonds Rd. (Rte. 7), Williamstown, MA 01267; (413)
458-5504. Rates are moderate. Children are welcome; no pets, please. Open
from April to November.

Shelburne

Parson Hubbard House. Richard and Jeanne Bole cordially welcome travelers to their charming old home, originally a parsonage
built in 1774. Situated on a quiet country road near Shelburne Center,
with nary a car passing at night and few during the day, the house
offers lovely views and a delightfully old-fashioned ambiance. For
guests there are three upstairs bedrooms, including two doubles and
one room with twin beds that can be used as a double or a single.
Two baths are shared. The very spacious Keeping Room with both a
fireplace and wood-burning stove is a cozy spot for relaxing, reading
or meeting other guests. There's also a large parlor with bay window,
piano and TV. A warm, friendly establishment, the Parson Hubbard

House is filled with antiques, including colorful quilts. Many of the windows have Indian shutters, inside shutters which could be quickly closed to protect against marauders, and the house is fronted by a broad porch with a swing and chairs. Another swing hangs from a huge maple tree. On the grounds are a few animals for young guests to admire, and right next door is a pre-Revolutionary cemetery to explore.

Breakfast is served in the country kitchen with a grand view, or out on the porch. The menu varies, depending on guests' wishes, and may include freshly baked muffins, omelets, berries in season and maple syrup from the Boles' own trees. You will need a car to reach restaurants and shops; Shelburne Falls is four miles away and Greenfield is five miles away. Historic Old Deerfield is about a seven-mile drive. The area also offers excellent weekend concerts and skiing in nearby Charlemont, and Amherst with its many colleges, museums and Fine Arts Center is only thirty minutes away.

Parson Hubbard House, Old Village Road, Shelburne Center, MA 01370; (413) 625-9730. (From Rte. 2 west, Mohawk Trail, 4½ miles from rotary in Greenfield; at sign for Shelburne Center on right, turn right on Little Mohawk Road. Go about ¼ mile and take first right onto Old Village Road; the house is the 4th on the left.) Rates are moderate. Children are welcome; pets are negotiable. No smokers, please. Open May–October.

Ware/Sturbridge

The Wildwood Inn. The Wildwood is a traveler's delight—a homey old inn offering an enthusiastic welcome, comfortable surroundings and delicious breakfast treats. Located in the small country town of Ware, approximately halfway between Northampton and Worcester, the Wildwood makes an ideal base from which to explore the many attractions of central Massachusetts. Margaret and Geoffrey Lobenstine and their twin daughters, Heather and Lori, are your cordial hosts.

Their handsome Victorian house, built in the 1800s, has five individually decorated upstairs bedrooms for guests, sharing three

baths. All of the rooms have been designed to display the family's collection of lovely antique quilts and handmade afghans, and are named after them, the name embroidered in a small frame on the door. As a sample there is the Old Embroidery Quilt Master Guest Room, featuring a striking blue and white quilt, a four-poster bed and a four-window bay. For extra comfort in chilly weather, all of the beds have dual control electric blankets. Downstairs a large, but very cozy, country parlor is furnished mainly with American primitives including a cobbler's bench coffee table, a spinning wheel and an unusual old pie safe. A magnificent "log cabin" quilt hangs on one wall, and a wooden carpenter's chest contains games and a variety of puzzles. There's an intriguing selection of books, too.

Breakfast at the Wildwood offers such good things as homemade applesauce bread, popovers or Peach Point muffins accompanied by homemade peach butter, juice, and coffee or tea. For a small extra charge guests can request some of Margaret's other specialties such as Puff Pancakes, Maple Cheese Square, Lemon Twist or Chipmunk Pie—which does *not* include chipmunks! In the afternoon or evening you are invited to sit beside the parlor's tiled fireplace and sip wine (BYOB) from antique pewter goblets or have a warming cup of mulled cider. Upon arrival, weary travelers are often greeted with a cup of hot herbal tea or refreshing ice water.

The inn is set on two acres of wooded grounds edged by stone walls. Some of the fir trees, Margaret Lobenstine confides, were smuggled (in the dark of night) out of the Quabbin Reservoir area before it was flooded. A grand old chestnut tree, one of the few remaining in the region, was purchased by a previous owner for twenty-five cents some sixty years ago. Directly behind the property are woods and a river for hiking and canoeing. The Lobenstines have their own canoe, which guests may use. Tennis courts are nearby, and a short drive will bring you to a deliciously icy, brook-fed swimming hole. In winter cross-country skiing and sledding are easily accessible. The scenic Quabbin Reservoir is close by and Old Sturbridge Village is twenty miles away. Northampton (of Emily Dickinson fame) and Worcester, with a superb art museum and an outstanding collection of medieval suits of armor, are both within an easy drive. Your hostess will be delighted to provide directions to these and other interesting sites for day trips from the inn.

The Wildwood Inn, 121 Church St., Ware, MA 01082; (413) 967-7798. (Take Exit 8 from the Massachusetts Turnpike; go left on Rte. 32 and follow to its end at Main Street in Ware. Bear right onto Main and go 3 traffic lights; bear left onto Church Street at the traffic light by the fountain. The house is ¾ mile on the right.) Rates are moderately expensive, lower for longer stays. Children over 6 are welcome; no pets, please. Smoking on porch and grounds only. Open year-round.

Colonel Ebenezer Crafts Inn. The town of Sturbridge has long

been famous for its historic Publick House, which has been offering delicious Yankee cooking since 1771. The Colonel Ebenezer Crafts Inn, part of a complex which includes the Publick House and a motor lodge, sits at the summit of Fiske Hill. The handsome old house, built in 1786 by David Fiske, Esq., has been renamed for Colonel Crafts, founder of the Publick House. There are six rooms in the inn and two suites, all with private baths. Four of the rooms are doubles; the others can accommodate four persons, more with cots. The large, airy chambers are individually furnished with Colonial antiques and period reproductions; all offer sweeping views of hills and country-side. The charming Cottage Suite, on the ground floor adjoining the main house via a short breezeway, includes a bedroom, living room and bath. For relaxing, guests will enjoy the inn's library, living room and sun porch.

Hosts Patricia and Henri Bibeau offer a continental breakfast daily, with juice, fruit, freshly baked muffins and coffee or tea, accompanied by the morning newspaper. Afternoon tea or sherry, with appropriate "sweets," is also provided. In the evening you'll find covers turned down on your bed and fruit and homebaked cookies on the night table. The Publick House, where the menu features baked lobster pie, Indian pudding with vanilla ice cream or deep-dish apple pie among a host of other good things, is just a short ride down the hill. Out behind the Publick House, the Bake Shoppe displays an array of treats including marvelous sticky buns. And famous Old Sturbridge Village is just a short drive away.

Colonel Ebenezer Crafts Inn, c/o Publick House, Main Street, P.O. Box 187, Sturbridge, MA 01566; (617) 347-3313. (Three miles from I-90 and I-84, on Rte. 131; guests must check in at the Publick House, and directions to the inn will be provided.) Rates are expensive, lower Jan. 2–June 30; special rates for renting entire house. American Express, MasterCard, Visa and Diners Club are accepted. Children are welcome; no pets, please. Open year-round.

Eastern Massachusetts
Lexington/Concord and Boston

Just west of Boston, the very attractive old towns of Lexington and Concord offer travelers an unmatched array of historic sites. The American Revolution began here more than two centuries ago. On the night of April 18, 1775, Paul Revere and two other patriots rode out from Boston to warn the colonists in Concord—where their cache of weapons was hidden—that the British were coming. At dawn on the following day the opposing forces first met on Lexington Green; the second battle took place at the Old North Bridge in Concord. There, in the words of Ralph Waldo Emerson, ". . . the embattled farmers stood, and fired the shot heard round the world." If you'd like to watch a dramatically realistic re-creation of those long-ago events, come on April 19. Each year on that day modern-day Minutemen and a regiment of "British Redcoats," all attired in authentic dress, re-enact the entire scene.

Concord is also renowned for its impressively long list of nineteenth-century literary and intellectual greats, including Emerson, Nathaniel Hawthorne, Henry David Thoreau and Bronson Alcott and his daughter, Louisa May. Among the town's many historic houses to be toured are the Old Manse, located beside the North Bridge and lived in by both Emerson and Hawthorne, and Orchard House on the Lexington Road (Route 2A), where Louisa May Alcott wrote *Little Women*. Don't miss the Hill Burying Ground, a steep incline on Lexington Road at Concord Center. The ancient, leaning, slate tombstones, topped with fearsome death's-heads, are engraved with fascinating legends and dire warnings. One of the most common, in one form or another, has this ghoulish message for passersby:

> Stranger, stop and cast an eye—
> As you are now, so once was I.
> Death is a debt by nature due;
> I've paid my debt and so must you.

Sleepy Hollow Cemetery, on Route 62, contains Authors' Ridge where Emerson, Hawthorne, the Alcotts and Thoreau are buried. And lovely Walden Pond, where Thoreau lived in his rustic cabin, is not far away; follow Walden Street across Route 2.

Boston, the capital of Massachusetts, is a walkable city with a number of distinctly different areas to explore. It is a city of scholars and politicians, of museums and seafood restaurants, and of ancient burying grounds resting in the shadow of ultramodern architecture. The old waterfront has been handsomely renovated and offers a wide variety of shops and restaurants, a fine view of the harbor and a pleasant waterfront park. Boston is also a city of confusing, narrow, one-way streets and eccentric motorists. Even the natives have problems navigating by car. If you can, stay outside—in Concord or on the North Shore, for instance—and take a train in. You'll be glad you did.

Start your tour of the city with a walk through the impeccable grounds of the Public Garden and a ride on a Swanboat. These charmers, which take passengers on a leisurely trip around the lagoon, have been operated by the same family for more than 100 years. Then cross the Common, originally a seventeenth-century cow pasture and training field. Hike up to Beacon Hill with its steep, narrow streets, brick sidewalks and the State House with its golden dome. At the red-brick information booth back down on the Common (on Tremont Street near the corner of Park Street) you can pick up a brochure describing Boston's Freedom Trail. Follow the trail down to the waterfront, paying a visit along the way to the Old Granary Burying Ground where so many early patriots lie including Paul Revere, John Hancock and Samuel Adams. Still farther down you will come to Faneuil Hall. Just beyond, three long, massive buildings have been turned into a colorful, bustling marketplace with ethnic foods of every kind, delightful specialty shops and fine restaurants. Musicians and magicians provide entertainment, and there are plenty of benches for sitting and people watching.

From Faneuil Hall Marketplace, continue on to the waterfront where you will find the New England Aquarium and boats for sightseeing cruises of the harbor. The North End, Boston's genuinely Italian neighborhood, is a short walk up the hill behind the waterfront. Italian restaurants and bakeries full of luscious pastries dot the area. Here also are Paul Revere's House, the city's oldest wooden structure, and the Old North Church. From the church's steeple the lantern message, "one if by land, two if by sea," was flashed to the waiting Revere, indicating the route the British were taking toward Concord and setting him off on his famous midnight ride.

Not far away, in Charlestown over the bridge, are the Bunker Hill Monument and "Old Ironsides," the U.S.F. *Constitution*. The oldest commissioned warship in the world, the *Constitution* is still operated by the U.S. Navy. The prestigious educational institutions of Harvard and M.I.T. (Massachusetts Institute of Technology) are located in Cambridge across the Charles River. Walk through venerable Harvard Yard and explore Harvard Square's multitude of shops and coffee-houses; it's a lively, collegiate scene.

Hawthorne Inn. History buffs will surely enjoy a stay at this handsome old house in Concord, set among huge maple and pine trees just across the road from Hawthorne's Wayside and the Alcotts' Orchard House. The land on which it stands was once owned by several of Concord's most famous residents, beginning with Ralph Waldo Emerson. Emerson deeded the property to Bronson Alcott in 1844, and during the following ten years Alcott, with the help of his daughter

Louisa and her sisters, grew fruit and vegetables here. Alcott also built a bathhouse, in what he considered to be the finest example of his own "Rustic Architecture." In 1855, Nathaniel Hawthorne purchased the property and planted a row of pine trees leading to the bathhouse. Two of the trees are still standing. Hawthorne sold the land to George A. Gray, who—in 1870—with his artist/genealogist son, built the house you see today.

Gregory Burch and Marilyn Mudry now own Hawthorne Inn and have seven guest rooms. Four are upstairs, two with private baths and two sharing a bath. The other three, all with private baths, are on the ground floor. All of the rooms are appointed with antique furnishings, colorful handmade quilts and Oriental or rag rugs. Magazines and books, AM-FM clock radios and flowers or a bowl of fresh fruit add to each room's charm and comfort. Guests are invited to enjoy the Common Room, too, with its fine wood floor, Oriental carpet, books and games, and a fireplace where a fire is lit on chilly evenings. The bay-windowed room, accented by cinnamon-colored walls, is furnished in antiques including an Empire secretary. Throughout the house guests will discover Greg Burch's own original art and sculpture, pre-Columbian curios, and a superb collection of Japanese *ukiyo-e* block prints, circa 1780–1850.

Hawthorne Inn

A continental breakfast, served in the dining room, features juice, homebaked breads and fresh fruit, sometimes including your hosts' own raspberries, and a selection of teas or freshly ground coffee. Afternoon tea is also offered. On the grounds guests will find a small pond with carp, vegetable gardens, fruit trees, grape vines and flowers, and—usually—two resident dogs and several cats. Restaurants and interesting shops are not far away, and all of the area's attractions are easily accessible including the Antiquarian Society Museum, the Old Manse and Old North Bridge, Sleepy Hollow Cemetery and Walden Pond.

Hawthorne Inn, 462 Lexington Rd., Concord, MA 01742; (617) 369-5610. Rates are expensive. Children are welcome; no pets, please. Open year-round except January.

The North Shore:
Salem/Marblehead/Gloucester/
Rockport/Newburyport

North of Boston, dozens of quaint, hilly little towns cling to the rocky coastline. To reach the North Shore, and Cape Ann, take Route 128 (I-95) north from the Concord/Lexington area, then Route 114 east to Salem. Salem's history is well known: in the witchcraft hysteria of 1692, nineteen men and women were hanged for supposedly practicing "the diabolical arts." Visitors can follow the intriguing story at the Salem Witch Museum and explore the Witch House where Judge Jonathan Corwin held preliminary examinations of some of the accused witches. The House of Seven Gables, setting for Nathaniel Hawthorne's novel of the same name, is also open to the public, as are a number of other seventeenth-century homes. The city's sea-going past is on view at the Salem Maritime Historic Site and in the superb Peabody Museum. Pickering Wharf, along the waterfront, offers a colorful complex of shops and restaurants.

Marblehead is a few miles south; its snug harbor is one of the prettiest anywhere and the best view is from Fort Sewell. Prepare to get lost; almost everyone does, trying to follow the town's narrow, twisting streets. Asking directions doesn't help much either, as the answers are too confusing. The best advice is to remain calm, and enjoy the special quality of Marblehead with its weather-beaten old houses and steep, rocky hillsides.

The most scenic route to Gloucester, northeast of Salem, is via Route 1A north to Beverly, then routes 127 and 127A out along Cape Ann. At Gloucester Harbor you will undoubtedly want to take a picture of the famous statue, "The Gloucester Fisherman," a memorial to fishermen lost at sea. Prowl around some of the wharves, too; they smell just as fishy today as they did in the days of *Captains Courageous.* Each year around the end of June the town holds a four-day fishermen's celebration called St. Peter's Fiesta, with parades, fireworks and the Blessing of the Fleet. Children will enjoy the Gloucester Fishermen's Museum, at Rogers and Porter Streets. Youngsters are invited to touch and operate the exhibits, listen to foghorns, and watch films. Working fishermen come to talk to the youngsters, show them how to mend nets, and even take them on tours down to the wharves.

Rockport, just beyond Gloucester, is an artists' colony, and art galleries are everywhere. Bearskin Neck, a tiny street off Dock Square, is lined with small shops and restaurants and is almost solidly packed with tourists in the summertime. In the early 1800s, Rockport boasted a flourishing granite industry. Huge blocks of granite were hauled by oxen from the quarries to the harbor. Most of the old, abandoned quarries are on private land today, but you can glimpse one or two from the road just past the bridge at Pigeon Cove. Shortly beyond the cove look for the turnoff to Halibut Point, the northernmost tip of Cape Ann. The entrance is not easy to find and is not always marked; ask someone for directions. A long, wooded path will take you out to the point, a spectacular site with tumbled granite ledges and crashing ocean surf.

To reach the salty old town of Newburyport, at the mouth of the Merrimack River, follow Route 127 from Rockport around Cape Ann then pick up Route 133 west to Ipswich and Route 1A north. Newburyport, even today, has the feeling and flavor of Colonial days, especially along the narrow streets near the restored Market Square District. High Street, with its row of magnificent nineteenth-century mansions, reflects Newburyport's later era as a bustling seaport and shipbuilding center. Signs with the hull of a clipper ship mark the Clipper Trail, a walking tour that will lead you to many of the town's sites of interest. Excellent restaurants and unique shops of every kind may be found here as well. For hiking, picnicking, bird watching, swimming and—in winter—cross-country skiing, head for Plum Island and Parker River National Wildlife Refuge three miles away.

The Suzannah Flint House/Bed & Breakfast. This wonderful old house in Salem was built around 1795 for Suzannah Flint, a widow. Today Charlotte and Richard Clemens are your hosts, with two very attractive rooms for guests. Both of the rooms are on the ground floor and have private baths. One has a double bed and a single bed, and a fireplace; the other guest room contains a double bed and a pretty Victorian painted bed. Guests are encouraged to enjoy the comfortably furnished downstairs living room, with a fireplace, and—in season—the exceptionally charming garden. In summer, your hostess picks flowers from the garden each day for guests' bedrooms. Breakfast, thoughtfully brought to your room, consists of fresh fruit, homemade breads, and coffee or tea. The house is conveniently located within easy walking distance of fine restaurants, shops and most of Salem's many attractions.

The Suzannah Flint House/Bed & Breakfast, 98 Essex St., Salem, MA 01970; (617) 744-5281. Rates are moderately expensive. Visa and MasterCard are accepted. Children are welcome; no pets, please. Open year-round.

The Stephen Daniels House. Mrs. Catherine B. Gill is the owner of the historic Daniels House in Salem. Built in 1667 by Stephen Daniels, a sea captain, the house was enlarged by his great-grandson in 1756 and remained in the Daniels family until 1931. Today the charming old home is a bed-and-breakfast guest house, appointed throughout with genuine antiques including canopy beds and a splendid assortment of Colonial furnishings. There are five spacious upstairs rooms for guests, all attractively decorated and all with private baths. Visitors will especially enjoy the huge, walk-in fireplaces on the ground floor, complete with age-scarred old wooden mantels and brick hearths. To the rear of the house is a lovely shaded terrace, paved with bricks and stone and bright with flowers and hanging baskets of greenery. The terrace is a fine place to sit and relax in complete seclusion. Complimentary morning coffee and tea are offered, and a full breakfast is available for an extra charge. In the afternoon Kay Gill serves her guests tea or iced lemonade, depending on the season. Dinner, on advance notice and at extra charge, can be provided for groups. Salem's shops, restaurants, historic houses, museums and waterfront are all within walking distance, and beaches are nearby.

The Stephen Daniels House, 1 Daniels St., Salem, MA 01970; (617) 744-5709. (At the corner of Essex and Daniels streets, about 3 blocks from the Hawthorne Hotel in downtown Salem.) Rates are moderately expensive. Children and pets are welcome. Open year-round.

10 Mugford Street. Located in Marblehead's historic Old Town, this splendid old house was built in 1837. For almost sixty years the house was a home for elderly women, but because of a lack of applicants it was sold in 1984 and turned into a charming bed-and-breakfast

establishment. Hosts Liz and Mike Mentuck have furnished 10 Mugford Street with antiques and have carefully preserved its hand-somely detailed woodwork and four fireplaces. Newly decorated in appropriate old-fashioned style, the house offers five comfortable double guest rooms, sharing three baths. One of the rooms is on the ground floor. A cozy parlor is available for reading or conversation, and outside there is a small yard with flower gardens for warm weather enjoyment. Breakfast, served buffet style in the attractive dining room, offers juice, fruit, cereal, homebaked muffins and coffee or tea. Occasionally, your hosts prepare boiled lobster dinners for guests, when arranged for in advance. All of Marblehead's historic sites and houses, and the harbor, are within walking distance of the house, as are restaurants and shops.

10 Mugford Street, Marblehead, MA 01945; (617) 639-0343. Rates are moderate to moderately expensive, lower November–May. Children over 6 are welcome; no pets, please. Parking is available in a lot a few yards down the street. Open year-round.

The Colonial Guest House. Bob and Barbara Balestraci cordially welcome guests to their beautiful, century-old Colonial in East Gloucester on Cape Ann. A lovely, tree-shaded lawn—with comfortable chairs for relaxing—offers a grand view of Gloucester Harbor. Guests may use the barbecue pit and picnic table, and one of the best beaches on the North Shore is a few minutes' walk away. Fishing and pleasure boats may be rented 1000 feet from the house; the famed Gloucester art colony, antique shops, restaurants and the intriguing Yankee General Store are just steps away. Your hosts will be pleased to suggest more activities for you to enjoy while staying in the area, including exciting whale-watching expeditions. The house contains eight bedrooms for guests, two of which are on the ground floor. All of the accommodations, furnished in Colonial and contemporary styles, are large and have private baths. Some rooms offer double beds, others a double bed plus trundle bed (which sleeps two) or a queen-size bed. A continental breakfast of coffee and toast is served each morning.

The Colonial Guest House, 28 Eastern Point Rd., East Gloucester, MA 01930; (617) 281-1953. (Between Niles and Rocky Neck; from Rte. 127 follow Western Avenue, Rogers Street, Main Street, then E. Main Street to lights; bear right up hill on E. Main.) Rates are moderate to moderately expensive. Visa and MasterCard are accepted. Children are welcome; no pets, please. Open year-round.

The Inn on Cove Hill. A classic Federal house in the heart of Rockport, the charming Inn on Cove Hill is conveniently close to shops, galleries and the harbor. Inside, beyond the exceptionally handsome doorway, architectural connoisseurs will delight in the Christian cross doors with "H" and "L" hinges, carefully preserved wainscoting and dentil molding, and wide pumpkin pine floors. Also notable are a fine ceramic tile fireplace and graceful spiral staircase, the latter built with thirteen steps, a common tribute to the original thirteen colonies.

Owners John and Marjorie Pratt have ten tastefully appointed rooms for guests, all with TVs. Restoration of the rooms is continuing in an effort to decorate in the Early American style of the almost two-century-old house. Two guest rooms each have a queen-size canopy Shaker bed; one room contains twin Sheridan four-posters, and two rooms in later wings of the house offer double brass-and-iron beds,

Laura Ashley wall coverings and fabrics. Three small bedchambers on the third floor, each with a double bed, share a hall bath; all of the other rooms have private baths. The color schemes throughout are based on predominant shades in the pretty print and floral wallpapers. Personal touches are everywhere: handmade pincushions for emergency mending, handmade afghans and quilts for nippy nights, vases of daisies in summer, pumpkins in autumn.

A third-floor porch offers a panoramic view of picturesque Rockport Harbor and the ocean beyond; whales may sometimes be sighted during migration. For quiet reading or chatting with other guests there is the house's original living room. Furnished in appropriate period style, the attractive room includes a cherry Winthrop desk and Windsor chair built by a family ancestor some 150 years ago. A well-stocked bookcase provides magazines and works by Longfellow, Dickens and other classic authors. In the service room guests may store snacks in the refrigerator or obtain ice buckets and cubes. An information table with maps and lists of local events is another thoughtful touch. Outdoors, guest may relax at umbrella tables set around a hand-operated (and working) water pump set atop an enormous granite capstone, surrounded by masses of yellow Marguerite daisies.

The Pratts offer their guests a continental breakfast, served outside on the lawn in summer or brought on a tray to your room in winter. Breakfast consists of freshly ground coffee or a selection of teas, orange juice and homemade muffins—blueberry, cranberry, blackberry or pumpkin, depending on the season—elegantly served on lovely Royal Doulton and Wedgwood English bone china. Your hosts bake each morning, just so guests may wake up to the delicious aroma of hot muffins! In wintertime, after a day of cross-country skiing in a nearby forest, guests will be offered a warming mug of hot mulled cider.

The Inn on Cove Hill, 37 Mt. Pleasant St., Rockport, MA 01966; (617) 546-2701. (Follow Rte. 127 into Rockport, then 127A to the house.) Rates are moderate to moderately expensive. Children over 10 are welcome; no pets, please. Open late February–late October.

Seven South Street, The Inn. A gracious old New England house, Seven South Street in Rockport was built in 1750. Owners Helene and George Waldschlagel are trying to trace the history of the place, but are back only to around 1820 so far. The inn, furnished with some antiques and period reproductions, including traditional wallpaper and Colonial curtains, has eleven rooms for guests; one of the rooms is on the ground floor. In addition, the inn offers several housekeeping suites and cottages. All but two of the rooms have private baths.

Guests are invited to enjoy the attractively furnished sitting room in the main house, with a fireplace, and the paneled common room in the annex, with TV, bridge table, cards and games. Outdoors are secluded gardens, sun decks and a flower-surrounded swimming pool. A continental breakfast is served each morning, offering orange juice, English or homemade bran muffins, good white bread or oatmeal bread, cream cheese, strawberry jam and orange marmalade, and coffee or tea. Rockport's wealth of attractions and fine restaurants, many of which remain open all year, are a short walk from the house. An excellent beach is also close by.

Seven South Street, The Inn, 7 South St., Rockport, MA 01966; (617) 546-6708. Rates are moderately expensive, lower April 1–June 15 and Sept. 15–Oct. 30. Children are welcome only in housekeeping units; no pets, please. Open April 1–Oct. 30.

Eden Pines Inn. Offering a spectacular view of the ocean, Inge Sullivan's Eden Pines Inn is about one mile from the center of Rockport. The gray-shingled house, featuring a Palladian window at the front, was built in 1900 as a private home. A curved brick walk, bordered by geraniums, leads to the door; a charming rock garden in the side yard overlooks the sea, as do the covered porch and open brick sun deck. Large, smooth rocks lead from the sun deck down to the ocean, where you will see lobstermen hauling in their catches, fishermen heading out to sea in their boats, and Thatchers Island with its twin lighthouses.

For guests there are six upstairs bedrooms, decorated in eclectic style with some modern, some wicker and some period furnishings. All of the guest rooms have private bathrooms (a few with marble baths) and sitting areas. Most of the rooms have ocean views and several are large enough to accommodate four people. In addition to porches and sun decks, there is a delightfully decorated living room with books and TV, where a fire is lit in the wood-burning

fireplace in the evenings. Breakfast, served on the latticed sun porch—done in fresh whites, blues, greens and yellows—consists of juices, fresh fruit compote, English muffins and some of Inge's delicious homemade pastries. Coffee and tea are available throughout the day and night, and at teatime guests are offered hot or iced tea, or coffee, and cookies. Cocktail hour (BYOB) begins at 5 p.m.; set-ups and a crunchy snack or cheese and crackers are provided.

Inge Sullivan also has a completely furnished guest cottage out on Rockport's Bearskin Neck, with a lawn directly facing the harbor; ask her for details if you're interested.

Eden Pines Inn, Eden Road, Rockport, MA 01966; (617) 546-2505; off season write to 8 Cakebread Dr., Sudbury, MA 01776; (617) 443-2604. (To reach Eden Pines, take Rte. 128 north to first set of lights and turn left on Rte. 127 to downtown Rockport; go right on Rte. 127A—toward Gloucester—for 1 mile and then turn left on Eden Road to the inn.) Rates are moderately expensive to expensive. Visa and MasterCard are accepted when there is not enough time to receive deposit by mail. Older children only are welcome; no pets, please. Open from mid-May to October.

Morrill Place. Newburyport reached its peak of prosperity as a commercial and shipping center in the late 1700s and early 1800s; trade with Europe and China made it the seventh largest port in the nation. It was during that period that many of the town's most beautiful homes were constructed. The Morrill mansion, one of Newburyport's finest, was built in 1806 by Capt. William Hoyt. In 1836, Henry W. Kinsman, a junior law partner of Daniel Webster's, bought the place, and Mr. Webster was a frequent visitor. Gayden Morrill, mayor of Newburyport, purchased the house in 1897; the

Morrill Place

Morrill family retained ownership for eighty-four years. Your gracious hostess today is Mrs. Rose Ann Hunter.

An elegant three-story Federal edifice, the twenty-two-room house boasts twelve fireplaces and ninety-three windows, as well as a host of fine architectural features such as lovely cornices, mantels, balustrades and a graceful hanging staircase. There are ten guest bedrooms, two with private baths. One room, with private bath, is on the ground floor. All of the rooms are furnished in antiques and several contain four-poster canopy beds. Guests are invited to enjoy the summer and winter porches (the latter with TV), the formal front parlor and the library. There's a rooftop widow's walk, too. The restored historic area, with scores of shops and restaurants and many more of Newburyport's marvelous old houses, is only a five-minute walk away. Plum Island and superb beaches are five minutes away by car.

Mrs. Hunter offers her guests a continental breakfast of juice, coffee and homemade muffins or breads, or English muffins with jam; afternoon tea is also served. For Newburyport visitors unable to stay at the house there are daily tours at 3 p.m. A nominal fee is charged, and the tour is followed by tea, served hot during the winter in the library by the fire, or iced in the summer on the porch or terrace. In 1985, Morrill Place was chosen to be the year's North Shore Decorators Showcase. Twenty of the area's finest interior designers redecorated the house for the week-long show.

Morrill Place, 209 High St., Newburyport, MA 01950; (617) 462-2808. (From I-95, exactly 2 miles on High Street.) Rates are moderately expensive. American Express is accepted. Children over 6 are welcome; well-behaved pets may be allowed but please call first. Smoking is restricted. Open year-round.

The Benjamin Choate Inn. Benjamin Choate (1770-1854) was a master shipbuilder; his Newburyport firm was renowned the world over for its fine workmanship. Choate was also interested in education and helped form a school in Salisbury across the river. (The prestigious Choate School in Connecticut was founded by distant relatives.)

Benjamin's exceptionally handsome house, situated on a quiet side street in historic Newburyport, was built in 1794. The three-story Federal mansion was designed as a "miniature" of the sixteen-room Federal across the street where Choate's inlaws lived; they gave the house to him and his bride as a wedding present. Today the mansion belongs to Herbert A. Fox and his wife Jeanne, and they cordially invite guests to share their beautiful home with its wealth of perfectly preserved architectural details. The rooms, appointed with fine antiques, retain their original woodwork with Indian shutters, rope and dentil moldings, beaded designs and nineteen-inch-wide pumpkin pine floorboards.

There are five double bedrooms for guests, one of which is on the ground floor. Two of the rooms have private baths; the others share a full bath and powder room. One of the guest chambers has a working fireplace. All are tastefully decorated with period furniture, elegant eighteenth-century draperies and Oriental and handmade Colonial rugs. Among the many thoughtful amenities offered are sheets all ironed by hand! Throughout the house you can enjoy an extensive collection of old master and contemporary works of art, accumulated by your host during his twenty years as Master Printer for many internationally known artists.

A beautiful front parlor, with a graceful Empire couch, floor-length satin drapes, exquisite hand-colored Japanese woodcuts and color cable TV, is a delightful room for relaxing or conversing with other guests. Each morning a complimentary full breakfast is served in the comfortable old kitchen, where a set of early nineteenth-century porcelain canisters over the massive fireplace may be admired, and the table is set with an antique handmade lace cloth. The hearty, homecooked meal consists of juice, fresh fruit, bacon and eggs or choice of hot or cold cereal, homebaked bread or pastry and coffee or tea. Sunday specials might be eggs Benedict, homemade waffles or Julia Child's crepes. Seasonal delicacies, such as Mr. Fox's smoked bluefish, may also be included. In addition, guests at the Benjamin Choate Inn are offered afternoon tea, and upon arrival you will be welcomed with a glass of wine or a soft drink.

Newburyport's restored downtown area is about a ten-minute walk along the river or past many of the town's magnificent old mansions. You'll find an excellent selection of restaurants, including several that offer native seafood dishes, and a wide choice of specialty shops and boutiques. Docking facilities are accessible at Waterfront Park and arrangements can be made for sailboat rentals and fishing trips. Bicycles are available at the inn for touring the area, and Plum Island is only five minutes away by car.

The Benjamin Choate Inn, 25 Tyng St., Newburyport, MA 01950; (617) 462-4786. (About 1½ miles from I-95, ½ mile from rtes. 1A and 1.) Rates are moderately expensive. MasterCard and Visa are accepted. Quiet, well-

behaved children are welcome. No cats, please; inquire in advance regarding dogs. Open year-round.

The South Shore and Cape Cod

The most direct route from Boston to Cape Cod is via I-93 and then Route 3 south to Route 6 east. A more leisurely way is to follow Route 3A, closer to the ocean, past wealthy South Shore communities with impressive homes, beautiful salt marshes and miles of beaches. Stop at historic Plymouth on the way. The first American settlement north of Jamestown, Virginia, Plymouth was founded by the Pilgrims in 1620. A replica of the original *Mayflower* is moored in the harbor and may be toured. The ship is amazingly tiny, only ninety feet long. Pilgrim Village and Plimouth Plantation both show visitors what life was like in the 1600s. And of course, Plymouth Rock is located here. It might well be called Plymouth Pebble, as it is not exactly as impressive as most people expect. But the rock is symbolic, and certainly something everyone wants to see.

Cape Cod begins after you cross the Sagamore Bridge over the Cape Cod Canal. About sixty miles in length, the Cape curves outward and upward around Cape Cod Bay. It is a flattish region of scrub pine and oak, beaches and freshwater ponds, rolling sand dunes and small, neat villages with houses shingled in silvery-gray cedar. There are also a few unlovely "touristy" areas, and—in mid-summer—the Cape often becomes thronged with visitors, creating traffic jams along its mostly narrow roads. To experience the true essence of Cape Cod, try to come in September when the weather is usually mellow, the crowds have left, and the real charm of the region is very evident.

The Mid-Cape Highway (Route 6) runs directly all the way to Provincetown. Route 28 follows the southern coast of the Cape, leading to the pleasant town of Falmouth and down to Woods Hole, then heading east and north to Orleans. Route 6A, a winding, scenic road, runs from the Sagamore Bridge along the Cape's northern shore. The Outer Cape, a sandy, narrow stretch of land lying between the bay and the Atlantic Ocean, begins approximately at Eastham and ends at Provincetown. On the ocean side is the Cape Cod National Seashore, with several visitor centers for information on the variety of activities and park ranger programs offered.

Woods Hole, the southernmost town on the Cape, is the home of the famed Oceanographic Institution, and ferries to the islands of Martha's Vineyard and Nantucket leave from the town dock. Hyannis, the Cape's commercial center, is approximately mid-Cape. The famed "Kennedy Compound" is in nearby Hyannisport, but none of the houses are open to the public. Chatham, at the southeast elbow of the Cape, is one of Cape Cod's oldest townships—settled in 1656 by a small group of Pilgrims. It is also one of the nicest towns on the Cape, with a large collection of fine shops and restaurants. At the

Chatham Fish Pier visitors can watch the fishing fleet unload its catch daily after 2 p.m., and on Friday nights during July and August the town presents a series of band concerts in Kate Gould Park. Offshore, the Monomoy National Wildlife Refuge is a wonderfully unspoiled wilderness area.

Sandwich, on Route 6A on the quiet northern shore of the Cape, is an exceptionally picturesque town with a scenic pond and several restored seventeenth-century buildings, including a working grist mill. Another interesting stop is the Sandwich Glass Museum, displaying more than 3000 pieces of the famous, brilliantly colored glassware created here between 1825 and 1888. The attractive villages of Barnstable and Yarmouth Port lie to the east. Barnstable's salt marshes once supplied salt hay for the early settlers' cattle. In Brewster a few miles beyond visitors can explore Stony Brook Mill, a working replica of America's first grist mill, and Sealand, where dolphins and sea lions entertain the public.

On the Outer Cape, the small communities of Wellfleet and Truro offer visitors a different perspective, much more old Cape Cod in appearance and feel. Blissful solitude may be found along the beaches and towering sand dunes. Brambly woods traced by dirt roads, hidden freshwater ponds and rolling moors add to the region's wild, untouched beauty. Provincetown, way out at the tip of Cape Cod, presents a colorful mixture of old New England seaport ambiance and contemporary tourism, spiced with a dash of Portuguese flavor. The two main thoroughfares, Commercial and Bradford streets, are intersected by narrow, winding byways. Looming above is the imposing granite Pilgrim Monument, which visitors can climb for a sweeping view of the entire Cape. The town offers a host of interesting restaurants (a few serve excellent Portuguese food), and there are scores of shops and art galleries. Whale-watching excursions sail several times daily from the harbor in season.

First-time visitors to Provincetown who expect a tranquil seaside village may be in for a shock, particularly at the height of the summer season. Then, the modern world collides with the town's seventeenth-century past, and the result may not be to everyone's taste. Restaurants, bars, galleries and shops along one-way Commercial Street—and the street itself—are mobbed with vacationers of every sort, including hordes of day-trippers and a large gay element. The gay culture predominates during the summer months and is very visible, sometimes flamboyantly so. You will have to decide for yourself whether or not you will appreciate the scene, or would rather come in fall, winter or early spring when the town is quieter.

Falmouth/Woods Hole

Mostly Hall, Bed & Breakfast. Even though situated on Falmouth's main street, just across from the village green, Mostly Hall is almost

Mostly Hall, Bed & Breakfast

invisible to passersby. The house, surrounded by thick shrubbery, is set well back from the road behind an impressive wrought-iron fence. But if you peer carefully through the trees, you'll see a most unusual structure. In this region of gray-shingled Cape Cod cottages and traditional sea captains' Federal or Victorian homes, this striking mansion is virtually unique. It is a classic example of Southern architecture, a typical New Orleans Garden District home.

Virginia Austin, who owns Mostly Hall with her husband, Jim, and their daughter, tells the tale of how such a house came to be constructed so far away from its native setting. In 1849, a Yankee sea captain named Nye planned to bring his New Orleans bride to Falmouth. She, however, announced that she would not come North unless he built a house similar to her own home. He did, and the result is this spacious edifice with high ceilings, airy rooms, long, narrow windows with louvered shutters, and exterior gallery extending all the way around the house. The living quarters are, in Southern fashion, set up off the ground on posts; the original kitchen and servants' quarters were on the ground floor/basement level. High at the top of the structure is a widow's walk—probably Captain Nye's personal addition.

The name "Mostly Hall," by the way, was given the place at a much later date. When the previous owners moved in, their young son—after glimpsing the expansive entranceway—cried: "Wow, it's mostly hall!"

The hospitable Austins, who opened the house to guests in 1980, have seven attractively decorated double rooms for visitors, five with private baths. Five of the rooms are on the upper levels, up the deep-gold-carpeted stairway, and two are on the ground floor. The accommodations include the Wicker and the French Room, the latter featuring two antique sleigh beds, Captain Nye's Room with a massive

152

four-poster—a favorite for honeymooners and anniversary couples—and the Widow's Walk, which has been converted into a guest bedroom. Laura's Room is done in pink, with a king-size bed.

Guest are invited to enjoy the large, elegant living room with its fourteen-foot ceilings, the woodwork done in Williamsburg blue, and a fireplace. A full breakfast is served in season at a dining table at the far end of the room. Ginny Austin arises early every morning to prepare homemade breads or rolls, and one of a dozen unique creations for her guests. Fresh fruit, juice and coffee or tea round out the repast, which may sometimes include house specialties such as Welsh rarebit served on English muffins with bacon, eggs Benedict, blintz souffle, frittatas, stuffed French toast or fruit soups. In the afternoon, tea or sherry are offered.

Outdoors, in addition to relaxing on the porch, guests have access to the lawn behind the house with flowers, many trees and a charming gazebo. The Austins also have four bikes for guests to use. Indoors or out, Mostly Hall is a quiet, secluded haven, yet the house is only a minute's walk from Falmouth's many shops and restaurants.

Mostly Hall, Bed & Breakfast, 27 Main St., Falmouth, MA 02540; (617) 548-3786. (Opposite the Village Green.) Rates range from moderate to expensive; lower off season and for longer stays. Children over 16 are welcome; no pets, please. Open year-round except for February.

The Marlborough. A charming "full Cape" house set on a wooded half acre in Woods Hole, the Marlborough is owned by Patricia Morris. There are six guest bedrooms; four, with private baths, are upstairs and two—sharing a bath—are on the ground floor. The individually decorated accommodations are furnished with wicker, brass, iron and old wood antiques; the comfortable beds are covered with colorful custom or handcrafted quilts and spreads. A parlor/library, decorated with a touch of the Edwardian—with antiques and balloon shades—offers books, magazines, games and first-run classic movies.

Outdoors, guests are invited to enjoy the pool, paddle tennis court and picnic facilities, play croquet or laze away a restful hour in a hammock. Mrs. Morris has been adding to the beauty of her grounds, installing a picket fence and arbor over which rambler roses will spill, and a small orchard with fruit trees and blueberry hedges that will provide fresh fruit for breakfast. In addition, she has established a flower garden outside the parlor, and an herb garden provides fresh flavorings for her *fines herbes* omelets. About one mile away are a private beach, with lifeguard on duty, nature walks on Quisset campus, the ferry docks for Martha's Vineyard and Nantucket and the Woods Hole Aquarium. For bicyclists there's a three-and-a-half-mile bike path that runs from Woods Hole to Falmouth.

Your hostess serves a full and delicious breakfast at two sittings (one for early risers), with juice, fruit, cereal, coffee and hot

153

homebaked pastries such as banana or zucchini bread, brioche or scones. There will also be a main dish house specialty, perhaps eggs Bechamel, *Apfelfannkuchen*, or English breakfast tarts. Mrs. Morris, a truly creative cook, says that one can stay at the Marlborough for a month and not have the same breakfast twice! In the evenings, sherry and cheese or hors d'oeuvres are offered, and afternoon tea on Sundays. For honeymooners, the Marlborough includes a split of champagne and breakfast in bed.

The Marlborough, 320 Woods Hole Rd., Woods Hole, MA 02543: (617) 548-6218. (Follow Rte. 28 south to Woods Hole.) Rates are moderately expensive. Older children are welcome; no babies, please. Well-behaved, quiet pets are accepted with a security deposit. Open April–November.

West Yarmouth/Bass River/
West Harwich/Chatham

The Manor House. Sherry Braun's pleasant guest house in West Yarmouth is a large Dutch Colonial, built in the 1920s. The house was originally constructed to provide additional guest quarters for the Englewood Hotel, owned by the Morin family. Your hostess has six rooms for guests, including five doubles and one that accommodates up to four persons. Two of the rooms are on the ground floor and all of the guest chambers have private baths, some of which feature stenciled claw-foot tubs. The large, airy rooms are bright with

plants, dried flower arrangements and quilts. For relaxing, there is a spacious, sunny sitting room with a fireplace, TV, many plants and comfortable furniture, including antiques. A continental breakfast is served, consisting of juice, coffee or tea, homebaked coffee cakes, breads and muffins, and homemade jams. House specialties include such delicious treats as sour cream or cranberry sour cream coffee cake and apple squares. Guests are encouraged to play badminton or volleyball on the grounds, and there are lounge chairs for sunbathing and a convenient outdoor shower for beachgoers. The house is within walking distance of the town beach and close to golf courses, tennis courts and boat ramp. Hyannis, with its many restaurants and shops, and boats to the islands, is less than ten minutes away.

The Manor House, 57 Maine Ave., West Yarmouth, MA 02673; (617) 771-9211. (From Rte. 6 take Exit 7 and go left; take first left, Higgins Crowell Road, and follow to Rte. 28. Go straight across to Berry Avenue, take right onto Broadway and 2nd right onto Maine.) Rates are moderate, lower from mid-May to mid-June and from mid-September to mid-October, excluding holiday weekends. Children are welcome; no pets, please. Open mid-May through mid-October.

The Old Cape House. Travelers who have been fortunate enough to visit England will feel right at home in this delightful bed-and-breakfast house in Bass River. Your hostess, Linda Arthur, is a native of London, and with her husband, George, she has nicely combined the flavor of Old England with that of New England. Their house,

built in 1815, is a fine example of the popular Greek Revival style of architecture of that era. It was constructed by the Baker family, farmers and seafarers who owned most of the land in the Bass River region. There are six guest rooms including one single and five doubles, and extra beds are available. Two of the rooms have private baths; one is on the ground floor. The other rooms share two hall baths. The charmingly decorated rooms are named after streets in London, such as Burlington Arcade, Knightsbridge, Leicester Square and Oxford Street. Bishops Court overlooks the garden and has its own private entrance, fireplace and small kitchen unit. All of the guest rooms feature beamed ceilings, and are attractively furnished in New England/English style with lacy white curtains, handmade quilts and flower print wallpaper. Linda's handcrafted latch hook rugs and stuffed calico geese and cats add further appealing touches.

For relaxing, guests will enjoy the spacious living room with its extensive library, a large porch, and a beautiful garden where roses and other flowers bloom in profusion. In the back patio area are several interesting old slate gravestones belonging to the Baker family. Linda Arthur says that they were apparently found by a previous owner in the rear garden; she assumes the graves were moved to the nearby church when it was built. Breakfast at the Old Cape House is served in the dining room, once the old kitchen, with the original fireplace and beehive oven. Homebaked muffins (blueberry, cranberry or the house specialty, chocolate chip) or coffee cake, special homemade preserves, fresh fruit, a selection of cereals, and plenty of tea or coffee are offered. During the week of the Wimbledon tennis matches in summer, your hostess keeps British tradition by serving fresh strawberries and cream!

Things to do in the area are many; just ask your hosts for suggestions. Two excellent beaches are nearby, and golf, tennis, marinas, fishing and much more are easily accessible. Ferries to Nantucket and Martha's Vineyard leave from Hyannis, four miles away.

The Old Cape House, 108 Old Main St., Bass River, MA 02664; (617) 398-1068. (From Rte. 6 take Exit 8; go south on Station Avenue 3 miles to house.) Rates are moderate to moderately expensive, lower from May 1 to June 15 and for longer stays. Children over 11 are welcome; no pets, please. Open May 1– October 31.

The Lion's Head Inn. This intriguing old house, in West Harwich, was built in the early 1800s by sea captain Thomas L. Snow. Originally a Cape "half-house," the Lion's Head had been expanded over the years but still retains many distinctive features such as the original pine floors, a root cellar and the "captain's stairs" leading to the second floor. According to present-day hosts Laurie and Djordje Soc, it is rumored that the ghost of Mrs. Snow sometimes appears on stormy nights on the widow's walk, awaiting her husband's safe return from the sea.

Three comfortable double rooms and one suite are available for guests. Furnished in period antiques and traditional pieces, they include the Rose Room and Map Room, which share a bath; the Morning Room with private bath, and Captain Snow's Suite, with private bath. The suite, which can be rented as two separate rooms, sharing a bath, is on the ground floor and once served as Captain and Mrs. Snow's living quarters. There are also two fully furnished

guest cottages on the grounds, which may be rented by the week. A living room in the main house, with a fireplace, games and cards, is a pleasant place to relax. A hearty breakfast with homebaked bread and fresh local eggs is served each morning, and your hosts offer a complimentary glass of wine or sherry in the late afternoon. The inn is just half a mile from the beach on Nantucket Sound, and close to golf, summer theater, shops and restaurants.

The Lion's Head Inn, P.O. Box 444, 186 Belmont Rd., West Harwich, MA 02671; (617) 432-7766. (Follow Rte. 28 through Dennisport into West Harwich and turn right on Belmont Road; the inn is just around the corner.) Rates are moderately expensive; special accommodations and meal packages may be arranged for groups of up to 10 people. Children are welcome in the cottages, but must be 12 or older to stay in the main house; no pets, please. Open year-round.

The Tern Inn. Originally a Cape half-house built circa 1795, with later additions, the attractive Tern Inn in West Harwich is owned by Bill and Jane Myers. Wide-board floors, antiques, and furniture handmade by Bill Myers grace the interior. For guests there are three upstairs bedrooms, with private baths, and two rooms on the ground floor, sharing a bath. Decorated in Early American and Victorian style, the rooms feature four-poster Jenny Lind or Hitchcock beds, braided or Oriental rugs, and lovely old quilts. Guests are invited to share the living room, with a fireplace and quiet corners for reading, and the Publick Room with TV, an organ for sing-alongs, books and games. Breakfast at the inn varies daily, with hot rolls or muffins, juice, fruit compote, French toast or eggs, bacon or sausage and coffee or tea. Or perhaps there will be one of the house specialties such as Egg Crisps, a form of shirred eggs, or berry, pecan or corn waffles served with Vermont maple syrup. In cold weather your thoughtful hosts may add hot cereal and cocoa! Occasionally, iced tea may be served on the patio in the afternoon, or a glass of wine before guests set off for dinner. The house is set on two acres of pine and huge old oak trees, on a quiet residential road. The patio and grounds are pleasant places to relax, sun and picnic. Nantucket Sound beaches are three blocks away, shops and restaurants are about a mile from the house and all of the Cape's attractions are within a thirty-mile drive.

The Tern Inn, 91 Chase St., West Harwich, MA 02671; (617) 432-3714. (From Rte. 6 take Exit 9; bear right on Rte. 134 to Rte. 28 and turn left. Follow 2.3 miles across Herring River to River Road, turn right and see house immediately right on Chase Street.) Rates are moderately expensive, lower from Sept. 15 to June 15, for longer stays and for children. Children are welcome; no pets, please. Open year-round.

The Captain's House Inn of Chatham. Tucked away behind tall hedges, the elegant Captain's House is owned by David and Cathy Eakin. Set on three secluded acres of lawns, gardens, open meadows and pine groves just outside of Chatham, the house and its two adjacent cottages much resemble Virginia's Colonial Williamsburg. The main house, a white Greek Revival-style structure, was built in 1839 by a packet skipper named Capt. Hiram Harding, and restored in 1983. The old random-width pumpkin pine floors, fireplaces, and other fine architectural features have been carefully preserved.

There are ten guest rooms, all with private baths; two of the rooms are on the ground floor and two have their own fireplaces. Named after the ships Captain Harding sailed—Hannah Rebekah, Eliza Jane, Trade Wind and others—the individually decorated rooms abound with antiques, among which are several 200-year-old four-poster canopied beds. Velvet wing chairs, reading lamps and Williamsburg wallpapers add further charming touches.

A cozy living room with a fireplace, appointed with antiques, provides a pleasant place for relaxing, reading and conversation. Breakfast is served to house guests in the all-white breakfast room, overlooking the gardens through floor-length windows. Guests are offered homemade coffee cakes or sweet breads, English muffins, cereals, and coffee or tea.

Additional accommodations are available in the two cottages on the grounds, rented only by the week. The Carriage House contains three bedrooms, a living room with fireplace, a dining room and a kitchen. The Captain's Cottage, a full Cape fronted by a garden and white picket fence, has three bedrooms, a large combination living and dining room with walk-in fireplace, a full kitchen and two baths.

Chatham Center, with its excellent restaurants and fine shops, is only half a mile away. Beaches, golf, tennis and boat charters are all accessible nearby, and all of Cape Cod's many attractions are within an easy drive.

The Captain's House Inn of Chatham, 369 Old Harbor Rd., Chatham, MA 02633; (617) 945-0127. (From Chatham Center follow the rotary out of town on Rte. 28 north toward Orleans; the inn's driveway will be on your left.) Rates are expensive, lower from Columbus Day through June 15. Visa, MasterCard and American Express are accepted. Children over 12 are welcome in the main house; younger children are welcome in the cottages. No pets, please. Open Feb. 15–Nov. 30.

Sandwich/Barnstable

The Summer House. The Summer House, in the attractive village of Sandwich, is owned by Pamela Hunt. Dr. Jonathan Leonard, Jr., built the handsome Greek Revival house in 1835; subsequent owners, the Dilloway family, owned the property until 1980. Hiram Dilloway was a mold-maker for the famed Sandwich Glass Company. Your hostess purchased the house in 1981 and restored it to use as her home and as a comfortable bed-and-breakfast for travelers.

The entire front section of the house is devoted to guests, with four bedrooms, one on the ground floor. Two of the rooms have

private baths; the other two share a bath. All of the rooms are strikingly and tastefully decorated in nineteenth-century style with lovely antiques. Fireplaces, the original woodwork and hardware and painted hardwood floors add to their charm as do fresh flowers, thick fluffy towels and freshly laundered and ironed bed linens. For relaxing, guests will enjoy the downstairs sitting room with a fireplace, the front porch, and a secluded patio surrounded by lawn and flower gardens. Books, magazines, newspapers and games abound for quiet moments.

A continental breakfast is served in the sunny Breakfast Room with its cherry-red walls and white woodwork, black and white checkerboard floor, black marble fireplace, many plants, and well-filled bookcases. Fresh fruit in season, hot French croissants, homemade cranberry or blueberry muffins or peach coffeecake, and freshly brewed coffee or a choice of teas are offered. Your hostess is happy to accommodate special dietary needs as well. Several restaurants, antique shops and all of Sandwich's many interesting activities and museums are within walking distance.

The Summer House, 158 Main St., P.O. Box 341, Sandwich, MA 02563; (617) 888-4991. (From Rte. 6 take Exit 2 to Rte. 130, turn left to Sandwich Village 1.3 miles and bear right onto Old Main Street for .2 mile.) Rates are moderate. Visa and MasterCard are accepted. Children over 10 are welcome; no pets, please. Open May–Thanksgiving.

Charles Hinckley House. Situated on the Olde King's Highway (Route 6A) and the corner of Scudder Lane in the historic district of Barnstable Village, the Charles Hinckley House was built circa 1809–1810. Charles Hinckley, a shipwright, purchased the house in 1821. Charles was the great-great-grandson of Thomas Hinckley, the last governor of the Plymouth Colony. An excellent example of Federal Colonial architecture, the Charles Hinckley House has been carefully restored to preserve its wealth of fine details including twelve-over-twelve windows with their panes of "purpling" glass, seven fireplaces, random-width pumpkin pine floors and exquisite paneling.

Hosts Les and Miya Patrick have three double rooms for guests, all with fireplaces and private baths. One of the rooms is on the ground floor, and all are furnished in period style with either queen-size or double four-poster beds, and easy chairs or chaise lounges. A pleasant common room, with sofas and comfortable seating arrangements around the fireplace, is an enjoyable place for conversation or reading, and an English country breakfast is served in the dining room, with its own fireplace. The breakfast, according to your hostess, "is an experience in itself!" Outdoors, a beautiful flower garden surrounds the house.

Your hosts make every effort to spoil their guests, with baskets of fruit, fresh flowers, and bedside chocolates in the evening. Tea and coffee or sherry, and cheese trays, are available at any time, and dinners are served on holidays and special occasions such as guests' honeymoons, anniversaries and birthdays. Cape Cod Bay is a five-minute stroll down the lane, and village shops and restaurants are within walking distance. Hyannis is four miles away, and all of Cape Cod's diverse attractions are easily accessible.

Charles Hinckley House, Box 723, Barnstable Village, MA 02630; (617) 362-9924. (Corner of Rte. 6A and Scudder Lane.) Rates are expensive, lower for longer stays. No children or pets, please. Open year-round.

Beechwood Inn. A Victorian fantasy come to life is one way to describe the delightful Beechwood Inn in Barnstable. Bea and Jeffrey Goldstein purchased the Queen Anne-style Victorian house, built in 1853 by a Barnstable hatter, in July, 1982. The old structure needed work, lots of it, and the Goldsteins estimate the time they spent in restoration as some 4000 labor hours. Easterners by birth, Jeff and Bea had previously been living in California where they owned and operated an antique store and Jeff had restored three other old houses.

Except for plumbing and wiring, the couple renovated and decorated the large old Barnstable house virtually by themselves—including jacking up the front of the structure, sanding the exterior to bare wood, finding or making matching moldings and making most of the fifty-five wooden storm and screen windows! Standing in the shade of two huge old beech trees, which give the house its name, Beechwood is now the Goldsteins' Victorian dream brought to reality. Even the exterior color scheme is historically accurate: yellow, jade green and gold.

Five individually decorated bedrooms are available for guests, all doubles with modern private baths. Two of the rooms, with working fireplaces, are on the ground floor and all capture the Victorian mood

161

to perfection. The Eastlake Room, which looks out at Cape Cod Bay in the distance through colored-glass windows, features William Morris wallpaper, a spoon-carved bed and matching marble-topped dresser. The charming Cottage Room contains a rare handpainted bedroom set, windows bordered by lavender and yellow church glass, and Victorian mauve walls.

Guests are invited to enjoy the parlor, Bea's favorite room, with a small marble-mantled fireplace and hand-silk-screened wallpaper. A traditionally hearty Victorian-style breakfast is served in the dining room, with its original tin ceiling, paneled walls, and fireplace. Guests sit at a large, round mahogany table and dine from Bea's collection of lovely Blue Willow china. Your hosts offer juice—grapefruit, cranberry or freshly squeezed orange, or apple cider, fresh fruit (melon, grapes, pineapple, kiwi, etc.), eggs in a variety of ways such as hard-boiled, scrambled or in a quiche, cheese, homebaked muffins and breads, and coffee, tea or espresso. Oatmeal may also be included, on appropriately chilly mornings. Afternoon tea, a happy custom, is also served, with cookies or tea sandwiches and hot tea or espresso or, in summer, iced tea and lemonade. In warm weather, breakfast and tea are served on the veranda. Restaurants and shops are within walking distance, and beaches, sports activities and museums are all easily accessible.

Beechwood Inn, 2839 Main St. (Rte. 6A), Barnstable, MA 02630; (617) 362-6618. Rates are expensive, lower from Nov. 1 to May 25 and for longer stays. Visa, MasterCard and American Express are accepted. No children or pets, please. Open year-round.

Yarmouth Port/Dennis/Brewster

The Wedgewood Inn and Gallery. An elegant, beautifully restored Federal house, the Wedgewood was built around 1812, the first home in historic Yarmouth Port to be designed by an architect. Set on two landscaped acres, the three-story white clapboard structure is surrounded by flower beds and greenery. Owners Jeff and Jill Jackson have decorated the inn with charm and flair, adding lovely antiques and handmade reproductions. Colonial print wallpapers, gleaming wide-board yellow pine floors, working fireplaces, freshly cut flowers and paintings and prints all contribute to the house's welcoming atmosphere.

Six spacious double rooms are available for guests, all with private baths. Two, with private screened porches and working fireplaces, are on the ground floor, and one has its own sitting room. Three of the guest rooms, each with sitting areas and two with fireplaces, are on the second floor, and the exceptionally large third floor room— with cannonball twin beds and a sitting area—offers a grand view of Cape Cod Bay. A nice added touch in each room are two stemmed glasses and a carafe of sherry. Newlywed couples are provided with a chilled bottle of champagne.

Breakfast at the Wedgewood Inn consists of fresh fruit or juice, baskets of freshly baked croissants and cranberry or blueberry muffins, homemade preserves and coffee or tea. The meal is served in the very attractive blue and white dining/common room, with French doors, a plant-filled bay window and your hosts' collection of English bone china tea pots. Other meals, such as a light luncheon served on the terraced garden patio, may be arranged by advance reservation for an extra charge.

The art gallery, situated in an old converted barn behind the inn, offers antiques, collectibles, prints and paintings. Many works created by your hostess Jill are on display, including paintings and handmade knitted and needlepoint items. A broad lawn beyond the barn is a pleasant place for strolling or enjoying the air at umbrella-topped tables. Several excellent restaurants and numerous antique shops are within walking distance of the house. Other nearby attractions include Yarmouth Port's stately old homes, the Botanic Trails and Gardens, golf, tennis and water sports. Your hosts have bicycles for guests' use, too, for exploring the area's country roads and salt marshes.

The Wedgewood Inn, 83 Main St. (Rte. 6A), Yarmouth Port, MA 02675; (617) 362-5157. Rates are expensive. Visa and MasterCard are accepted. No children or pets, please. Open year-round.

Isaiah B. Hall House. Isaiah Baker Hall built this spacious old farmhouse in Dennis in 1857. Of Greek Revival architecture with Victorian overtones, the house is connected to a large, white clapboard barn. In 1948 an artist and craftswoman named Dorothy Gripp purchased the property to operate as an inn, with a craft shop in the barn. Some of her famous apple dolls are now in museums, and much of her delightful artwork remains in both the main house and barn.

Your present-day hosts, Marie and Dick Brophy, have eleven rooms

for guests. Most of the rooms share baths, and one room—in the main house—is on the ground floor. The guest quarters in the main house are decorated with white iron beds and antique bureaus, small print country wallpaper, handmade quilts, Oriental, hooked or rag rugs, and airy eyelet curtains. Most also feature antique prints or paintings, or some of Marie's embroidery or needlepoint. The first floor guest room boasts matching log cabin quilts. The spacious barn bedrooms are all upstairs; most have knotty pine walls, quilts and rag rugs. Downstairs is the Great Room, done in blue and white and offering games and TV.

In the main house, both a parlor and a library are available for quiet reading or good conversation. The parlor contains some nice antiques including lovely Persian rugs on the old wide-board pine floor, "mammy" rockers and a dragonfly stained-glass lamp. Hand-crafted tiles surrounding the fireplace portray the ships captained by past owners of the house and their relatives, and the old beehive oven and a cupboard for raising bread (or hiding liquor from the pastor, as your hostess suggests!) are still in evidence. The library, with Oriental rugs, wing chairs and an interesting collection of antiques including tin photos, is very popular with guests. Many, according to your hostess, enjoy listening to music or the "Prairie Home Companion" on the turn-of-the-century radio. A side porch with rockers offers more space for relaxing, and an acre of land to the rear of the house offers badminton and croquet, lounge chairs and several small gardens.

Breakfast is served in the paneled dining room, originally the old summer kitchen, in the main house. Guests dine at a long Sheraton table. Offered are a choice of three juices, fruit, a variety of cereals, a selection of homebaked breads, muffins and/or coffee cake or English muffins, jams and preserves and coffee or tea. The house is a short walk from restaurants, shops and beaches. Dennis is the geographical center of Cape Cod, so all of the region's attractions are easily accessible.

Isaiah B. Hall House, 152 Whig St., Dennis, MA 02638; (617) 385-9928. (From Rte. 6 take Exit 8, go left 1.2 miles to Rte. 6A, turn right and go 3.4 miles to Hope Lane opposite cemetery and church. Turn left on Hope and at the end turn right on Whig; the house will be on the left.) Rates are moderately expensive, lower from Sept. 16 to May 14 and for longer stays. Visa and MasterCard are accepted. Children over 6 are welcome; no pets, please. The main house is open year-round; the barn is open June–October.

The Captain Freeman Inn. John and Barbara Mulkey are your hosts at this elegant old sea captain's mansion in Brewster. William Freeman, an aristocratic shipmaster who attained his wealth from the clipper trade, built the house in 1860. A painting of his ship, the *Kingfisher*, hangs in the hall, and memorabilia belonging to the Captain are on display in an antique cabinet in the parlor. Among the items are his personal flag, footrests he made while at sea and an invoice for hauling lumber on one of his voyages.

During his sailing career Captain Freeman traveled first in clipper ships and later in steamers. He survived mutiny and fire at sea and

lived to recount a 2100-mile voyage in a small open boat. The Captain married twice. During his second marriage a daughter, Phoebe, was born. It is said that upon his daughter's arrival the Captain came from the birthing room and announced to those in attendance that Phoebe had been born. When questioned about the name Captain Freeman sternly repeated, "Phoebe has been born." Phoebe was also the name of the Captain's first wife!

Fine architectural details may be noted throughout the house such as the plaster moldings, imported from Italy, on the first floor's ten-foot ceilings. The main hall floor is laid in a herringbone pattern in light and dark woods; the parlor and six of the guest rooms have hardwood floors. Four of the rooms have random-width pine floors. All of the ten guest bedrooms are doubles; five have private baths and five share baths. Two of rooms, both with private baths, are on the ground floor. All are beautifully furnished with antiques and collectibles, including several four-poster beds with canopies. Quilts and country comforters cover the beds. The first-floor parlor, with a handsome marble fireplace, is available for guests' use for reading, listening to music, playing games or watching TV. There's also a cozy reading corner in the second-floor alcove.

A continental breakfast of juice, muffins and coffee, tea or milk is served around the large oak table in the parlor or, in summer, on the side porch by the pool. Barbara Mulkey bakes the muffins herself and says that guests' favorite are Mormon Muffins (made with bran, dates and nuts) and Zucchini Nut. Wine, juice or cider are offered in late afternoons, either around the fireplace in the parlor or on the porch.

Across the town green from the inn is the First Parish Church with

165

its ancient burying ground established in 1700, and an old-time country store with a potbelly stove and penny candy is nearby. Breakwater Beach on Cape Cod Bay is a short walk away, as are restaurants, antique shops and tennis. The town of Brewster, first settled in 1656 and named in honor of Elder Brewster, a Pilgrim Father, was the home of many of Cape Cod's nineteenth-century seafaring families. Their well-preserved houses are still to be seen along Main Street.

Captain Freeman Inn, 15 Breakwater Rd., RR 2, Brewster, MA 02631; (617) 896-7481. (From Rte. 6 take Exit 10, Rte. 124, north to Brewster. At intersection of Rte. 6A turn right and take first left onto Breakwater Road.) Rates are moderately expensive, lower from November through April. Visa and MasterCard are accepted. Children are welcome; no pets, please. Open year-round.

North Truro/Provincetown

The Summer House at Pond Village. Back in 1620, the Pilgrims spent their second night ashore camped near the small pond a few hundred yards away from the site of this charming old house in the center of North Truro. Built in the 1820s, the Summer House has

been nicely renovated by owners John and Sara Parker as a bed-and-breakfast establishment. The original pine floors, quilts on all the beds and turn-of-the-century photographs of the local fishing industry—as well as paintings by local Truro artists—all create a warm Cape Cod atmosphere.

There are five bedrooms for guests, including four doubles and one triple, sharing two baths. Two of the rooms are on the ground floor. A broad front porch is a delightful place to sit, and at the side of the house there is a large lawn with a hammock, small gardens and fruit trees. A continental breakfast is served each morning, featuring delicious homemade Cape Cod specialties such as cranberry cheese bread or blueberry muffins, and cranberry orange marmalade.

Several excellent restaurants are close by, as are the small but intriguing Truro Historical Museum and fine golf course. Cape Cod Bay and the Atlantic Ocean are only a mile apart at this narrowest strand of the Cape; both the National Seashore and the bay are within walking distance. Highland Light can be seen from the house and Provincetown is visible from the end of the road.

The Summer House, Pond Road, North Truro, MA (mailing address: P.O. Box 724, Truro, MA 02666); (617) 487-2077; (From Rte. 6, take Exit 6A to North Truro and turn left onto Pond Road. The house is the second on the right.) Rates are moderate, lower from May 1 to June 15 and after Sept. 9, and one night free for a week's stay. Children are not encouraged; no pets, please. Open May 1–Oct. 31.

Bradford Gardens Inn. James Logan welcomes guests to his interesting old Provincetown house, built in 1820 and noted for its beautifully landscaped gardens. Original oil paintings and stunning antiques abound throughout the house, and there are seven working fireplaces. The main house has eight double rooms and apartments for guests; additional accommodations are available in separate lodges. Each of the guest quarters is uniquely different in character, and all have private baths and color TV.

The delightful Chimney Nook offers water and garden views and an old fireplace nook; the Sun Gallery Suite, with its own private entrance, also has a fireplace and a garden view. The Honeymoon Suite, with a bedroom and sitting room, boasts an old Franklin stove and a view of the garden, and the Alcove Room, with a fireplace, is named for the charming alcoves that overlook garden and sea. Both the Cherry Tree Room and Cherry Tree Apartment have views of your host's famous Japanese cherry tree; the apartment offers a private entrance, a fireplace, and ten windows overlooking the garden. The Beloved Toad, a cozy lodge for four. features a cathedral ceiling and

a unique corner beehive fireplace, a loft bedroom and a full kitchen, and a patio off the rose garden.

A full gourmet breakfast, which may include shirred eggs with tarragon Mornay sauce, eggs Benedict, quiche or perhaps blueberry crepes, is served in wintertime in the attractive Morning Room with its central fireplace and large bay window overlooking the garden. In spring and summer, breakfast is served in the gardens among flowering fruit trees and rose bushes; in May the splendid Japanese cherry tree is a spectacular sight to behold. The grounds also offer a large outdoor barbecue where guests are encouraged to broil their own lobster or steak dinners. All of Provincetown's many attractions are easily accessible.

Bradford Gardens Inn, 178 Bradford St., Provincetown, MA 02657; (617) 487-1616. Rates are expensive, 10 percent off for weekly stays. Visa, MasterCard and American Express are accepted. No children or pets, please. Parking is available. Open April 1–Dec. 1.

Richmond Inn. This handsome house, built by a Provincetown ship captain in 1860, is owned by James Hay Richmond and James Pardy. Located in the quiet West End of town, Richmond Inn is decorated with period furnishings and many paintings, including period works and those of modern Provincetown artists, and a large collection of Southeast Asian and Chinese art. There are twelve guest bedrooms, two with private baths; all face either the water or the gardens. Four

of the rooms are on the ground floor. A common room and TV lounge are pleasant places for relaxing, as are the gardens and a large sun deck that overlooks the harbor. Coffee and tea are offered each morning; on weekends your hosts also provide homebaked coffee cakes or other pastries. Restaurants, shops and galleries are a short walk away, and the house is on the shuttle bus line. The National Seashore is also within walking distance, and special whale-watching boat trips through Greenpeace can be arranged.

Richmond Inn, 4 Conant St., Provincetown, MA 02657; (617) 487-9193 or 487-1921. (On the harbor just west of town center.) Rates are moderate to moderately expensive, lower off season. Visa and MasterCard are accepted.

Children are welcome; no pets, please. Parking is available. Open year-round.

Asheton House. One of Provincetown's most elegant guest houses, Asheton House is superbly appointed—down to the last detail—with antiques from the owners' private collection. Built as a whaling captain's home around 1840, the house stands behind a Nantucket-style white fence; a graceful double set of steps leads to the front door. Hosts Jim Bayard and Les Schaufler encourage their guests to enjoy the formal English boxwood garden, with rare Japanese Temple trees and brick walks, and the sheltered terrace at the rear of the house. An "eye-opener" of juice and coffee or tea is served each morning.

Asheton House has three upper-level guest rooms, each spacious, airy and individually decorated. One is a suite consisting of a bed/sitting room with French furnishings, a dressing room with wardrobe wall, a fireplace and a private bath. The other two, equally attractive, share a bath. The Captain's Room, with American antiques, includes a queen-size nineteenth-century four-poster bed; the Safari Room, with two double beds, is furnished in natural wicker and bamboo and handsome campaign chests.

In addition, a charming early 1800s Cape on the adjoining property offers four more distinctively decorated guest rooms, sharing baths, and a three-room apartment. The double-bed Deck Room with Oriental accessories and the double-bed Bay Room (with Chinese Chippendale arm chairs and a planter's chaise) both overlook the bay. The Lattice Room features wallpaper of white lattice on a brown background; the Paisley Room is American antique with a documentary pattern framing walls and ceiling; both have double beds.

Asheton House, 3 Cook St., Provincetown, MA 02657; (617) 487-9966. (In the West End.) Rates are moderately expensive. No children or pets, please. Parking is available, and if you come by plane your hosts will meet you at the airport. Open year-round.

The Islands: Martha's Vineyard and Nantucket

Bartholomew Goswold, an English explorer, discovered Martha's Vineyard in 1602; he named it after one of his daughters and for the wild grapes that grew so abundantly. They still do. The Vineyard, seven miles across the water from Woods Hole, is about twenty miles long and ten miles wide. Inland are moors, ravines, forests and a number of freshwater ponds. At Gay Head, spectacular multi-colored clay cliffs tower 145 feet above the surging ocean. Excellent roads lead to beaches, swiftly crisscross the island, or meander leisurely through lovely, hilly countryside past old farms, stone walls and fields of wildflowers.

The Vineyard's major communities are Edgartown, Vineyard Haven (Tisbury) and Oak Bluffs. The others are West Tisbury, Chilmark, Gay Head and Menemsha. Edgartown, the county seat since 1642, is pretty enough to be framed, blooming with flowers and dotted with chic shops and restaurants. Back in the days of the whaling fleet, sea captains built stately homes here that are just as handsome now as they were then, with their classic fanlights and roofs topped with widow's walks. Chappaquiddick Island is just off Edgartown; a ferry will take you over for a drive or bicycle ride. It is a beautiful, serene little island of tangly wooded thickets, broad marshes and secluded beaches.

Vineyard Haven, an attractive town with tree-lined, hilly streets, offers a number of excellent restaurants and several fine shops, including an outstanding bookstore, the Bunch of Grapes. Oak Bluffs, which began as a tent camp run by the Methodist Church in the mid-1800s, is famed for its collection of American Gothic cottages. These quaint "gingerbread" houses look rather like large versions of children's cutouts, their ornate jigsaw scrollwork painted in bright colors or pastels. Band concerts are performed near the cottages on summer evenings and the Camp Ground is the scene for Illumination Night, when all the cottages are decorated with Japanese and Chinese lanterns.

Ferries carrying both cars and passengers run to Martha's Vineyard from Woods Hole. Boats carrying passengers only run from Hyannis, Falmouth and New Bedford. Since some of the vessels dock at Vineyard Haven and others at Oak Bluffs, check to be sure you are taking the right one. Space for cars is booked up weeks in advance in summer; if you must bring one make your reservation early. Your guest house proprietor will tell you where to call or write. Guest houses, too, overflow with visitors during the summer season so try to reserve accommodations as far in advance as possible.

Nantucket, "the Far-Away Island," lies thirty miles out to sea, far removed from sight of the mainland. It is an island of roses, moors and beaches, sunshine and fog, cobblestoned streets and elegant eighteenth- and nineteenth-century sea captains' homes. The Indians believed that Nantucket was created by a giant, a mighty chief, who tossed a great moccasin-full of sand out into the ocean. In truth, the island is a terminal moraine—a glacial deposit—about fifteen miles long and five miles wide.

The largest community, Nantucket Town, was settled by Quakers in 1659. For almost a century, from 1740 to 1830, Nantucket was the greatest whaling port in the world. The town retains much of the character of those early days, with its cobblestoned main street and collection of beautiful old houses. More than 400 of the homes in Nantucket's historic district have been lived in continuously from the time they were built. A number are open to the public, including the oldest, the 1686 Jethro Coffin House. To experience a taste of the island's nautical past visit the Whaling Museum, near the ferry landing.

Nantucket also offers many interesting shops for browsing, and plenty of good places to dine. Like Martha's Vineyard, the island is edged by beaches, and inland, has miles of rolling green moors. The atmosphere is quiet and decidedly restful; no traffic lights or neon signs disturb the tranquility. You don't really need an automobile for exploring; many visitors bring bicycles or rent mopeds or bikes and go off by themselves . . . or walk. The less athletic can take bus tours. And buses run between Nantucket Town and Siasconset ("Sconset") on the other side of the island.

Guest houses are the traditional places to stay on Nantucket, and there are few other forms of accommodation. Most of the houses are historic, antique filled and very charming. Most are also small, with a limited number of rooms, and it is imperative to make reservations as far in advance as possible, especially in summer. Planes fly to the island, and there is regular car and passenger ferry service from Woods Hole all year. In summer, the ferries also run from Hyannis and Martha's Vineyard.

Edgartown/Vineyard Haven/Chilmark

The Dr. Shiverick House. Edgartown's tree-shaded streets are lined with elegant nineteenth-century houses, many of them once the homes of whaling ship captains. The Dr. Shiverick House, however, was the home of Dr. Clement Shiverick, an eminent Edgartown physician. Originally a simple, two-story residence built in 1840, the house was added onto and modified over the years. Dr. Shiverick's daughter, Anna Josepha, recalled that her mother—who was from New York—was horrified when neighbors would call at the back door in typical New England fashion. "I—I—have a front door," she would gasp in consternation. The problem was solved when Dr. Shiverick had a wing built for his office, and the old back door became the side door, "altogether proper for neighborly calls." In the early 1870s, Mrs. Shiverick began to spend winters in the South and became intrigued with the Southern

The Dr. Shiverick House

style of homes, built with a broad central hall running from the front of the house to the back. A few years later, in 1875, she had her house rotated, an addition built on, and the interior restyled so that she, too, now had an impressive entrance hall.

The Dr. Shiverick House, after remaining a private residence for 144 years, was carefully restored to its original nineteenth-century beauty and opened as an unusually stunning bed-and-breakfast inn in 1984. Still owned by descendants of the Shiverick line, Dr. Paul Rogers and his family, the house is managed by innkeeper Tena McLoughlin. For guests there are eleven spacious, high-ceilinged rooms, all with private baths, and two suites each with a bedroom, sitting room and private bath. Four of the rooms are on the ground floor. All of the guest quarters in the exquisitely appointed house were individually decorated with great taste and charm by a noted Vineyard interior designer. Authentic antiques, perfectly coordinated wallpapers and fabrics, fresh flowers, and wide, glowingly polished pine floorboards grace the house. A solarium, a living room/reading area and porches on several levels offer quiet relaxation and opportunities for meeting other guests. There's even a hammock for lazy afternoon dozing.

A continental breakfast is served at the inn, highlighted by home-made breads baked by innkeeper McLoughlin, a baker by profession. On Sundays guests are treated to French toast, with island blueberries. Homemade cookies or brownies are provided in the afternoon or evening. Excellent restaurants are within an easy walk, as are museums, a movie theater and performing arts center, and fine shops. Bicycles may be rented nearby, and bus tours of the island are available. Martha's Vineyard is a delight to visit at any time of the year; off season, in fact, is an especially pleasant time to come. At Christmas, Edgartown's inns and shops hold open house, and the town celebrates in old-fashioned Victorian style.

The Dr. Shiverick House, Box 640, Edgartown, MA 02539; (617) 627-8497. (Corner of Pent Lane and Pease's Point Way.) Rates are expensive, lower off season. Visa and MasterCard are accepted. Children are welcome; no pets, please. Open year-round.

Chadwick House. This handsome Greek Revival-style house, built in 1840 for an Edgartown whaling captain and recently redecorated, is owned by Gene and Jean DeLorenzo. The Garden Wing was added to the original structure in 1981. Fourteen large, airy rooms are available for guests, all tastefully appointed with antiques. In addition, there is a comfortable suite with a bedroom and living room. Twelve of the rooms have private baths, and six are on the ground floor. A spacious covered first-floor veranda is a popular spot for summertime relaxing; for cooler weather there are a large front parlor and a smaller second parlor. The DeLorenzos say that the larger parlor, with a beautiful staircase at one end, is perfect for weddings. A continental breakfast is served in the attractive dining room, where a crackling blaze in the fireplace greets guests on chilly mornings. Juice, homemade coffee cake, rolls or muffins and coffee or tea are offered. The house is located in the center of Edgartown, one block from Main Street and two blocks from the harbor.

Chadwick House, Winter Street and Pease's Point Way, P.O. Box 1035, Edgartown, MA 02539; (617) 627-4435. Rates are expensive, lower off season. Visa and MasterCard are accepted. Children over 10 are welcome; no pets, please. Open year-round.

The Victorian Inn. The Victorian, an early eighteenth-century whaling captain's home now owned by Marilyn and Jack Kayner, is just across from Edgartown's famed old Pagoda Tree. Your hosts have fourteen rooms for guests, all with private baths. Two of the guest bedrooms are on the ground floor. Furnished with family pieces and antiques, including four-poster canopy beds, the rooms are tastefully decorated with coordinated wallpaper and linens, eyelet and hand-crocheted dresser scarves, and fresh flowers. Some open onto balconies, overlooking the garden or harbor. Guests are invited to use the comfortable sitting room with a fine marble fireplace and TV, and outdoors an enchanting English Garden offers a peaceful, secluded haven. The Kayners provide guests with an ample breakfast: a choice of juice, fresh fruit in season, homemade granola and preserves, breads and muffins, and freshly ground coffee or English or herbal teas. There will also be a different main dish each day, such as the house specialty,

The Victorian Inn

Eggs Victorian. The meal is served in the Breakfast Room, with a fireplace, or—in warm weather—in the English Garden. The house is a block above the town dock and harbor, a short walk away from Edgartown's many restaurants and shops.

The Victorian Inn, S. Water Street, P.O. Box 947, Edgartown, MA 02539; (617) 627-4784. Before April write or call: P.O. Box 251, Wilmington, VT 05363; (802) 464-3716. Rates are expensive. Visa, MasterCard and American Express are accepted. Children 16 or older are welcome; no pets, please. Open April 1– Nov. 1.

The Lothrop Merry House. Built in the mid-1700s, The Lothrop Merry House was moved from West Chop two miles away to its present location in Vineyard Haven overlooking the harbor. A typical eighteenth-century structure, the house has a central chimney and six fireplaces. John and Mary Clarke, a very friendly couple, have seven double rooms for guests, four with private baths. All are decorated with antiques, including a handsome four-poster bed, and fresh flowers. Four of the rooms are on the ground floor, and several offer working fireplaces with a supply of wood. Most of the guest chambers have views of the harbor and ocean beyond; the sunrises are magnificent, and at night guests drift off to sleep to the wind-chime sound of harbor bell buoys.

A continental breakfast, with delicious homebaked sweet breads and freshly brewed coffee or a selection of teas, is served out on one

of the shady, flower-bedecked brick terraces in summer. In wintertime, breakfast is offered by a blazing fire in the living room/reception area. At the rear of the house a green lawn with trees, flowers and lawn chairs slopes down to the harbor. The Clarkes have their own sandy beach, with dinghies and Sunfish for guests' use. In addition, their 38-foot boat *Irene*—an authentic 1917 Friendship sloop—is moored in view of the house and is available for charter by the day or overnight. John Clarke, a licensed U.S. Coast Guard captain, skippers the *Irene* and will take you on cruises among the many coves and small harbors around Martha's Vineyard and the Elizabeth Islands, on evening harbor sunset sails, overnight to Cuttyhunk, or on longer charters to Nantucket.

The Lothrop Merry House is within easy walking distance of Vineyard Haven's restaurants and shops. It's a grand place to visit in summer, but the Clarkes feel that autumn is the best season of all. The water is still warm enough for swimming; boating, biking, tennis and golf are excellent, and on chilly evenings the house's fireplaces will warm you. Even wintertime is pleasant on the Vineyard: the weather is usually milder than on the mainland, several good restaurants remain open, and the beaches are blissfully deserted, ideal for brisk walks or jogging. *The Lothrop Merry House, Owen Park, P.O. Box 1939, Vineyard Haven, MA 02568; (617) 693-1646. (Just off Main Street or a short distance along the beach from the ferry dock.) Rates are expensive, lower off season. Visa and MasterCard are accepted. Children are welcome; extra cots and cribs are available. No pets, please. Open year-round.*

The Captain Dexter House. Beyer and Lara Parker are your cordial hosts at the Captain Dexter House in Vineyard Haven. The three-story Victorian home, built in 1843 by sea captain Rodolphus Dexter, has served as a bed-and-breakfast inn for almost half a century. The Parkers,

The Captain Dexter House

who purchased the dignified old house in 1983, have completely restored and refurbished it in the style of the early 1800s. There are nine rooms for guests (three on the ground floor) including eight doubles and one suite; three of the doubles are also suitable for an added rollaway bed. All of the rooms have private baths. Each of the guest chambers is distinctively decorated with family furnishings and eighteenth- and nineteenth-century antiques, including handmade quilts and several four-poster canopy beds. Some of the rooms have fireplaces and harbor views; all provide an atmosphere of warmth and comfort. The cheery living room/library with a large fireplace is a pleasant spot for reading or meeting other guests. Breakfast, served each morning in the elegant dining room, offers freshly squeezed orange juice, a variety of homebaked goods such as banana, cranberry or strawberry bread or blueberry muffins, homemade preserves, coffee and herbal or regular teas. The house is conveniently located in the center of Vineyard Haven, one and a half blocks from the ferry and within easy walking distance of many excellent restaurants.

The Captain Dexter House, 100 Main St., P.O. Box 2457, Vineyard Haven, MA 02568; (617) 693-6564. Rates are expensive, lower off season. Visa and MasterCard are accepted. Children over 11 are welcome; no pets, please. Open year-round.

Haven House. The Haven, owned by Karl and Lynn Buder, is a pleasantly secluded guest house just beyond Vineyard Haven village.

A classic "craftsman bungalow," the house was built in 1918 by a Chicago grain merchant named J. Herbert Ware as a wedding present for his son. The elder Ware owned a splendid oceanfront estate across the street, and the smaller, newer structure became known in the family as the "little house." In later years the "little house" served as a home for the elderly, and then a summer guest house. The Buders purchased the property in 1981 and began a painstaking restoration which included adding private baths and complete redecoration. They now offer ten double bedrooms for guests, all with private baths. Some of the baths still feature the original turn-of-the-century fixtures and clawfoot tubs. The individually—and romantically—decorated guest rooms are predominantly Victorian and Colonial, with many antiques including four-poster beds and three matched Eastlake and carved Renaissance suites. Two of the rooms have decks, and one offers a

private porch and entrance. There are a Victorian reading parlor, with a fireplace, and a TV den for relaxing. A full breakfast is served in the formal Victorian dining room. The menu includes almond French toast, quiche Lorraine, spinach-sausage-cheese pie, buttermilk pancakes and bacon, and croissant-ham and cheese omelet sandwiches. Your hosts, who know the island well, will be pleased to suggest restaurants, good shopping choices and interesting excursions either within walking distance or via bike or car. An added amenity: for guests who wish to enjoy the beaches after check-out time, the Buders have a spare bath available for use before departure.

Haven Guest House, 278 Main St., P.O. Box 1022, Vineyard Haven, MA 02568; (617) 693-3333. (One mile from ferry dock.) Rates are expensive, lower Oct. 17–May 13. Visa, MasterCard and American Express are accepted. Children over 12 are welcome; no pets, please. Open year-round.

The Captain R. Flanders House. Over in Chilmark, in the southwestern portion of Martha's Vineyard, visitors to the island will find a most delightful guest house. This region of the Vineyard, called "up-island" by the inhabitants, has managed to retain its rural serenity, far away from the crowds and summertime bustle of the larger down-island towns. And the Captain R. Flanders House offers an ideal haven for anyone searching for a quiet, relaxed island holiday. The restored farmhouse is situated on sixty acres of rolling hills and pastureland, overlooking Bliss Pond. Built by whaling captain Richard Flanders in 1754, the house is part of an original island homestead. Architecturally, it is a large Cape that has grown throughout the years. Recently returned to the Flanders family (Elizabeth Flanders is your hostess), the historic old place is being restored.

Wide pine floors, spacious rooms, many windows and a collection of fine antiques and country primitives create a warm and welcoming atmosphere. Among other notable features are a set of handpainted bird windows imported more than seventy years ago from the Orient, and pine pieces dating from 1760 to 1800. There are six rooms for guests, including two singles and four doubles. Two have private baths; the others share two baths. Four of the rooms are on the ground floor. Several of the guest chambers have fireplaces, and all offer a view of the pond or garden. A large living room, with a fireplace, also overlooks the pond and contains a stereo and games (backgammon, chess and Scrabble) for guests to enjoy. Breakfast, served on the sun porch, consists of fresh fruit, cereal, home baked muffins and breads, locally made jams and honey, and coffee, tea or hot chocolate.

Outdoors, guests are welcome to roam the fields, relax and enjoy the air or play lawn games such as volleyball, badminton and croquet. There are outdoor grills for guests' use, too, and a refrigerator is available for storing food. An old windmill on the property is intriguing to see; its inner works were brought by ship from Holland in the early 1900s. And there are the duck houses. A previous owner had replicas of his Edgartown homes constructed for his ducks; placed along the edges of the pond they create an optical illusion when viewed from the house of vast mansions beside a lake! Just across the road a conservation preserve offers running trails and nature walks.

Menemsha, a small, exceedingly picturesque fishing village with interesting shops and several fine seafood restaurants, is minutes away. The town of Chilmark offers square dancing, chamber concerts, and a restaurant serving Haitian-French cuisine. Beach passes provided by your hostess entitle guests to the use of private surfside beaches a mile away, and the spectacular cliffs at Gay Head are an easy drive.

The Captain R. Flanders House, North Road, Box 252, Chilmark, MA 02535; (617) 645-3123. Rates are expensive, lower off season. Visa and MasterCard are accepted. Children and pets are welcome. Open April–October.

Nantucket Town

Fair Gardens. Claire Murray has an especially deep love for Nantucket; she chose the island as the ideal place to open her English-style bed-and-breakfast establishment. Built in the early 1800s, Fair Gardens was previously owned by an elderly clockmaker and antique restorer. Claire, who is herself an artist and craftsperson, spent a year restoring the house, making sure the antique flavor was kept intact. Among its many delights are six working fireplaces; a parlor stove keeps the kitchen toasty warm on chilly days. A porch and charming brick terrace out back are wonderfully relaxing places to sit, and the classic Shakespearean Herb Garden adds to guests' pleasure. On rainy days, books and games are available indoors in the parlor/breakfast room, where a continental breakfast with homebaked muffins or breads is served each morning. Freshly made scones are a specialty of the house, and afternoon tea is also offered.

There are ten spacious guest rooms, furnished with antiques including several canopy beds. Claire's handmade quilts grace most of the beds, and some have European-style down comforters with duvet covers. All of the rooms have private baths; five guest bedrooms are on the ground floor.

For those readers interested in Colonial crafts, Claire Murray offers a variety of workshops at Fair Gardens in the spring and fall, including

classes in quilting, stenciling, needle art, rug making and herbs. She will be delighted to provide details on dates and other pertinent information. Her own work—including quilts, soft sculpture, silk-screened items and potpourri—is on display (and for sale) in the Studio Gallery, a charming small cottage on the premises.

Fair Gardens, 27 Fair St., Nantucket, MA 02554; (617) 228-4258. Rates are expensive. Visa and MasterCard are accepted. Children are welcome on a limited basis; no pets, please. Open May–October.

Corner House. This handsome old whaling captain's home in Nantucket's Historic District is owned by Sandy Knox-Johnston and her British husband, John. They have, as Sandy puts it, "brought their 1790 house very gently into the twentieth century." The several-stage restoration, while keeping and enhancing original details such as the wide-board pine floors, paneling and fireplaces, has added three rooms under the eaves and a wealth of pleasant amenities.

There are nine individually decorated guest bedrooms, one of which is on the ground floor. All of the rooms have private baths and all are furnished with English and American antiques including several canopy beds, designer linens, down comforters for cool nights, plenty of pillows and large, thick towels. Guests are encouraged to enjoy the entire house, including a sitting room with a fireplace, and a porch and patio for warm-weather relaxation. The screened-in porch, which overlooks the garden, is particularly inviting with its antique wicker furniture and hanging baskets of flowers. Books, magazines, games and puzzles are available for guests' enjoyment.

A hearty continental breakfast, featuring homemade muffins, coffee cakes and breads, a choice of fruit juices, and coffee, English tea or cocoa is served each morning on the sideboard of the sitting room, or in your room if you wish. Afternoon tea, with delicious fruit bread and biscuits, is also provided. Excellent restaurants and fine shops are within easy walking distance from Corner House.

Corner House, 49 Centre St., Nantucket, MA 02554; (617) 228-1530. (Across from the Old North Church.) Rates are expensive, lower off season except for Christmas week. Visa and MasterCard are accepted. Children over 8 are welcome; no pets, please. Open generally from Easter to New Year's; at other times please call and ask.

The Carriage House. Once this attractive bed-and-breakfast establishment really was a carriage house, built in 1865 as part of a whaling captain's estate. The newly refurbished Victorian structure, just a block off cobblestoned Main Street on a quiet "country lane," is owned by Bill and Jeanne McHugh. They have seven beautifully appointed guest rooms, all with private baths. One of the rooms is on the ground floor. A large, recently redecorated Common Room and a game room with cable TV and books are comfortable places for reading and relaxing. A continental breakfast with homebaked muffins, juice and coffee, tea or milk is offered, served outdoors on the patio in warm weather.

The Carriage House, 4 Ray's Court, Nantucket, MA 02554; (617) 228-0326. Rates are expensive. Children over 5 are welcome; no pets, please. Open year-round.

Phillips House. A typical Nantucket whaler's home, the late eighteenth-century Phillips House is centrally located in the town's historic district. Abounding with antiques and fireplaces, Phillips House boasts a wonderful old kitchen which your cordial hostess, Mary Phillips, will be delighted to show you. She has five comfortable bedrooms for guests, including one with a private bath. Each morning a continental breakfast of homemade muffins and coffee is served.

Phillips House, 54 Fair St., Nantucket, MA 02554; (617) 228-9217. Rates are moderate, lower off season. Children are welcome; no pets, please. Open year-round.

The Four Chimneys. This gracious old mansion is situated on historic Orange Street, where no fewer than 126 sea captains built their homes. Capt. Frederick Gardner constructed Four Chimneys, the largest house on the island, in 1835. Present-day owner Betty Gaeta has ten double bedrooms for guests, all with private baths. One of the rooms is on the first floor. All of the accommodations are furnished with period pieces; six original "Master Rooms" have been authentically restored and decorated with antiques, four-poster or canopy beds, Oriental rugs and handmade quilts. Each of these handsomely appointed rooms has a fireplace; several offer harbor views, and one has its own porch. For relaxing there is an elegant double drawing room with twin fireplaces, comfortable chairs and antique Chinese rugs and porcelain. The room also offers TV, a game table and a piano for guests' enjoyment. Outdoors are lovely grounds and a secluded garden, and porches on three levels of the house provide grand views of the harbor. A continental breakfast is offered daily, served in your room, in the drawing room, or on the first-floor porch with its collection of antique white wicker. Crackers and cheese, glasses and ice are provided each afternoon at five, and there is an extensive selection of island restaurant menus on hand to help you make a choice for dinner.

The Four Chimneys, 38 Orange St., Nantucket, MA 02554; (617) 228-1912. Rates are expensive. Visa, MasterCard and American Express are accepted. No children or pets, please. Open April–November.

Connecticut

In 1614, six years before the Pilgrims landed in Massachusetts, a Dutch navigator named Adriaen Block sailed along the Connecticut coast and discovered the Connecticut River. The Indians called the river *Quonecktacut*; some say the word means "long river of the pines" and others interpret it as "long tidal river." Whichever, it certainly is long. The Connecticut starts in northern New Hampshire, forms the boundary between New Hampshire and Vermont, runs down through the center of Massachusetts and then angles across the state of Connecticut, emptying into Long Island Sound at Saybrook.

Eventually the river's name was applied to the region now known as Connecticut. Colonists from Massachusetts arrived there in 1634, establishing settlements during the next few years in Wethersfield, Saybrook, Windsor, Hartford and New Haven. The settlers were not well received by the local Indians. The Pequots resented the takeover of their land and, in 1637, killed several of the newcomers. In revenge, the colonists struck back and killed some 700 Indians, almost wiping out the tribe.

In 1638, Connecticut's settlers drafted a constitution, believed to be the first ever written by a self-governing people. The British governor-general of the New England colonies, Sir Edmund Andros, tried to end Connecticut's self-rule in 1687. Andros demanded that the colony's charter be surrendered and went to Hartford in person to get it. The wily colonists meekly entered the council chamber and proceeded to debate the matter. Suddenly the lights were blown out and a wild melee resulted, during which the charter was said to have been whisked to a hiding place in a great oak tree. Andros was deposed shortly after that and sent back to England. The famous "Charter Oak," said to be 1000 years old, fell in a storm in 1856.

Despite its proximity to New York City, Connecticut is still very much a New England state—historic and very scenic, with many picturesque, small Colonial towns. Hartford, the capital, is a bustling insurance center; insurance and industry are the state's major sources of income. There are, however, many farms even today, and tobacco fields stretch for miles along the banks of the Connecticut River. The land is seventy percent wooded; the landscape ranges from gentle highlands in the west to sandy beaches and fine harbors along the Atlantic. Stone walls ramble through fields and alongside roads, and each spring the state's flower, mountain laurel, blooms in delicate

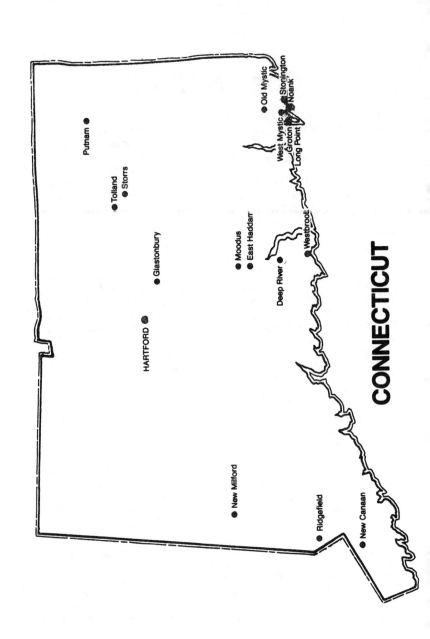

CONNECTICUT

profusion. In autumn, Connecticut presents a typically brilliant New England display of foliage.

Northeastern Connecticut

The Putnam Area

Putnam is way up in the northeastern corner of Connecticut, not far from the borders of Massachusetts and Rhode Island. This rural region of the state, as yet undiscovered by most travelers, offers a number of interesting and unusual attractions. Putnam itself, named for Revolutionary War hero Gen. Israel Putnam of Bunker Hill fame, is situated on the falls of the Quinebaug River; the town spreads over four hills. One of the country's earliest textile mills was established here in 1806; in the mid-1800s, after the advent of the railroad, the town became for a time a busy industrial center.

One of Connecticut's most intriguing historic houses is in Woodstock, about five miles away. Roseland Cottage, a sprawling Gothic Revival structure, was built in 1846 by Henry Bowen, a wealthy publisher and silk importer. The "cottage," adorned with ornate gingerbread detailing, is painted salmon pink with magenta trim. Formal gardens, spectacular in summer, form patterns on the grounds; inside, visitors will find a fascinating clutter of typical nineteenth-century furnishings, and the color pink. Pink is everywhere, incorporated into the carpets, walls, and even the stained-glass windows!

In Pomfret, a few miles southwest of Putnam, the Hamlet Hill Vineyards offers tours and free wine tasting. And in Brooklyn to the south the New England Center of Contemporary Art presents different gallery displays each month—paintings, sculpture and art glass—in a lovely rural setting. Resident artists are on hand for conversation and illumination.

The Felshaw Tavern. Back during the turbulent days of the American Revolution this historic old tavern, which sits beyond an ancient stone wall, was a popular gathering place for the local militia. The village green on which the men trained is about one and a half miles away. A typical New England Colonial with center chimney and five fireplaces, the Felshaw Tavern was built in 1742. Expertly restored by present-day owners Herbert and Terry Kinsman, the venerable structure now appears much as it did in the eighteenth century, with all of that era's warmth and charm. Your hosts have furnished the house throughout with antiques and superb reproductions, many of the latter made by Herb himself.

Three comfortable bedrooms on the second floor, all doubles, are available for guests. The two most often used are exceptionally large, seventeen by twenty feet; each has a working fireplace and a sitting area, and features a four-poster bed. All of the guest chambers have private baths. For the exclusive use of guests (though you are encouraged to explore the whole house) there is a cozy, oak-paneled sitting room on the second floor adjacent to the guest quarters. The Kinsmans keep the room well supplied with books, magazines, sherry and port, and there is a TV. A hearty English-style breakfast is served in the formal dining room, with a working fireplace. The meal consists of fruit juice, scrambled eggs with beef sausage or perhaps ground round, homemade muffins and marmalade, and coffee or tea. Terry, by the way, says that she and Herb very much enjoy socializing with their guests but if you prefer to be alone at breakfast you have that option! Your hosts will also serve dinner, by pre-arrangement and at extra cost.

There are several excellent restaurants in the area, just a short drive away, and the Kinsmans will be happy to offer suggestions. Things to do in this region of rolling hills and rural countryside include roaming the grounds, on which stands a classic red barn built in 1710, and following the scenic back roads. Other enjoyable pursuits might be horseback riding, or swimming and boating at nearby lakes. And if you would like to make Felshaw Tavern a base from which to explore farther afield, Mystic Seaport is an hour's drive and Old Sturbridge Village in Massachusetts is only about twenty-five miles away.

The Felshaw Tavern, Five Mile River Road, Putnam, CT 06260; (203) 928-3467. (From Exit 96 on I-395, turn east—left if coming south on 395, right if coming north—and go 1½ miles to blinking traffic light at Rte. 21. The house is the first on the left across Rte. 21. From Rte. 44, turn south onto Rte. 21 and go 2 miles to blinking traffic light; turn left and the house is the first on the left.) Rates are expensive; special rates are available for a week's stay. Well-behaved children and small, well-trained pets are welcome. Open year-round.

Central Connecticut

Storrs/Tolland
and the Hartford Area/Glastonbury

Storrs, about halfway between Putnam and Hartford, is the home of the University of Connecticut. In nearby Gurleyville, travelers can visit the state's only remaining stone grist mill. Built circa 1830 on an early eighteenth-century mill site, the mill is open to the public as a museum. Coventry, just south of Storrs, has the Nathan Hale Homestead, built in 1776, and Caprilands Herb Farm. The fifty-acre farm with thirty-two herb gardens surrounding a rustic eighteenth-century farmhouse offers gardens tours, usually led by Caprilands owner and master herbalist, Adelma Grenier Simmons, and 360 varieties of herbs for sale. Luncheon is served Monday through Saturday, and on Sundays, afternoon tea. Tolland, a few miles northwest of Storrs, offers several historic houses and an old jail, now a museum.

In Hartford, Connecticut's capital, history buffs will find a number of interesting museums and storied old houses. The Butler-McCook Homestead, built in 1782, contains some excellent collections of eighteenth-century furnishings, Chinese bronzes and Egyptian statuettes, antique dolls and toys. Nook Farm offers both the 1874 Mark Twain house (where he wrote several of his books, including *Tom Sawyer* and *Huck Finn*) and the 1871 Harriett Beecher Stowe House. The Wadsworth Atheneum, a nationally renowned art museum, has galleries covering every major period.

In Hartford's Bushnell Park, children and grown-ups alike will enjoy the Carousel, a 1914 merry-go-round with forty-eight ornately carved wooden horses. And the Elizabeth Park Rose Gardens, at their peak in June, bloom with 450 varieties of roses. Glastonbury, a few miles southeast of Hartford, has a number of beautiful old historic homes. The area also offers travelers a chance to experience an entertaining ferry ride, crossing the Connecticut River to Rocky Hill. The ferry, which began operating in 1655, is the country's oldest still in continuous use.

Farmhouse On the Hill Above Gurleyville. William and Elaine Kollet are your friendly hosts at this pleasant bed-and-breakfast establishment just outside of Storrs. Mrs. Kollet's father built tobacco barns in the Connecticut River Valley, so she is quite knowledgeable about the construction business; she designed the traditional New England farmhouse herself. A white center-chimney Cape with connecting breezeway and garage, the house was built in 1979 but appears to have been standing here for at least a century. Farm buildings and pastures lie to the rear. The Kollets have three comfortable rooms for guests, and a rollaway bed is available for an extra person in the room. Two of the rooms have private baths; one of the guest bedrooms is on the ground floor and shares a bath. There are some family

antiques, and the blankets are woven from wool obtained from your hosts' own Columbia purebred sheep.

Breakfast includes freshly made muffins and eggs from the farm. Dinner is also offered, by reservation only, and bag lunches will be provided on request. The Kollets encourage their guests to feel at home in their house and on the farm. Cross-country skiing is excellent right on the property, and there are good walking trails nearby. Gurleyville village, a five-minute walk from the house, offers a historic grist mill to explore and an antique shop; trout fishing is great in the Fenton River behind the mill. The University of Connecticut is only 1.9 miles from the house.

Farmhouse On the Hill Above Gurleyville, 418 Gurleyville Rd., Storrs, CT 06268; (203) 429-1400. (From Rte. 84 take Exit 99, Rte. 195, to University of Connecticut campus. Take left at Congregational Church and go 1.9 miles on Gurleyville Road to house.) Rates are moderate, lower for longer stays. Children are welcome; no pets, please. Open year-round.

Old Babcock Tavern. Travelers searching for the essence of eighteenth-century New England will find it at the charming Old Babcock Tavern in Tolland. Hosts Barbara and Stuart Danforth, "Barb and Stu" as they prefer to be called, purchased the handsome building with its typical center chimney and four fireplaces in 1967. Then known as the Sgt. John Cady House, built in 1720, the historic structure was in sad disrepair. The Danforths, with the help of their two children, worked for seventeen years to authentically restore the house to its original elegance. They were rewarded when their home became one of two buildings in Tolland to be listed on the National Register of Historic Places.

In 1984, the Danforths opened the house to the public as a bed-and-breakfast country inn. There are four attractive upstairs rooms for guests, three doubles and one single, sharing two baths. All of the tastefully decorated rooms, with glowing wide-board floors, are appointed with Early American antiques. One of the guest bedrooms, originally the ballroom, features a fireplace and a canopy bed. For relaxing, reading or conversation there are the tap room with polished paneled walls and reconstructed early bar, the keeping room and the parlor. Each contains a large stone working fireplace and fine antiques. Many of the latter may be for sale; just ask.

A hearty old-fashioned country breakfast is served each morning, with juice (or fruit cup in summertime), scrambled eggs or omelets, sausage or bacon and homefried potatoes seasoned with herbs. Homemade muffins and all the coffee or tea you can drink accompanies the meal and then—your hosts bring out hot apple pie or some other homemade dessert! In addition to all this pampering, the Danforths offer arriving guests a welcoming snack of tea and crackers, or possibly some wine. Ice and glasses are provided for evening drinks in the tap room; guests bring their own liquid refreshment.

Occasionally, in emergencies or in bad weather, dinner is also available.

For visitors intrigued by the house's restoration story, a "Before and After" slide presentation is offered in the evenings. Activities in the area are many, including exploring the scenic countryside with its stone walls, woods and streams. According to Barb Danforth, there is a beaver in nearby Cedar Swamp. Bicycling, swimming, fishing and boating are all available nearby as are golfing and country auctions. In winter there are ski touring and ice skating, weather permitting. Restaurants and shops are a five-minute drive, Caprilands Herb Farm is three miles away, and the University of Connecticut is ten miles away. Farther afield but within an easy drive are Old Sturbridge Village in Massachusetts and Mystic Seaport.

Old Babcock Tavern, 484 Mile Hill Rd. (Rte. 31), Tolland, CT 06084; (203) 875-1239. (From I-84 between Hartford, Conn., and Sturbridge, Ma., take Exit 98 and follow Rte. 31 south 2 miles to first stop sign; the tavern is on the right at the corner of Cedar Swamp Road.) Rates are moderately expensive, lower for longer stays. No children or pets, please. Open year-round.

Butternut Farm. Glastonbury, a small town not far from Hartford, traces its ancestry to the 1600s. An eminent early landowner, Samuel Hale, gave a large tract of land to his son Jonathan when the young man married in 1717 at age 21. Three years later Jonathan Hale built a house on the land, and the property remained in the Hale family for more than a century. In 1840, however, a Hale descendant purchased the *Alert*, a whaling vessel made famous by Melville's *Moby Dick*. A mutiny aboard ship, combined with an unsuccessful whaling voyage, lost both ship and the house to creditors.

Today, historic Butternut Farm is one of Connecticut's most interesting bed-and-breakfast guest houses. Owner Donald B. Reid has authentically restored the early eighteenth-century home to its original Colonial ambiance and charm. For guests there are four comfortable upstairs rooms, one with twin beds and three with four-poster double beds. Two of the rooms share two baths and two (actually small apartments) have their own baths. All are beautifully appointed with period furnishings, including handwoven bedspreads and other items from your host's extensive collection of antiques.

The house offers a wealth of intriguing architectural details, too, such as the large summer beams in the first- and second-story front rooms, and wide floorboards, handsome original paneling and sheathing throughout. An oversize fireplace with rear bake oven is particularly noteworthy, and an eighteenth-century portrait of Jonathan Hale looks down upon a gateleg table surrounded by bannister-back chairs and period accessories. A continental breakfast is served to guests each morning either in the breakfast room or in the dining room.

Butternut Farm's grounds are just as appealing as the house, and guests are encouraged to explore. Don Reid, an herb grower and designer of herb gardens, maintains his own large herb garden on the property. Another garden near the barn produces flowers and vegetables. And your host's flock of fancy chickens and pigeons will most likely be observed wandering in the barnyard near his herd of dairy goats!

Butternut Farm, 1654 Main St., Glastonbury, CT 06033; (203) 633-7197. Rates are moderately expensive. Children are welcome; pets are not generally accepted and smoking is discouraged. Open year-round.

Southeastern Connecticut

The Mystic Area: Old Mystic/West Mystic/ Noank/Groton Long Point/Stonington

Mystic is a nice town all by itself, but Mystic Seaport is fabulous. A superb maritime museum, the seaport is located on the site of a bustling nineteenth-century shipyard along the banks of the Mystic River. The complex comprises three sections: the shipyard, the restored village and waterfront, and various exhibit buildings. Visitors can roam through a ship chandler's establishment, a sail loft, a hoop shop, a tavern, a newspaper office, a drug store and many other structures typical of a busy seaport community of the 1800s. One of my favorite exhibits is the collection of old carved ships' figureheads, which includes a number of weather-beaten yet strikingly beautiful ladies of the sea.

More than 200 boats are on view including the last of the wooden sailing vessels, the *Charles W. Morgan*, built in 1841. The *L.A. Dunton*, a Gloucester fishing schooner that was once part of the sailing fleet that fished on the Great Banks, and the square rigger *Joseph Conrad*, may also be explored from stem to stern. Guides called "interpreters" are on hand to explain what is going on throughout the seaport. And plenty is—there's a long list of daily events ranging from sail setting and furling, whaleboat demonstrations and steamboat cruises to chantey singing. Plan to spend half a day at least, more if possible. If by some chance you arrive in late afternoon, your ticket will be validated to include the next day as well, for a small additional fee.

At Christmastime Mystic Seaport celebrates with colorful Lantern Light Tours; a guide carrying a lantern leads visitors through a number of houses, shops, ships and exhibits. The interpreters demonstrate old Christmas customs, including cooking foods on an open hearth. And the entire seaport is bedecked with Christmas greenery and old-time decorations.

Submarine fanciers can stop in nearby Groton and walk through a World War II sub, the U.S.S. *Croaker*. Bus tours will take you through the U.S. Naval Submarine Base, and a boat tour cruises in summer down the Thames (pronounced Thames, not "temmes") River past the submarines and other points of interest such as the U.S. Coast Guard Academy in New London. Visitors may also wander about the academy's campus on foot. New London, by the way, has an old cemetery dating to 1653 with the enchanting name of "Ye Ancientest Burial Ground." Ferries to Block Island leave from New London, as well as from Rhode Island ports.

The town of Old Mystic is just north of Mystic; West Mystic, Noank and Groton Long Point are just to the south via Route 215 along the ocean. Stonington, a few miles east of Mystic on Route 1A off Route 1, is one of Connecticut's most appealing seventeenth-century towns. Settled in 1649, Stonington was a thriving shipbuilding village in the old days and still has an active fishing fleet today. The Stonington Historical Society is housed in Whitehall, a beautifully restored country mansion. The Old Lighthouse Museum offers an excellent display of whaling gear and ship models, and the town's streets are lined with charming old houses. One of the nicest aspects of Stonington is its serene, untouched air. Its homes are very much lived in, not part of a museum collection, and the "touristy" atmosphere of so many historic villages is happily missing.

Red Brook Inn. In Old Mystic, two miles from the seacoast, travelers will find the delightful Red Brook Inn, set among seven and a half acres of woods and old stone walls. Owned by Ruth Keyes and Verne Sasek, the inn is actually two historic Colonial structures, faithfully restored, and standing side by side. The Haley Tavern, an early Connecticut stagecoach inn, was built in 1761 and recently moved to the Old Mystic site. Notable for its museum-quality paneled rooms and original early eighteenth-century tap room, the building contains six bedrooms for guests. The charming Crary House, circa 1770, stands on its original site; the center-chimney Colonial offers three guest bedrooms.

All of the guest quarters are doubles, located on the upper level.

Each is furnished with Early American antiques, and has a fireplace and a private bath. Firewood is provided for chilly nights. Parlors with cable TV, a library and a sitting room are comfortable places for quiet reading or conversation by the hearth. Your hosts' personal collections of early lighting devices, pewter and ivory may be seen throughout the inn, and old wide-board floors and the original hardware enhance the authentic Colonial atmosphere.

Breakfast at the Red Brook Inn is ample and delicious. Served family style, the meal includes juice, fresh fruit and coffee or tea. Depending on the cook's preference, there will also be walnut waffles, quiche or perhaps blueberry pancakes, corn bread, zucchini-pineapple cake, banana bread or another of the inn's specialties. Tea and coffee are always available, and in summer your hosts offer lemonade or iced tea as an afternoon or evening cooler. On weekends from December 1 to April 1, guests are treated to Colonial dinners, cooked in an open hearth fireplace and the original bake oven!

All of the area's attractions including Mystic Seaport, the Mystic Marinelife Aquarium, ocean beaches, the New London Submarine Base and Nautilus Submarine Museum and the Coast Guard Academy are easily accessible.

Red Brook Inn, P.O. Box 237, Old Mystic, CT 06372; (203) 572-0349. (From I-95 take Exit 89, Allyn Street, and go north 1.5 miles to Gold Star Highway, Rte. 184. Then head east .2 mile to Welles Road; the inn is on the northwest corner of the intersection.) Rates are expensive. Visa, MasterCard and American Express are accepted. No children or pets, please, and no smoking. Open year-round.

Leventhal Bed & Breakfast. A local boat builder, George Owen Lamb, constructed this Victorian-style house in West Mystic in 1872. Some of the half hulls made by the original owner are today owned by the house's present occupants, Bob and Natalie Leventhal. Bob enjoys building ship models, many of which are on display, along with models of airplanes, trains and trolleys. Three upstairs rooms are available for guests, including one single, one double and one triple, sharing a bath. For relaxing, there are a living room with TV and a porch overlooking the Mystic River. Throughout the house guests will note the Leventhals' daughters' craft work of quilting and basketry, and memorabilia from Bob and Natalie's extensive travels. A continental breakfast is served daily, consisting of juice, rolls, bagels or English muffins, cereal for children, and coffee, tea or milk. Your hosts also offer iced tea on warm summer afternoons. Restaurants and shops are within walking distance, and Mystic's multitude of attractions are easily accessible.

Leventhal Bed & Breakfast, 40 W. Mystic Ave. (mailing address: Box 105), West Mystic, CT 06388; (203) 536-1341. (Exit 89 off I-95, head south onto Allyn Street which becomes W. Mystic Avenue. The house is 1.8 miles from the highway.) Rates are moderate; a small extra fee is charged for a child sleeping on a cot. Well-behaved children are welcome; no pets, please. Open year-round.

The Palmer Inn. The columned Palmer Inn, surrounded by tall hedges, is in Noank, a short drive southwest of Mystic. The elegant Southern-style structure, unusual in New England, was built in 1907 for Robert Palmer, Jr. Palmer, the story goes, wanted his home to resemble a plantation manor he had seen while traveling in the South, and he hired a Knoxville, Tennessee, architect to design it. Robert Palmer and his father operated one of the larger wooden shipbuilding firms on the East Coast, and skilled craftsmen from the shipyard constructed the house. Present-day owners Patricia and Donald Cornish, who with the help of local artisans painstakingly restored the mansion to its turn-of-the-century ambiance, have a copy of the original blueprint.

Guests enter the inn through the magnificent main hall. Carved mahogany woodwork, the original brass fixtures, thirteen-foot ceilings and stained-glass windows are only some of the striking architectural details to be seen throughout the house. A curving staircase leads to the six guest bedrooms, attractively furnished with antiques and family heirlooms. Four of the spacious, individually decorated rooms have private baths. The accommodations include the Master Bedroom with its own fireplace, the Oak Suite with a private sitting room, and the Wicker Room with a cozy sitting area. The Brass Room was originally the servant's chamber, the Mahogany Room features a pineapple four-poster bed, and the Cherry Room offers a private balcony with a spectacular view of the water.

For relaxing, there are the Grand Salon, a Victorian parlor with a working fireplace for chilly nights, and the library/sitting room where board games and reading areas offer quiet entertainment. There's also a broad veranda for warm-weather enjoyment. A continental breakfast is served each morning, with homemade muffins and breads, your hosts' own jams and jellies, and coffee or herb teas. Afternoon refreshments of hot or iced tea or mulled cider, depending on the season, are also offered.

The Palmer Inn is within walking distance of Fisher's Island Sound, an open-air lobster house, and tennis courts. Mystic, with shops, restaurants and Mystic Seaport and Marinelife Aquarium, is two miles away, and all manner of year-round sports activities are easily accessible.

The Palmer Inn, 25 Church St., Noank, CT 06340; (203) 572-9000. (From Mystic take Rte. 215 southwest to Noank, and turn onto Main Street; Church Street is off Main.) Rates are expensive. Visa and MasterCard are accepted. Children 16 or older are welcome; no pets, please. Smoking is permitted only in the parlor. Parking is available behind the inn, reached from Cedar Lane. Open year-round.

Shore Inne. Out on Groton Long Point, a peninsula extending into Fisher's Island Sound just southwest of Mystic, the Shore Inne has been welcoming guests since the turn of the century. The attractive old Colonial house, directly overlooking the water, is in a quiet residential area. Owner Helen Ellison, who renovated and improved the house, has seven comfortable upstairs rooms for guests. All are pleasantly furnished and brightened with handmade patchwork coverlets. Three of the bedrooms have private baths; the other four share two baths.

Guests may relax in the pleasant living room with white wicker furniture and a fireplace, or in the combined TV/library/sun room, both with spectacular ocean views. Outdoors, a handsome copper beech provides shade for summertime visitors. A homecooked continental breakfast, perhaps with Shore Inne Buttermilk Bran Muffins, is served each morning in the dining room overlooking the water. Your friendly hostess will gladly suggest some good restaurants in the area for other meals.

Mystic Seaport, the Mystic Marinelife Aquarium, Fort Griswold and the Coast Guard Academy and U.S. Submarine Base are just a few miles away. Excellent private beaches are only a short walk from the

inn's front door; a fishing dock, biking and tennis are also easily accessible. Boats may be anchored immediately offshore, and day cruises are available.

Shore Inne, 54 E. Shore Ave., Groton Long Point, CT 06340; (203) 536-1180. (From Rte. 1, take Rte. 215, then first left after Yankee Fisherman Restaurant onto E. Shore Ave. Park in rear off Middlefield Street.) Rates are moderate. Visa and MasterCard are accepted. Children are welcome; no pets, please. Open April 1–Nov. 1.

Farnan House. Farnan House, on a quiet, dead-end street in historic Stonington, is a family homestead built in 1906. The present-day Farnans have restored their antique-filled old home, maintaining its original New England flavor and charm. Your hostess, Ann Farnan, says that her guests particularly like the house's homey atmosphere. Outdoors, massive maple trees give the grounds a parklike beauty.

There are four upstairs rooms for guests, all doubles. Three rooms share a bath; the fourth has a private half bath. A sitting room and large open outdoor deck are pleasant places for sitting and chatting. Breakfast, of orange juice, sweet rolls and muffins and coffee or tea is served daily. Stonington Village is a short walk from the house, and Mystic Seaport and the Mystic Marinelife Aquarium are four miles away.

Farnan House, 10 McGrath Court, Stonington, CT 06378; (203) 535-0634. (From Rte. 1 heading towards Westerly, RI, take Rte. 1A, go past Don's Dock and turn right on McGrath Court.) Rates are moderate, lower from November to April. Children are welcome; no pets, please. Open year-round.

Westbrook/Deep River/East Haddam/Moodus

Westbrook lies down the coast from Mystic, a few miles past the mouth of the Connecticut River and the attractive towns of Old Lyme and Old Saybrook. A scenic drive inland up along the Connecticut River will bring you to the historic village of Essex, founded in 1645, and the small communities of Deep River and East Haddam. Just beyond Deep River, on the other side of the Connecticut in Hadlyme, is the 190-acre Gillette Castle State Park.

William Gillette was one of America's greatest actors, famed for his portrayal of Sherlock Holmes. A native of Connecticut, Gillette decided to build a home there in 1913 . . . a dream house, as it were. The site, atop lofty ridges of rock amid wooded hills, has a sweeping view of the river and surrounding countryside. The Castle—resembling a medieval fortress—took five years and more than a million dollars to build. Some of the furniture was built in; other pieces slid on metal tracks. There are twenty-four rooms in all, a rather haphazard sprawl notable for the actor's attention to the smallest detail and offering evidence of a somewhat whimsical mind. Or possibly, a monumental ego. But Gillette didn't stop there. He constructed his own man-sized railroad outdoors, with a depot near the front entrance and a three-mile stretch of track winding its way through forests and glens. Unfortunately, the railroad has long since been dismantled. The Castle and its beautiful grounds are open daily from May 21 to Columbus Day, weekends only from mid-October to mid-December.

In East Haddam, a visit to the famed Goodspeed Opera House is a must. Critically acclaimed musical productions are presented in the splendid Victorian-style structure from April through November. The town also offers handsome old homes, a fine selection of antique, craft and gift shops, the Historical Society Museum and several good restaurants. In Moodus, a few miles north, there is an unusual crafts center called Down On the Farm; the artisans' studios are in renovated chicken coops on an old poultry farm.

The Captain Stannard House. Capt. Elbert Stannard, a native of Westbrook, built this handsome old New England home in 1850 when he was 21. After a notable career at sea, Captain Stannard retired here in 1871. In later years the house served as an inn, under several different names, and as a private residence. In 1970 a fire seriously damaged the building, but the Captain Stannard House—now a charming bed-and-breakfast inn—has been completely restored. Floor-to-ceiling windows, a beautiful foyer staircase and a widow's walk are only a few of the house's interesting features.

Hosts Arlene and Ed Amatrudo have seven rooms for guests, each with a private bath. The tastefully decorated bedrooms, all upstairs, are furnished in antiques with many homey touches such as hand-made crafts, wicker and calico. Each offers individually controlled heat and air conditioning, and one of the rooms features a canopy bed. Your friendly hosts provide welcome extra amenities, too, such as a fruit and cheese basket and fresh flowers in each room. There is a cozy lounge for relaxing, with a piano, TV, books, cards and board games. A bar set up and guest refrigerator with snacks and ice are also available. Outdoors, the spacious lawn is a nice place for sunbathing or enjoying the sea breezes. Breakfast offers a choice of fruit juices, hot or cold cereals, homebaked muffins and breads, and coffee or a selection of teas. The meal is served in the attractive dining room or, in warm weather, outside at umbrella tables. If desired, guests may also choose a tray in bed.

Westbrook's private town beach is one and a half blocks away, and beach passes are available. Excellent restaurants and shops are nearby, and all of the area's many attractions are easily accessible including Mystic Seaport, Gillette Castle and the Goodspeed Opera House. In addition, the inn has its own country store and antique shop, with a good selection of New England furnishings and accessories.

The Captain Stannard House, 138 S. Main St., Westbrook, CT 06498; (203) 399-7565. (From I-95 take Exit 65 to Rte. 1 west.) Rates are moderately expensive to expensive. Visa, MasterCard and American Express are accepted. Children over 6 are welcome; no pets, please. Open year-round.

Riverwind. Several years ago, Riverwind was a dilapidated old building with no apparent charm. That was before Barbara Barlow found the 1850 house on Main Street in the small Connecticut River Valley town of Deep River. Ms. Barlow, a native of Smithfield, Virginia, came to Connecticut in 1983. She explains that she became disenchanted with her profession of teaching, fled north, and saw the possibilities of Riverwind. Having some past experience in restoring old houses, she plunged bravely into a year's renovating work, which included stripping and repapering walls, hand sanding the pine board floors, tiling bathroom showers, uncovering fireplaces and doing most of the electrical wiring. In July, 1984, Riverwind—transformed into a decidedly appealing, antique-filled home—was ready for bed-and-breakfast guests.

Many of the furnishings and accessories in the house are family antiques, including a collection of stoneware and Barbara's great-grandfather's desk; others are from her own extensive collections. Imagination and whimsical creativity are evident everywhere. There are four very attractive rooms for guests, three upstairs and one down, all with private baths and each with its own personality. The Colonial period dominates in three of the rooms, the decor taken from the

197

colors and patterns of antique quilts. The Barn Rose Room has stenciled walls, a fishnet canopy bed and a clawfoot tub in the bath; the Smithfield Room features a high maple bed, once a rope bed; and the Havlow Room, named for Barlow's family, contains an early pine bed with handpainted rose panels on the headboard. Zelda's Room, decorated quite differently with an F. Scott Fitzgerald–era flair, has a bed with a massive carved oak headboard and an antique hall tree. A parlor with a fireplace, piano and guitar offers a comfortable place for guests to relax, play or sing, and the game room on the second floor contains a wonderful old game table and a pie safe full of games; books to read fill shelves in the hallway. There's also a wraparound porch with white wicker furniture for guests' enjoyment.

Breakfast at Riverwind has a distinctively Southern flavor, with delicious Smithfield ham and freshly made baking powder biscuits. Served in the dining room at an antique trestle table, the meal also offers fruit compote or juices, coffee cake, jams, and coffee or tea. A pot of coffee awaits early risers in the game room, and a decanter of sherry in the living room provides afternoon refreshment. Riverwind's kitchen is at guests' disposal, and there are hibachis for backyard cookouts. Menus from area restaurants are on hand for perusal and your hostess will be delighted to make reservations for you. Tempting to collectors, there is an antique shop on the premises at the rear of the house in the old summer kitchen. The region offers a wealth of things to do and see, including riverboat rides and a trip on the Essex Steam Train, Gillette Castle and the Goodspeed Opera House.

Riverwind, 209 Main St. (Rte. 9A), Deep River, CT 06417; (203) 526-2014. Rates are moderately expensive. Visa and MasterCard are accepted. No children or pets, please. Open year-round.

Bishopsgate Inn. This delightful old house, an exceptionally handsome Colonial, was built in 1818 by Horace Hayden, an East Haddam merchant and shipbuilder. Your friendly hostess, Julie Bishop, has six double rooms for guests, each with its own decor and name, such as the Jenny Lind Room, Sweet Adeline Room and Blue Heaven. Four of the beautifully appointed guest chambers have private baths; the other two share a bath. The Director's suite has its own private entrance, a dressing room and sauna bath, and an outside deck. Two of the rooms are on the ground floor and all are furnished with period pieces and family antiques.

A comfortable sitting room on each floor offers a pleasant place to read or chat with other guests. Breakfast, featuring delicious freshly baked scones, blueberry or apple crisp, homemade preserves and excellent coffee, is served each morning in the spacious old country kitchen. The Goodspeed Opera House, restaurants and shops are

within walking distance of the house. Swimming, boating, riding, tennis and golf are all accessible nearby and your hostess will be delighted to help you plan a day's activities in the area. Julie will also act as concierge, making dinner reservations or obtaining theater tickets for guests.

Bishopsgate Inn, Goodspeed Landing, Rte. 149, East Haddam, CT 06423; (203) 873-1677. (From the Goodspeed Opera House take Rte. 149 to the crest of the first hill; Bishopsgate's drive is on the right.) Rates are expensive, lower for longer stays. Children over 6 are welcome; no pets, please. Open year-round.

The Fowler House. The Fowler House, an imposing Queen Anne Victorian set on the town green in tiny Moodus, was built in 1890 by Dr. Frank C. Fowler. Known as the "Medicine Man of Moodus," the doctor was a manufacturer of patent medicines. He was also renowned as a sportsman and world traveler. During the last decade of the nineteenth century his patent medicine mail order business became so successful that the Moodus Post Office was forced into rapid growth in order to accommodate it.

Dr. Fowler then acquired a hotel, a newspaper and extensive real

estate holdings. A true "sport," the doctor enjoyed gambling and sailing on his steam yacht *The Huntress,* one of the largest yachts on the Connecticut River. His forty-five acre Moodus estate, Oak Grove Farm, included a fish and game preserve, a famous stable, a racetrack and a kennel. Generous to a fault, the good doctor was constitutionally unable to refuse requests for money by his so-called friends and acquaintances. In time he lost his business and his personal fortune; Dr. Fowler left Moodus and retired to New London, where he died in 1919.

The Fowler House, now an elegant bed-and-breakfast inn operated by Barbara Ally and Penny Davidson, is just as handsome today as when Dr. Fowler was in residence. The handcarved woodwork and grand staircase, eight Italian ceramic fireplaces, and stained-glass windows and skylight are still intact, as are many of the original light fixtures and two floor-to-ceiling pier mirrors. The six guest rooms, each with its own personality, are comfortably and tastefully furnished with antiques and family heirlooms. Afghans, handmade by Penny's mother, warm the beds on chilly nights. Dr. Fowler's Study has a brass queen-size bed and a handcarved fireplace mantel with a sportsman theme; the doctor's old bedroom, now called the Enanttha T. after his wife, contains a carved tall oak bed and oak treadle sewing machine. The Turret, the Harry M., Frederick B. and the Silva are similarly furnished, and the last three offer working fireplaces. One of the rooms is on the ground floor, and four of the guest bedrooms have private baths, one of which boasts the original clawfooted tub, marble sink and tin ceiling.

Guests are invited to enjoy the library with a fireplace, stocked with books and games, the living room/parlor, a sitting area on the second floor and the large wraparound porch with lounge and rocking chairs. Breakfast, served in the dining room, consists of freshly squeezed juice, fruit, cold cereals, homebaked breads and muffins with homemade jams, and coffee or a variety of teas. Afternoon tea is also served, on the porch or in the library, with freshly baked pastries or cookies and tea or lemonade. Fine restaurants, shops and antiquing are within an easy drive, as are the Goodspeed Opera House and Gillette Castle. All manner of summer sports activities are available nearby, and ice skating and cross-country skiing in winter.

The Fowler House, Plains Road, P.O. Box 432, Moodus, CT 06469; (203) 873-8906. Rates are moderately expensive to expensive, lower for longer stays and from January to April. Visa, MasterCard and American Express are accepted. Children over 12 are preferred; no pets, please. Open year-round.

Western Connecticut
New Canaan/Ridgefield/New Milford

New Canaan, in southwestern Connecticut, is a quiet village in a pretty setting. The New Canaan Bird Sanctuary and Wildlife Preserve offers eighteen acres of trails, ponds and brooks for outdoor roaming. This area of the state, with its appealing small towns, many excellent restaurants and antique shops galore is fun to explore. Ridgefield, to the north, a pleasant, tree-shaded community, is the site of the famous Keeler Tavern, headquarters for Colonial patriots during the American Revolution. The authentically restored stagecoach inn, which may be toured, is noted for a British cannonball embedded in a corner post, lodged there during a battle in April, 1777. The tavern also boasts a hidden staircase and a charming walled garden.

New Milford lies farther north, just past beautiful Candlewood Lake. From there, follow Route 7 to Kent. A delightfully meandering road, Route 7 leads all the way north to the Berkshires, following the tumbling Housatonic River much of the way. Kent Falls State Park offers a spectacular 200-foot cascade, and picnicking and recreation facilities. Swimming is available in nearby Lake Waramaug; in winter there is skiing at the Mohawk Ski Area farther north. At the Sloane-Stanley Museum travelers will find an outstanding collection of Early American crafts and domestic tools, many dating from the seventeenth century. The ruins of the old Kent iron furnace, part of Connecticut's nineteenth-century iron smelting industry, may also be seen on the grounds.

A jog to the east will bring you to Litchfield, one of the finest surviving examples of a late eighteenth-century Colonial village. The town claims to have more old Colonial homes still being lived in than any other community in New England. As they *are* inhabited, most are not open to the public except for Litchfield's annual Open House Day which falls in July, on a different date each year. The renowned White Flower Farm is also in Litchfield; its eight acres of beautiful gardens are open daily from mid-April through October. Back on Route 7, heading north, travelers will come to the Cornwalls, a cluster of tiny upland towns surrounded by thickly forested hills. One of the state's few remaining covered bridges crosses the Housatonic at West Cornwall, on Route 128 just off Route 7.

The Maples Inn. A large, many-gabled building with an open wraparound porch, the Maples in New Canaan was constructed as an inn and opened for business in 1908. The gracious turn-of-the-century structure is surrounded by spacious grounds landscaped with shade trees, shrubs and an abundance of colorful flowers in spring and summer. Cynthia T. Haas purchased the inn in 1982 and has totally restored and refurbished the Maples, returning it to its original elegance and charm.

There are fifteen good-sized bedrooms for guests, including one single, eleven doubles and three suites. Nine of the rooms have private baths and some have fireplaces or porches. All of the guest quarters are on the upper levels and contain firm new mattresses, comfortable chairs, air conditioning and TV. The individually decorated rooms, furnished with antiques and fine quality period reproductions, include some canopy and four-poster beds.

In addition, the Maples offers eight relocation apartments, ideal for couples or families moving into the area and needing accommodations while waiting to move into their new homes. The apartments are fully appointed with living/dining areas, kitchens, and one to four bedrooms. Each has color TV, a private phone and private entrance. Four of the apartments are on the ground floor and a playground across the street is available for children.

Inn guests may relax or await friends or business associates in the elegantly furnished sitting/reception area with a wood-burning fireplace or out on the broad porch. A continental breakfast, served with fine china and silver, consists of juice, cereal, pastries and coffee or tea. Guests may help themselves and chat with other guests, or return to the privacy of their rooms. There is an excellent restaurant next door to the inn, and just across the way the nature center offers walks and hiking trails. The pleasant, quiet village of New Canaan, a fifteen-minute walk from the inn, is only an hour by train from New York City and twenty minutes from the busy corporate center of Stanford-Greenwich. Antique shops and factory outlets are plentiful in this attractive region of Connecticut.

The Maples Inn, 179 Oenoke Ridge, New Canaan, CT 06840; (203) 966-2927. (Please contact Kathy Whisenhunt, asst. innkeeper.) Room rates are moderately expensive to expensive; nightly rates for apartments are expensive, but monthly rates are available. Visa, MasterCard and American Express are accepted. Children are welcome; no pets, please. Open year-round.

West Lane Inn. Ms. Maureen M. Mayer is the gracious proprietor of West Lane Inn, a splendidly appointed bed-and-breakfast establishment in Ridgefield. A large white Colonial with black shutters, the house was built in the early 1800s. In the early 1900s West Lane became a hotel/boardinghouse; later it was converted into apartments, and finally into an elegant guest house. There are twenty spacious, air-conditioned rooms for guests, with queen- or king-size beds and color TV. All are tastefully decorated in traditional style and have private baths, some with bidets. Seven of the rooms are on the ground floor. Several boast working fireplaces, and all include such luxurious amenities as extra thick towels and blankets. Each landing holds a lounge area with comfortable chairs.

Downstairs there is a large, attractive foyer/sitting area with a fireplace and an impressive spindle-type staircase. Note the handsome woodwork, especially at the top of the stairs. Guests may relax in the foyer, in wicker chairs on the delightful veranda with its hanging pots of flowers, or sit on the lawn. Situated on a quiet, tree-lined street, the house is surrounded by one and a half acres of handsomely landscaped grounds.

A complimentary continental breakfast is served in a pleasant small dining room or—in season—on the porch. Your hostess will also provide a full breakfast of eggs, fruit and cereal if you wish, for an extra charge. A light lunch and snacks are available too, at extra cost. The West Lane Inn is close to several good places to eat (The Inn at Ridgefield is right next door) and also to various area points of interest including the Keeler Tavern. Bicycles may be rented at the house. And there is wheelchair access via a ramp in the back.

West Lane Inn, 22 West Lane, Ridgefield, CT 06877; (203) 438-7323. Rates are expensive. Major credit cards are accepted. Children are welcome; no pets, please. Open year-round.

The Quid. Far off the beaten path, on thirty secluded acres of meadows and woods, this charming bed-and-breakfast house in New Milford is a true haven for weary travelers. Gardens surround the dark brown cedar-sided house, and rolling hills can be seen in the distance. Wildflowers abound in the meadows; deer, foxes and chipmunks may often be observed. Susan Borie Rush, your cordial hostess, says that her parents built The Quid in 1939, using lumber from an old tobacco barn—hence its name. Various additions have been made since then, all in keeping with the house's rustic Colonial style. Wood paneling, wide oak flooring, antiques and old paintings enhance the warm Colonial ambiance.

Two double rooms are available for guests; one can also accommodate a rollaway bed. The upstairs guest room, with a shared bath, is furnished with antiques and has twin beds covered with Navajo bedspreads. The low-ceilinged dormer room looks out over hills, a small pond, woods and gardens. The downstairs guest room, with handloomed Irish wool bedspreads, has its own entrance, deck and private bath, and the same delightful view.

Guests are welcome to share the living room, on an invitational basis. The spacious room has a cathedral ceiling, walk-in stone fireplace with wrought-iron cooking crane, and a ten-foot-high picture window. Breakfast is served in the sitting room; its brick wall (the back of the living room fireplace) holds a display of Colonial copper and brass utensils. A woodstove supplies extra warmth when needed. Guests are offered freshly squeezed juice, homemade granola and breads, and coffee or tea along with a view from the windows of gardens and birds breakfasting at the birdfeeders. In summer, breakfast is sometimes served outdoors under the wisteria. Your hostess, a professional chef, also enjoys preparing dinner for her guests, with advance notice and at extra charge.

Exploring The Quid's grounds is encouraged. Susan will tell you how to find an old spring, once a camping place for Indians of the Naugatuck tribe. The spring feeds a heated swimming pool which guests may use when invited. The town of New Milford is about halfway between Danbury and Kent, each approximately a half hour away.

The Quid, 245 Second Hill Rd., New Milford, CT 06776; (203) 354-6143. (Specific directions will be given when you write or phone for reservations.) Rates are moderately expensive to expensive, lower in winter. Children and pets are welcome, but must be well behaved and housebroken! Open year-round.

Rhode Island

Although it is the smallest state in the Union, tiny Rhode Island—named after the Greek island of Rhodes—has the longest title. Its proper name, dating from its early days as a royal colony, is "The State of Rhode Island and Providence Plantations." The state also boasts an imposingly impressive history, marked by religious dissension, boundary fights and slave running, not to mention smuggling and privateering. The state bird is, inappropriately, a chicken: The Rhode Island Red. A more fitting symbol is the statue atop the dome of the State House in Providence, "The Independent Man," a male figure defiantly brandishing a spear.

Giovanni da Verrazano was the first known European to visit Rhode Island; the Italian navigator discovered Narragansett Bay in 1524. In 1636, an English clergyman named Roger Williams had a serious disagreement over religion with the narrow-minded Puritans in Massachusetts. Williams was forced to flee to neighboring Rhode Island, where he purchased land from the Narragansett Indians and founded the city of Providence. Other dissenters followed. But they didn't exactly join hands in peace; it wasn't until 1654 that Williams managed to bring the various settlements together. Nine years later, King Charles II of England granted them a charter. Sir Edmund Andros, that disagreeable Colonial governor who tried to take back Connecticut's charter in 1687, attempted the same thing with Rhode Island a year earlier. He failed in both instances.

Newport, down at the tip of Aquidneck Island in Narragansett Bay, was also founded in the 1600s. The town grew rapidly, and by the 1760s the seaport almost equalled Boston in trade. Like Boston, Newport made its money through the triangular system of trading in rum, molasses and slaves. Ships carried rum to Africa and exchanged it for slaves. The slaves were sold both to the Southern colonies and to the sugar plantation owners in the West Indies—from whence came the molasses for the rum. A notoriously raffish community, Newport in those days was also a haven for pirates and smugglers.

Rhode Island bickered almost continuously with the other colonies over boundaries during the 1700s. The problems were finally resolved in the late 1800s. Rhode Island was not exactly a favorite among the other New England colonies at any time; they considered it a pernicious place, a refuge for nonconformists and heretics. During the American Revolution Newport was occupied by the British from 1776 to 1779, and the town suffered widespread damage from looting and

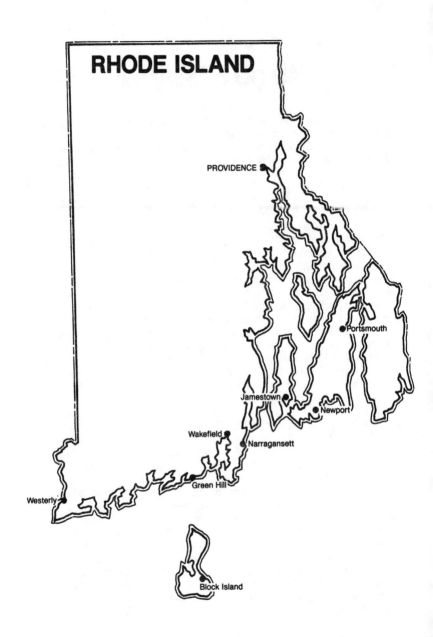

RHODE ISLAND

PROVIDENCE

Portsmouth

Jamestown

Newport

Wakefield

Narragansett

Green Hill

Westerly

Block Island

burning. Even after the Revolution Rhode Island tried to maintain its independence—not from England, but from the other ex-colonies. It refused to send delegates to the Constitutional Convention and later rejected the newly drafted Constitution. But in 1790, when the government threatened to sever relations entirely with the fractious region, Rhode Island voters finally, grudgingly, ratified the Constitution—by a two-vote majority.

Rhode Island is a hilly state, although it has no real mountains. The state's small land mass curves around beautiful Narragansett Bay; its shoreline includes both rugged rock and fine beaches. Inland are quiet country roads and old historic towns. Block Island, a famous summer resort, lies twelve miles out to sea. Providence, the state capital, is an attractive city with a number of historic houses and churches to tour. The city is also the home of Brown University and the Rhode Island School of Design. Providence's founder and namer, Roger Williams, is buried in the North Burial Ground on North Main Street.

Most of Rhode Island's bed-and-breakfast guest houses are located near or on the coast and out on Block Island. As the state is so small, any of the mainland houses may be used as a base from which to explore other areas, including the coastal regions of neighboring Connecticut.

The Narragansett Bay Area

Portsmouth

Narragansett Bay, which almost divides Rhode Island in half, extends inland for twenty-seven miles. Providence is at the head of the bay; below lie the small islands of Prudence and Conanticut. Aquidneck Island to the east is connected to the mainland by several bridges. Portsmouth, at the northern end of the island, was settled in the 1630s by sympathizers of Anne Hutchinson. Another of the religious liberals banished from Boston, Hutchinson—after being tried and convicted on the charge of "traducing the ministers"—lived for a time in Portsmouth.

Off Route 114 in Portsmouth, on Cory's Lane, visitors will find the enchanting topiary gardens called "Green Animals." The gardens were begun around 1880 and now include some eighty sculptured trees and shrubs, beautiful formal flower beds and vegetable gardens. The "animals," including a seventeen-foot giraffe, a camel and an elephant, are droll creatures carefully manicured into amusing shapes by skilled gardeners. Non-animal shapes are on view, too, such as a two-masted schooner and several armchairs.

In nearby Middletown, a few miles to the south, the Prescott Farm and Windmill House are interesting to tour. The restored buildings include a working windmill, circa 1812, that still grinds cornmeal which is sold at the adjacent country store, built around 1715. Gen. Richard Prescott's guardhouse, now a museum, contains furniture from the Pilgrim period. Prescott was the commander of the British forces in Rhode Island. His rule came to an ignominious end one night in 1777 when the Continental Army captured him—in his nightshirt.

Brown's Bayview Guest House. Dorothy and Roger Brown are the owners of Bayview, a handsome three-story Dutch Colonial home built around the turn of the century. Located just outside of Portsmouth, the natural shingled house with green trim stands on three acres of lawn and overlooks beautiful Narragansett Bay. There are six rooms for guests, all with water views, some more spectacular than others.

Five of the guest bedrooms are on the second floor. The Lavender Room, with mahogany furnishings, has twin beds and a private bath. The Blue Room, with white Provincial furniture, contains a full-size bed, and the Yellow Room, with mahogany furnishings, has twin beds. The Green Room, with satinwood furniture, offers a full-size bed, and the large Red, White and Blue Room, decorated with white Provincial pieces, contains a full-size and twin bed and a queen-size Colonial sleeper couch. These last four rooms share baths. The downstairs guest room, with a library and water view, offers a single and a double bed and a private half bath.

For relaxing, guests may use the formal parlor with TV, and the Solarium, a screened or glassed-in sun porch looking out over the lawns to the bay. Breakfast at Bayview offers toasted Portuguese sweet rolls with butter and jams and homemade blueberry muffins, or an assortment of pastries, and tea, regular or decaffeinated coffee or milk. There will also be orange or grapefruit juice and—in season—fresh fruit or fresh fruit salad. Your accommodating hostess gives her guests all they want to eat, at whatever hour of the morning they choose to come downstairs. Portsmouth, with several excellent restaurants, is only five minutes away, and historic Newport is a fifteen-minute drive.

Brown's Bayview Guest House, 502 Bristol Ferry Rd., Portsmouth, RI 02871; (401) 683-0155. (Rte. 114 near Mt. Hope Bridge.) Rates range from inexpensive to expensive, lower from November to April and for longer stays. A two- or three-night stay is requested for holiday weekends. Children are welcome; no pets, please. Open year-round, but only two rooms, both with their own bath, are available in winter.

Newport

Newport's first settlers came from Massachusetts in 1639. Quakers from England soon followed, and in 1658 a number of Jewish families arrived from Holland. The small colony grew over the next century into a thriving seaport. During the American Revolution, however, much of the town was destroyed by the British, and Newport never regained its former maritime prosperity. The town's fame as a summer watering place for the very, very rich began after the Civil War. Many of the mansions built in the last half of the nineteenth century by such wealthy families as the Vanderbilts, Astors, Belmonts and the like are open to the public, and they are truly breathtaking.

One of the simpler establishments is Hammersmith Farm, where Jacqueline Bouvier married John F. Kennedy. Built in 1887, the twenty-eight-room shingled "cottage" is set on fifty rolling acres of pastures, lawns and gardens. Kennedy memorabilia are on view, and the estate was used in filming the movie *The Great Gatsby*, as Robert Redford's ("Gatsby's") home. Chateau-Sur-Mer, a superb example of lavish Victoriana, was built for William S. Wetmore in 1852. The mansion contains a delightful children's toy museum, in addition to its other charms.

Cornelius Vanderbilt's "The Breakers" is located out on Ochre Point Avenue, overlooking the Cliff Walk and the ocean. Richard Morris Hunt designed the structure to resemble a sixteenth-century Italian palace; with its seventy rooms and stunning grounds the Breakers is Newport's grandest. Marble House, completed in 1892 for another Vanderbilt (William) is named for its sumptuous use of many kinds of marble, and Rosecliff, designed by Stanford White, is modeled after the Grand Trianon at Versailles.

Belcourt Castle, built for Oliver Hazard Perry Belmont, is another Richard Hunt extravaganza. It was styled after Louis XIII's palace in France; Europe's finest craftsmen and artists were brought over to work on the sixty-room residence—at a cost of about $3 million. Each room is in a different period—French, English or Italian; the grand staircase is all handcarved. Among the many beautiful objects on view is a 23-karat-gold coronation coach, weighing four tons. In case you're feeling a bit peckish after viewing all these splendors, the tour of Belcourt includes tea. And at Caroline Astor's Beechwood, visitors are greeted by a liveried footman and a host of other "servants," and "Mrs. Astor's friends," played to the hilt by costumed actors.

In mid-July, the Newport Music Festival presents a series of concerts of nineteenth-century music performed in several of the mansions. Later on in the summer are the famed Jazz Festival, held in historic Fort Adams State Park, and the Opera Festival. At Christmastime, Newport offers a full month of activities, with concerts, house tours, pageants and bazaars. Included are an elegant medieval mass at St. George's School Chapel in nearby Middletown, a candlelight tour of Newport's historic district, a Festival of Trees, a "Traditional Stirring of Christmas Plum Pudding" and much more. The town is also an internationally renowned sailing port and, since 1930, has hosted the prestigious America's Cup Race. Held every few years the races, which began in 1851, were consistently won by the United States until 1983, when Australia took the Cup. The next series of races will take place in Australia, and will not return to Newport until the United States wins again.

All visitors to Newport, whatever the time of year, should follow scenic Ocean Drive for its nine-and-a-half-mile length, or better still, hike along the Cliff Walk. You can see some of the mansions and enjoy the ocean view and rugged coastline at the same time. In town, visit the Touro Synagogue and Quaker Meeting House, both the oldest structures of their kind in America, and wander through Newport's restored historic district with its superb collection of seventeenth-, eighteenth- and nineteenth-century houses. You will also find shops and galleries galore for browsing, and a number of excellent restaurants.

The Willows of Newport. These two adjoining townhouses in the oldest part of historic Newport were built 100 years apart, one in the 1700s and the other in the 1800s. When owner Pattie Murphy set out to restore them, she left each house in its own time. Both are listed on the National Register of Historic Places and are among the very few homes in this section of Newport that are open to guests. Since Pattie, as she says, is a true believer in the theory that a vacation should be a fantasy, she created four delightful period rooms for guests, each with its own private bath.

In the 1740 house are the Colonial Wedding room, decorated in several tones of off-white with lace accents, with a king-size solid brass cannonball bed, a corner sitting area, a fireplace and four windows, and the Canopy Room, done in rose tones and off-whites, with a double brass canopy bed, the original skylight, a sitting area and three windows. The 1840 house contains the Victorian Wedding Room and the French Quarters. The first is done in pastel greens and rose tones, with a queen-size canopy bed, handpainted Oriental teak furniture, a corner sitting area, a non-working fireplace and five windows. The pastel French Quarters contains a double brass canopy

210

bed, a corner sitting area, a skylight and two windows. All of the charming rooms have matching comforters and draperies, lots of pillows, fresh flowers, and champagne glasses and silver ice buckets. In the evenings guests return to their rooms to find the lights turned low, the beds turned down, and mints on the pillows.

The Victorian parlor, done in romantic soft pinks, is a comfortable place to unwind after a day's sightseeing; a wet bar for guests' use is located on the second floor. Outdoors there are secluded gardens to enjoy. Reminiscent of nineteenth-century Newport's Gilded Age, continental breakfast at the Willows is served in bed, black tie, on bone china and silver services! Your hostess, whose name should be "Pamper," not "Pattie," exerts every effort to coddle her guests. And as a native Newporter, she will be pleased to share her knowledge of the town with you.

The Willows, 8/10 Willow St., Historic Point, Newport, RI 02840; (401) 846-5486. Rates are moderately expensive to expensive, lower from Oct. 15 to May 15. No children or pets, please. Garage parking is available. Open year-round.

Admiral Benbow Inn. Arlene McKenna welcomes guests to the bed-and-breakfast Admiral Benbow Inn in Newport. The recently restored Victorian house was built in 1855 by a retired sea captain. His gravestone rubbing hangs in the first floor hallway and reads: "Capt. Augustus N. Littlefield . . . An experienced and careful Master Mariner who never claimed any loss on his underwriters." Ms. McKenna believes that the structure has always been an inn, for Littlefield actually lived in a large house farther down the street.

The inn is furnished with antiques, including brass beds and candelabras, and decorated with attractive old-fashioned print wall-coverings and drapes. There are fifteen double rooms for guests and two efficiencies, all with private baths. Each of the rooms is different in style: one has a four-poster canopy bed, some have views of the harbor, and one has a deck. Four of the rooms are on the ground

floor, and the common room, with a wood-burning stove and TV, is a pleasant place for guests to gather for conversation or quiet reading.

A continental breakfast is served daily, with zucchini or raisin bread, bran, blueberry, corn or English muffins and jellies, fresh fruit and orange or grapefruit juice. In wintertime breakfast is served by the fire. The house is two blocks from Bannister's Wharf and a short walk from most of Newport's varied attractions including the Cliff Walk and the mansions.

Admiral Benbow Inn, 93 Pelham St., Newport, RI 02840; (401) 846-4256. Rates range from moderately expensive to expensive, lower from Nov. 1 to May 16. Special Winter Mansion Tour/Dinner Packages are available. Visa, MasterCard and American Express are accepted. Children over 10 are welcome; no pets, please. Open year-round.

The Brinley Victorian Inn. Actually two Victorian homes, built in 1850 and 1870 on the land where the historic Filmore Hotel once stood, the Brinley in Newport is owned by Edwina Sebest and Amy Weintraub. The buildings are classic examples of late Victorian architecture with clapboard siding, mansard roofs, high ceilings, polished wood floors and curving staircases. The seventeen guest bedrooms, each individually decorated, carry out the romantic Victorian ambiance with antique satin and lace window treatments and handsome antique furnishings. These include several high-posted pineapple beds, a brass bed and a magnificent six-foot carved mahogany bed, mahogany bureaus, desks and armoires. Each room has at least one comfortable reading chair and a good reading light; several rooms offer loveseats and one has a Victorian "fainting couch." Added amenities include mints on the pillows, fresh flowers, antique candlesticks with candles you may burn, and miniature kerosene lamps. Thirteen of the rooms are doubles and four are triples. Seven have private baths; the others share ten baths. Seven of the guest chambers are on the ground floor.

For relaxing, guests will enjoy the parlor with its antique lamps, period chairs and tables, Oriental rugs and an interesting selection of books about Newport, photography and art. There are also a library, with game table and antique checkerboard, and two porches for guests' pleasure. Breakfast features homebaked muffins, cakes and breads, orange juice and coffee or tea. On summer afternoons your hostesses serve iced tea or iced coffee, and if given advance notice they will supply wine for a special occasion.

The Brinley is within walking distance of the town's many attractions, and Edwina and Amy, who gave up careers as a psychologist and television producer to move to Newport, will be delighted to share their love and knowledge of the old seaport with their guests.

The Brinley Victorian Inn, 23 Brinley St., Newport, RI 02840; (401) 849-7645. (Take Rte. 138 or 114 to Broadway, go left on Ayrault, right on Kay and left on Brinley.) Rates are moderately expensive to expensive, lower for longer stays and from Nov. 1–May 27. Children over 12 are welcome; no pets, please. Open year-round.

Jamestown

Jamestown, on Conanticut Island in Narragansett Bay, was almost destroyed by the British in 1775. A few eighteenth-century houses, the Quaker Meeting House and a windmill still stand, however. The island, connected to Newport on the east and the mainland on the west by bridges, is an interesting place to explore, with a tranquil, un-touristy atmosphere. There are an old lighthouse and fort along the rugged coastline, and a museum in the Jamestown Historical Society building opposite Town Hall on Narragansett Avenue displays local historical items. The Sydney L. Wright Museum on North Main Road offers early Colonial and Indian artifacts. The island also has three state parks and five public beaches.

The Calico Cat—Bed & Breakfast. A recently restored Jamestown house, circa 1860–1870, the Calico Cat is only 250 feet from East Harbor with its grand view of the Newport Bridge and Newport Harbor. Hosts Donald and Patricia Fleming have ten rooms for guests including two singles, seven doubles and one triple, sharing four baths. Two of the double rooms are on the first floor. A comfortable common room with a fireplace and a desk for writing is a nice place to relax, read or play cards and other games. State parks and beaches are easily accessible; shops and restaurants are a short walk from the house, and Newport is minutes away by car or bus. The Calico Cat offers guests a continental breakfast featuring orange juice, homebaked muffins and breads selected from your hosts' collection of more than sixty recipes, and "the best coffee on the island!" The meal is served on the large enclosed front porch, appealingly deco-

rated with blue and white checked tablecloths and ice cream parlor chairs.

The Calico Cat, 14 Union St., Jamestown, RI 02835; (401) 423-2641. (Specific directions will be given when you make your reservation.) Rates are moderately expensive, lower off season; midweek specials, 5 nights Sunday–Thursday, are available. Rollaway beds are also available for a modest extra charge. Visa, MasterCard and American Express are accepted. Children are welcome; no pets, please. Open May 1–Oct. 1.

West of Narragansett Bay
Narragansett/Wakefield/Green Hill

Narragansett, or Narragansett Pier as it is commonly known, has been a popular summer resort since the late nineteenth century. Not as grand as it was in its heyday, the town is still very inviting, and the surrounding areas offer superb beaches and fishing. A short drive south will bring you to Galilee, a busy fishing village, and the rocky headland of Point Judith. The town of Wakefield is just to the west of Narragansett, and Green Hill is off Route 1 farther down the coast, facing Block Island Sound.

The Phoenix. Dave and Joyce Peterson are your hosts at the Phoenix, an exceptionally attractive bed-and-breakfast guest house in Narragansett. The rambling old Victorian "cottage," designed in 1888 by Stanford White, is included in the National Register of Historic Places. Joyce Peterson, a realtor who enjoys photography and swimming, has some marvelous tales to tell about the couple's restoration work on the house—such as their bitterly cold first winter there when they discovered that the place was not on the town sewer lines. Today, the Phoenix is a comfortable, informal home with, as your hostess puts it, "a brightened-up Victorian ambiance," offering soft colors, glowing refinished floors and flowers.

There are five double upstairs guest rooms, one of which can accommodate three people; the others are also available as singles. One has a private bath, the others share two baths and one of the bathrooms features a high, long tub on a marble stand. Some of the tastefully decorated, spacious guest chambers are graced with lovely antique bed coverings; all contain fresh flowers and a decanter of sherry. For relaxing there are a large living room with a fireplace, books and games, a broad wicker-furnished veranda and a private lawn.

In the morning guests can walk to the beach and return to a full breakfast of fruit or juice, muffins or homemade breads such as Russian coffee cake, and freshly ground gourmet coffee. Depending on the day there will also be eggs Benedict, cheese blintzes with strawberries, lobster quiche or perhaps omelets with shrimp and avocado or other fillings. The delicious meal is served on fine china in the always open kitchen. Afternoon sherry, menus of area restaurants, maps of the region and tokens for the Newport Bridge are also supplied by the thoughtful Petersons. The fishing village of Galilee is just down the road and you can take a ferry from there out to Block Island for a day's excursion; fine beaches are close by and Newport is twenty minutes away. Dave Peterson, who is involved with energy management and local politics, is always eager to play tennis, golf or go fishing with guests.

The Phoenix, 29 Gibson Ave., Narragansett, RI 02882; (401) 783-1918. (The Petersons will give you directions when you call or write for reservations.) Rates are moderately expensive. Well-behaved children over 10 are welcome; no pets, please, and smoking is restricted to the living room or porch. Open year-round.

Steven and Nancy Richards/Bed and Breakfast. The Richards's comfortable house in Narragansett was built a half century ago as a summer home. Your hosts have remodeled the place themselves, refinishing floors, roofing and insulating, adding more rooms and a new kitchen, and decorating with new wallpaper and attractive furnishings. The ambiance is pleasantly "country," a "kick-your-shoes-off" kind of place, as Nancy Richards describes it. There are three quiet bedrooms for guests, all on the first floor off the living room. The accommodations include two rooms with double beds and one with king-size bed or two twin beds. One of the rooms has a private bath; the others share a bath. Rag rugs, chintz fabrics and flowers brighten the guest quarters, and the attractive living room is always available for relaxing. There are also a deck, where in the evenings guests may have the opportunity of meeting the neighborhood raccoon family, and a brick patio. Flowers abound from spring to fall on the nicely landscaped grounds.

A hearty breakfast is served each morning, with juice, fresh fruit, homemade breads and tea or freshly ground coffee, and the house specialty, a delectable baked apple pancake with breakfast meats. Steven and Nancy's home, on a dead-end street in the center of town, is within walking distance of restaurants and shops. Beaches and tennis are close by, and Newport is a twenty-minute drive.

Steven and Nancy Richards/Bed and Breakfast, 104 Robinson St., Narragansett, RI 02882; (401) 789-7746. Rates are moderate; cots are available for children at a modest extra charge. Children are welcome; no pets, please, and no smoking in the house. Open year-round.

Blueberry Bush. A large Cape Cod house on a scenic road not far from the center of Wakefield, Blueberry Bush is owned by June and Peter Nielsen. Two upstairs rooms are available for guests; both can accommodate up to four persons. A full bath is shared if both rooms are occupied. The house, furnished with antiques, contains a pleasant living room with Oriental rugs and a fireplace for guests to enjoy. A full breakfast is served each morning, with homebaked treats and your hosts' own blueberries and peaches in season. Spacious grounds surround the house, including a fenced-in back yard, with lawn furniture and charcoal grills for guests' pleasure. Bicycles are available, excellent beaches are nearby, and both Newport, Rhode Island, and Mystic Seaport in Connecticut are an easy drive. Block Island, too, is easily accessible via a ferry ride.

Blueberry Bush, 679 South Rd., Wakefield, RI 02879; (401) 783-0907. (From I-95 take Exit 3A, go 10.6 miles on Rte. 138 and 3.2 miles on South Road.) Rates are moderate, lower for longer stays and from October to March. Children are welcome; no pets, please. Open year-round.

Fairfield-By-The-Sea. Set on four acres of land just up the road from the beach, this delightful bed-and-breakfast guest house in Green Hill is owned by Jeanne Ayers Lewis. Of contemporary architecture, the house was designed and built by Jeanne's artist husband. The

open, airy structure is filled with art and charming handcrafted items ranging from dolls to colorful quilts. Your hostess, a home economist who has traveled extensively, worked many years for the pattern division of *McCall's* and other large corporations as a consumer consultant. Now retired from teaching home economics in Arsdley, New York, Jeanne can devote all of her time to enjoying her guests.

Fairfield-By-The-Sea has two upper-level guest bedrooms, sharing one and a half baths. There is also an outdoor shower for beachgoers. Guests are invited to enjoy the screened balcony and deck, the comfortable living room with a fireplace—which offers a welcome blaze in chilly weather—and several outdoor picnic areas. Your hostess also maintains a superb library with many interesting books and magazines.

Breakfast, which always includes homebaked goodies, may be either continental or more elaborate. Afternoon tea may be provided, too. Sometimes, guests are offered a seafood feast, sharing the costs, and gourmet box lunches will be supplied upon request. Nearby activities include swimming or sunning at beautiful Green Hill Beach, fishing, catching blue crabs, golfing, bird watching, tennis and sailing. Block Island is a ferry ride away, and the University of Rhode Island offers year-round events. Newport is twenty-five miles away; Mystic Seaport in Connecticut is a twenty-mile drive.

Fairfield-By-The-Sea, 861 Green Hill Beach Rd., Green Hill, RI 02879; (401) 789-4717. (Rte. 1, halfway between Wakefield and Westerly; 16 miles from I-95 south.) Rates are moderate; special rates are available Sunday–Thursday in winter. Well-behaved children are welcome; no pets, please. Babysitters are available. Open year-round.

Westerly

Westerly, in southwestern Rhode Island, offers a number of unusual items for curious travelers. A lacy nurse's cap that belonged to Florence Nightingale is displayed in a glass case in the Westerly Hospital lobby. And on the front lawn of the town's public library is a bench presented to the town by television personality Ralph Edwards in honor of TV star Ruth Buzzi, a native of Westerly. If you'll recall, Buzzi played the role of dowdy, hair-netted Gladys Ormphby on the show "Laugh-In." The Gladys Ormphby "Trysting Bench" commemorates those wonderful scenes in which Gladys/Buzzi sat on a park bench and smacked the Dirty Old Man, played by Arte Johnson, with her purse. Adjacent to the library lovely Wilcox Park extends for eighteen acres, including a fragrant scented garden for the visually impaired and handicapped.

Tiny Watch Hill, six miles west of Westerly out on a peninsula, is another interesting place to visit. An old, serene community cooled by sea winds, Watch Hill offers a number of century-old houses, excellent beaches and great swimming, sailing and fishing. The town also has the famous Flying Horse Carousel, one of the country's oldest, dating back to the late 1800s. Drive out to Watch Hill Light for a grand view of Block Island Sound. A working lighthouse, its beacon is visible thirteen miles out to sea. Even so, shipwrecks have occasionally occurred. Local records report that in 1962 the ship *Leif Viking* ran aground just a few hundred feet off the light; her captain radioed the lighthouse and calmly announced: "You have a ship in your front yard."

Another local story tells of Albert Einstein's visit to Watch Hill in the 1930s. Although utterly hopeless at navigating a small boat, Einstein came up with a simple solution: he set sail each morning and headed due west until he ran aground at sandy Napatree Point. There, some helpful soul would go out and turn him around. Back he'd go, but unless someone leaped into the water and stopped him, the brilliant physicist would crash into the dock!

Woody Hill Guest House. Ellen L. Madison designed her Colonial reproduction gambrel-roofed home to be built on land that has been in her family for several generations. The inviting house, which sits on a hill in the countryside outside of Westerly, features wide-board floors and a blend of country antiques and reproductions—most of them made by your hostess. Tab curtains, handmade quilts and charming informal gardens add to the "country" atmosphere.

A recent addition to the house has added two new bedrooms for guests, for a total of four. Two baths are shared. One of the upstairs rooms has also been redecorated, with a Victorian theme including an old pump organ which has been repaired to tip-top condition. The other airy, spacious guest rooms are decorated in an earlier period, and all contain comfortable sitting chairs. One of the two new ground floor rooms opens directly into the back yard and gardens. The other room is also the library. For relaxing, reading or conversation, guests are welcome to enjoy the living room, library, large porch and lovely grounds.

Ellen Madison is an English teacher, working on her doctorate, and the house overflows with books, which visitors are welcome to borrow. Gardening and cooking are two of your hostess's chief interests, and the results are likely to appear on the breakfast table! Breakfast will be a surprise, as it consists of whatever Ms. Madison feels like serving—perhaps fruits of the season, homemade muffins and the like. You will need a car to reach restaurants and shops, but historic Watch Hill, Newport and Mystic Seaport are all within easy drives. And the best beaches in Rhode Island are two miles away.

Woody Hill Guest House, RR 3, Box 676E, Woody Hill Road, Westerly, RI 02891; (401) 322-0452. (Woody Hill Road is ¼ mile on left heading north on Rte. 1 after intersection at Dunn's Corners.) Rates are moderate, lower from Columbus Day to Memorial Day, and 1 day free for every 6 days' stay.

Well-behaved children are welcome; no pets, please, and no smoking. Open year-round.

Inn on the Hill. Set high on a terraced hill three blocks from downtown Westerly, Dave and Amy Merritt's bed-and-breakfast house was built circa 1870. When the Merritts purchased the Victorian-style structure, which had formerly been run as an apartment house and then as a boarding house, they discovered that its interior had been badly neglected. So, Amy says, their first nine months were spent "Spackling, sanding, sheetrocking, hammering and painting their way through thirteen rooms, four bathrooms, and a large hallway." The Merritts still have lengthy lists of projects to complete, but the Inn on the Hill is now welcoming guests and offering them a comfortable, happy stay.

The house's many fine architectural details are still intact, including the original plaster ceiling moldings and medallions, five unique hearths and some handsome hardwood flooring. The furnishings throughout are antique mixed with family pieces. There are seven double rooms for guests, sharing baths. Three of the bedrooms are on the ground floor. Each of the guest rooms has been stenciled with a different, original design, and all contain either a double bed or twins, a bureau or wardrobe, plenty of good books, and fresh flowers. As there is so much wall space in the house, your hosts have invited area artists to hang their works, available for purchase. Your inventive hostess is even exploring the possibility of offering stenciled nightshirts for guests to buy!

For relaxing, there are the public room with color TV, games and magazines, the breakfast room, and a combination library/sitting room. Breakfast consists of juices, including freshly squeezed orange juice, fresh fruit salad, cold cereals, and coffee or tea accompanied by a different selection of homebaked treats each day such as muffins, coffee cake, cinnamon buns or popovers. The grounds include a spacious back yard and newly planted gardens. A small blueberry patch is already producing berries for muffins. A children's play area with a wading pool, sandbox and playhouse is on the Merritts' list for early completion, along with picnic tables, and barbecue and outdoor game areas for adults.

Excellent restaurants are within a five- to fifteen-minute drive away; Westerly's Wilcox Park is a five-minute walk and water slides, beaches and golf are easily accessible. Mystic Seaport in Connecticut is a fifteen-minute drive, Newport is forty-five minutes away, and the ferry to Block Island is a half hour's drive.

Inn on the Hill, 29 Summer St., Westerly, RI 02891; (401) 596-3791. (From I-95 take exit for Rte. 3, follow south to junction with Rte. 1, turn left up hill—North Rte. 1—for 3 blocks; the inn is at the corner of Rte. 1 and Summer Street.) Rates are moderately expensive, lower for longer stays and from Labor Day to Memorial Day. Children are welcome. Pets may be allowed by prior arrangement but must be housebroken and not left alone in guest rooms. Open year-round.

Block Island

Located twelve miles out to sea, Block Island lies approximately south of Narragansett Bay. Ferries take passengers to the island from Newport and Point Judith, Rhode Island, and from New London, Connecticut. The island was originally inhabited by the Narragansett Indians, who called it "Manisses," or the Isle of the Little God. The Florentine explorer Verrazano may have discovered the island in 1524, when he sailed along the coast. The Dutch explorer Adriaen Block, for whom it is named, landed there in 1614; English settlers arrived in 1661. Once a haven for pirates and smugglers, and the site of more than 200 shipwrecks, Block Island began to attract summer vacationers in the 1800s. Today people come to sun, sail, fish and swim, or simply unwind.

With its rolling moors, miles of stone walls, sandy roads, wildflowers, freshwater ponds and fine beaches, Block Island is a delightful place to explore, on foot or by bicycle. It is a small island, about six miles long and three and a half miles wide. From Mohegan Bluffs, spectacular clay cliffs rising 185 feet above the Atlantic on the southern side, there is a superb view of the ocean and distant mainland. On the west side of the island are pebble beaches and quiet coves; the east side offers beautiful, sandy beaches, and Sandy Point, at the northern end of Block Island, has a bird sanctuary and an old lighthouse.

Old Town Inn. Ralph and Monica Gunter are your hosts at this attractive bed-and-breakfast inn on Block Island. Centrally located in a quiet country setting at the junction of Old Town Road and Center Road, the inn nicely combines old with new. The old section, built circa 1830 as a homestead, was moved to the Old Harbor site in 1900, and the east wing was added in 1981. There are twelve rooms for guests, eight with private baths. Two of the rooms, with private baths, are on the ground floor. All are comfortably furnished, some—in the old section—with antiques.

For relaxing, there is a lounge with color TV and a fireplace. Early morning coffee or tea will be brought to your room, if requested, and a full breakfast is served daily in the inn's traditionally decorated dining rooms. There will be juice, cereal, hot blueberry or other muffins, eggs, pancakes or French toast with bacon or sausage, and coffee, tea or Sanka. Afternoon tea, another of the Gunters' pampering touches, is served between 4 and 4:40 p.m. in the lounge, complete with cakes and pastries.

The spacious grounds, about four and a half acres, offer well-tended

flower beds and shade trees, lawns and a patio, lounge chairs and picnic tables. Beaches and the town are about a mile away, and bicycles can be rented at the inn. An interesting added note about the old house: Monica Gunter says that it was the setting for a novel called *Only in New England.* Author Theodore Roscoe wrote the book at the inn; the subject was the murder of a nineteenth-century owner of the house, one of whose sons was tried for the crime but not convicted. There are also, she says, rumors of ghosts and buried money!

Old Town Inn, Old Town Road, Box 351, Block Island, RI 02807; (401) 466-5958. Rates are moderately expensive to expensive, lower for longer stays. Children over 5 are welcome; no pets, please. Open Memorial Day–mid-September.

The Sea Breeze. Originally an old Block Island fishing house, this interesting building was enlarged in the 1920s to provide extra accommodations for an adjacent boarding house. Today, the New England-style shingled cottage has an airy, open look with old island furniture combined with contemporary art from a gallery on the property. The site is spectacular, overlooking colorful gardens and a swan pond, and with a panoramic ocean view.

Hosts Alisa Newhouse and Kevin Scanlan, who live in the old boarding house, offer five rooms for guests. Four are doubles and one has twin beds. All of the rooms have sitting areas; baths are shared. Three of the rooms are on the ground floor. Sitting areas on each floor provide books, games and writing tables, and there are a porch and patio outdoors for relaxing. Breakfast at the Sea Breeze consists of juice, fruit, homemade muffins, croissants, and tea or Viennese coffee. Guests may use the refrigerator for storing wine, cheese or snacks. The ferry, shops and restaurants are a three-minute walk; beaches, fishing, boating and biking are all easily accessible.

The Sea Breeze, Spring St., Box 141, Block Island, RI 02807; (401) 466-2275.

Rates are moderately expensive, lower for longer stays. Children are welcome; no pets, please. Open Memorial Day–late September.

The 1661 Inn and Guest House. Two separate buildings set amid flower-splashed meadows and overlooking two ponds and the Atlantic Ocean, the 1661 Inn and Guest House are owned by the Abrams family. On a 1969 sailing trip to the island the Abrams discovered an old hotel, which they purchased, renovated, and reopened to guests a year later. Named The 1661 Inn in honor of the year Block Island was settled by colonists from New England, the building's rooms have been done over in authentic New England decor, with antiques and Early American paintings. Each of the guest chambers, which are all appointed with antique Colonial furniture and wallpaper, is named after an original island settler. The Abrams acquired the adjacent Guest House in 1972; the charming old structure (circa 1900) has also been completely remodeled.

Hosts Joan and Justin Abrams and Steve and Rita Draper have a total of twenty-five rooms for guests: fifteen in the inn and ten in the guest house. Most are double rooms, and twelve have private baths; the others share thirteen baths. Nine of the rooms are on the ground floor, and eleven have private decks and ocean views. A beautifully decorated lobby offers a comfortable place to relax, as does a sunny deck. Breakfast is served in the ocean view dining room or under umbrella-topped tables on the deck. The lavish meal, served buffet style, may include fruit, eggs, quiche, corned beef hash, breakfast meats, two daily hot specialties of the house, potatoes, beans, muffins, and coffee or tea. Complimentary wine and "nibbles" are offered each evening.

For other meals, the Abrams also operate the nearby Hotel Manisses, a landmark structure from the Victorian era which they restored to its original grandeur. There you will find a turn-of-the-century bar, dining rooms and a garden terrace offering delicious

lunches and dinners, afternoon high tea served in the lobby, and much more. All of Block Island's activities are easily accessible from the inn; shuttle service to the beaches is provided along with beach towels. For shoppers, the Manisses Attic Antique Shop one block from the Manisses Hotel offers a variety of art, furniture and cut glass. But as your hostess, Joan Abrams, says: "Our best asset is the beautiful view!"

The 1661 Inn and Guest House, Spring Street, Block Island, RI 02807; (401) 466-2421 or 466-2063. Rates range from moderately expensive to expensive, lower off season. Visa, MasterCard and American Express are accepted. Children over 10 are welcome; no pets, please. The 1661 Inn is open in summer until Columbus Day; the Guest House is open year-round.

Index

New Hampshire

ABOUT THE AUTHOR

Corinne Madden Ross, a freelance writer living near Boston, stays in bed & breakfast homes whenever possible on her frequent travels. She has had published numerous travel articles and is the author of *The Southern Bed and Breakfast Book* and *The Mid-Atlantic Bed and Breakfast Book* (The East Woods Press). With husband Ralph Woodward, she co-authored *New England: Off the Beaten Path* (The East Woods Press), and she has also written *To Market, To Market: Six Walking Tours of the Old & New Boston* (Charles River Books).

Bed & Breakfast Books From
The East Woods Press

Quantity	Title	Each	Total
	THE NEW ENGLAND BED & BREAKFAST BOOK, Ross Guide to the finest B & B lodgings in Maine, Connecticut, Massachusetts, New Hampshire, Rhode Island and Vermont.	$8.95	
	THE MID-ATLANTIC BED & BREAKFAST BOOK, Ross Guide to the finest B & B lodgings in New York, Pennsylvania, New Jersey, Delaware, Maryland and West Virginia.	$8.95	
	THE SOUTHERN BED & BREAKFAST BOOK, Ross Guide to the finest B & B lodgings in Alabama, Florida, Georgia, Louisiana, Mississippi, North Carolina, South Carolina, Tennessee, Virginia and the District of Columbia.	$8.95	
	THE CALIFORNIA BED & BREAKFAST BOOK, Strong Sample the diversity of this great state in this comprehensive guide to its varied and delightful B & B accommodations. More than 350 listings!	$8.95	
	THE CARIBBEAN BED & BREAKFAST BOOK, Strong Visits more than 150 charming B & B establishments and includes much information on traveling to these beautiful islands.	$9.95	
	THE BEST BED & BREAKFAST IN THE WORLD, UNITED KINGDOM, 1986-87, Welles & Darbey A fascinating collection of more than 800 lodgings with a special section on B & B in London.	$10.95	
	Subtotal		
	Shipping		
	Total Enclosed		

Prices subject to change.

Send order to:
THE EAST WOODS PRESS
429 East Boulevard
Charlotte, NC 28203

ALLOW 4 TO 6 WEEKS FOR DELIVERY

Please send my order to:

Name _____

Street _____

City _____ State _____ Zip _____

My check for $_____ is enclosed. Or charge my MasterCard or Visa

☐ Please send me your   Account No. _____
   Free book catalog.   Expiration Date _____

For charge orders only, call our toll-free number: (800) 438-1242, ext. 102. In North Carolina (800) 532-0476. We will refund your money, excluding shipping costs, if you are dissatisfied for any reason.

Notes